# SLAVERY AND THE BRITISH
# EMPIRE

# Slavery and the British Empire

*From Africa to America*

KENNETH MORGAN

# OXFORD

UNIVERSITY PRESS

Great Clarendon Street, Oxford OX2 6DP

Oxford University Press is a department of the University of Oxford.
It furthers the University's objective of excellence in research, scholarship,
and education by publishing worldwide in

Oxford New York

Auckland Cape Town Dar es Salaam Hong Kong Karachi
Kuala Lumpur Madrid Melbourne Mexico City Nairobi
New Delhi Shanghai Taipei Toronto

With offices in

Argentina Austria Brazil Chile Czech Republic France Greece
Guatemala Hungary Italy Japan Poland Portugal Singapore
South Korea Switzerland Thailand Turkey Ukraine Vietnam

Oxford is a registered trade mark of Oxford University Press
in the UK and in certain other countries

Published in the United States
by Oxford University Press Inc., New York

British Library Cataloguing in Publication Data

Data available

Library of Congress Cataloging in Publication Data

Morgan, Kenneth, 1953–
Slavery and the British empire : from Africa to America / Kenneth Morgan.
p. cm.
Includes bibliographical references and index.
ISBN-13: 978–0–19–289291–1
ISBN-13: 978–0–19–923899–6
1. Slave trade—Great Britain—History. 2. Slave trade—Africa—History.
3. Slave trade—America—History. 4. Slavery—Great Britain—History. 5. Slaves—Great
Britain—History. 6. Slaves—Great Britain—Social conditions. I. Title.
HT1162.M67 2007
306.3′620941—dc22                2007036888

Typeset by Laserwords Private Limited, Chennai, India
Printed in Great Britain
on acid-free paper by
Biddles Ltd, King's Lynn, Norfolk

ISBN 978–0–19–289291–1 (Pbk)
ISBN 978–0–19–923899–6 (Hbk)

1 3 5 7 9 10 8 6 4 2

To Leigh Sharon Morgan

# Preface

This short book provides an overview of slavery, the slave trade, and abolitionism in the British Empire over a period of two hundred years from the mid-seventeenth century to the mid-nineteenth. These are subjects of perennial historical interest and, moreover, ones that have accumulated a vast historiography. It is no exaggeration to say that over the past forty years some of the finest scholarship published in any historical field has been devoted to these topics. Historians have used interdisciplinary techniques and have unearthed much new data in an effort to come to grips with a diasporic experience that had wide geographic scope, vast numeric scale, and deep human impact. My book is aimed at the educated reader with no detailed knowledge of the subjects discussed. Accordingly, I have provided only light referencing, mainly identifying direct quotations embedded in the text. Some of these are taken from manuscript sources consulted in relation to more detailed projects. A select bibliography of major works on British slavery and abolitionism is appended for readers who want to follow up this book with more detailed reading.

As is always the case with a broad overview, the book depends on the labours of many fine historians. My debts to the leading scholars of slavery and abolitionism can be seen throughout my chapters. At the same time, the book reflects my long teaching and research experience of the subjects discussed, especially in lectures and classes delivered over many years to students at Brunel University. In a relatively short book, I have had to present concentrated arguments without many digressions, but I hope this does not mean that my analyses are too tight or too abbreviated. Plenty of statistics, ratios, and percentages underpin the arguments presented, so that the reader is aware of the scale and dimensions of the topic discussed. But I have often expressed the statistics in words rather than in tables and graphs because that seemed appropriate for a general text of this nature. Specialists will note omissions and inevitably there will be errors of commission. I hope they find something useful, however, in what I have written.

One important strategic decision affects the coverage of the book. It concentrates more on slavery and the slave trade in the British Atlantic world than on British involvement in slavery in other parts of the globe such as the Cape Colony, Mauritius, and India. This is largely because of the word length of the total text, but secondarily because my expertise lies more in the Atlantic aspects of slavery rather than in slavery in other locations. But where it was possible to integrate comparative material into the text, comparing and contrasting slavery in the British Atlantic world with that elsewhere, I have done so. The book appears in the year of the bicentenary of the abolition of the British slave trade, though it was not written to coincide with that landmark. Nevertheless, I would hope that it provides an intelligent summation of a thriving historical field at a time when the remembrance of slavery is prominent in public life.

In 2005 an Andrew W. Mellon Fellowship at the Henry E. Huntington Library, San Marino, California, gave me the opportunity to check many sources cited in this book. I am grateful for the support of P. G. M. Dickson, Richard S. Dunn and Jacob M. Price in securing this appointment, and I would like to thank the staff of the Huntington for their friendly assistance during my stay in southern California. The City of Pasadena Public Library kindly offered me computer facilities when my laptop was damaged. In 2006 a Visiting Professorship in the School of Philosophical and Historical Inquiry at the University of Sydney, though awarded for another project, enabled me to use the resources of the Fisher Library to carry out final editing and checking. I should like to thank Richard Waterhouse for acting as my academic patron while I was in Sydney. Stanley Engerman of the University of Rochester offered a helpful commentary when I was revising my original draft of the book. In finalizing the script for publication, I am grateful to archives cited in the notes below for granting me permission to quote from manuscripts in their possession. A final word of thanks should be given to my wife, Leigh, who has assisted my work in more ways than she realizes.

# Contents

# Maps

# Introduction

Slavery as an institution and as an important phenomenon in the transatlantic world was well established before England began its involvement in slavery and the slave trade. Various forms of slavery flourished in the ancient and medieval worlds. The Egyptians, Greeks, and Romans all used enslaved labourers in construction work, the armed forces, agriculture, industry, and domestic service. Most captives were recruited through war or kidnapping from outside of the societies where they were placed in bondage. Throughout the Middle Ages slaves could be found in the Mediterranean world, in Russia and other Slavic lands, within Africa, and throughout large parts of Asia, especially in areas where Islam prevailed. Slaves within Islamic territories were non-Muslims because the Qur'an forbade the enslavement of co-religionists. Slavery within Africa was one form of dependency that flourished in societies based on kinship. By the eighth century slaves from African sources were readily supplied to Islamic societies in the Persian Gulf and Indian Ocean.

Slave markets existed throughout the ancient and medieval worlds. Bonded workers were bought and sold by middlemen and sometimes transferred over long distances. The Greeks and the Romans recruited slaves from their own and neighbouring societies around the Mediterranean. Within Africa slave routes existed for the supply of slaves to Tunisia, Libya, Morocco, and Egypt. Cairo, in particular, was a large emporium for the slave trade to the Mediterranean world. During the eighth and ninth centuries the Vikings plundered for slaves in Iceland, Greenland, Scotland, Ireland, and territories around the Baltic Sea. Some were absorbed into Norse society; others were sold to the Byzantine and Muslim empires. Between the eighth and the eleventh centuries slave routes from the area around Kiev stretched westwards towards Slavic lands and southwards to Constantinople and the Black Sea. By the fifteenth century Arabs had established slave posts on the East African coast whence they shipped the enslaved to the Persian Gulf and India. Slavery and the slave trade were thus widespread phenomena on several continents for centuries before Christopher Columbus discovered the New World in 1492.

After the Iberian powers began to colonize Central and South America and the Caribbean in the sixteenth century, slavery soon became transplanted there. Thus the Portuguese and the Spanish dominated the early phase of transatlantic slavery. Portugal shipped Africans to its settlements in Brazil. Spain took slaves to its viceroyalties in New Spain and New Granada, to what are now Peru, Colombia, and Chile, and to the Caribbean territories of Hispaniola, Puerto Rico, and Cuba. By 1650 the Dutch and the French had followed suit in the shipment of enslaved Africans to their American territories, but their involvement in the early transatlantic slave trade was on a much smaller scale than that of the Spanish and Portuguese. Apart from their seizure of Brazil from Portugal between 1630 and 1654, the Dutch had a toehold in America only in tiny Caribbean islands such as Curaçao and St Eustatius and along the 'wild coast' of South America, primarily in Surinam, Demerara-Essequibo, and Berbice. The French had Caribbean possessions mainly in Guadeloupe, Martinique, and Saint-Domingue, and also claimed land around Cayenne on the northern mainland of South America.

The forms of slavery in existence before the European discovery of America were radically different from the type of slavery that developed rapidly and on such a large scale on the western shores of the Atlantic. One crucial difference was that the latter was essentially a racialized version of slavery. Another significant difference was that most slaves in the Americas lived and worked on plantations devoted to the production of staple crops intended mainly for marketing to Europe. Black slavery flourished in the Americas because it was difficult permanently to employ white workers in semi-tropical agricultural labour. High costs were involved in attracting free white workers to the Americas. Moreover, European venturers overseas did not conceive of fellow Europeans as being fit to enslave. European countries, of course, included many people whose working lives were not totally free in the early modern period. There were thousands of servants, with or without contracts, and agricultural workers employed and housed on the basis of their social and economic ties to landowners. But these workers did not experience permanent bondage. Nor was it thought appropriate that they should do so. Enslaving Africans was a different matter. Africans were regarded as heathens, as racially and culturally different from Europeans, and as people lacking legal rights; they were prime candidates for enslavement.

Portugal was the first European nation to become involved in slavery in the Atlantic world. Voyages sponsored by Prince Henry the Navigator raided the West African coast in the 1440s. These ventures brought black Africans to Portugal. The trade then became transformed into a peaceful traffic in acquiring slaves from African chieftains, mainly in Mauretania and Upper Guinea. Some of these slaves were absorbed into Portuguese society, especially in Lisbon, but many were re-exported to Spain. Papal blessing was given to this traffic in a bull of 1442, which proclaimed that enslaving Africans fell within the limits of a 'just war'. This was extended in a further edict of 1452 which gave Portugal the right to enslave captives taken in such a war. After news of Columbus's discovery of America reached the Iberian peninsula, Portugal moved swiftly to protect its burgeoning maritime interests in the Atlantic world. At the Treaty of Tordesillas, signed in northern Spain in 1494, Portugal claimed the right to possessions south and east of a line 270 leagues west of the Azores while Castile reserved the right to claim dominion north and west of the line. This was a definitive turning point in determining which possessions in the New World would be Spanish-speaking and which would claim Portuguese as their mother tongue. The treaty also made Africa a commercial sphere of the Portuguese. In Gambia and along the Gold Cost the Portuguese built forts to protect their presence in West Africa, where they traded in gold and slaves.

During the sixteenth century, the Portuguese shipped African slaves to several of their Atlantic island possessions—to the Azores, Madeira, the Cape Verde archipelago, and Príncipe and São Tomé, in the Gulf of Guinea. Each of these destinations employed slaves in sugar or cotton production and each served as an entrepôt for reshipment of slaves to Brazil. Portugal gained a claim to Brazil in 1500 through the arrival there of the explorer Pedro Alvares Cabral. The Portuguese thereafter dispatched settlers to Pernambuco, in north-east Brazil, via a system of land grants. Settlement soon extended throughout Bahia. The first African slaves were introduced to Brazil in 1538. Between 1551 and 1650 around 250,000 slaves arrived in Brazil. Salvador and Rio de Janeiro were the main ports of disembarkation. Most of the African slaves were employed in sugar production. By 1570 sixty sugar mills were in operation in Brazil. Having tried to use local Indian labour for sugar cultivation, Portuguese settlers found this was insufficient for their requirements; in addition, it was opposed by local Jesuit priests.

They therefore turned to African slaves as the main source of enforced labour.

Cane sugar can be cultivated only in tropical or semi-tropical conditions. Though it was grown in Cyprus and the Iberian peninsula in the medieval period, it was a marginal crop. It had not penetrated European consumer markets to any great degree before the end of the Middle Ages, which is why archaeological findings of teeth from cemeteries of that era rarely show signs of tooth decay arising from sugar consumption. During the sixteenth century, however, the growth of sugar production in Portugal's Atlantic islands demonstrated that there was an extensive market for sugar as a sweetener for food and beverages. Moreover, sugar could be imported in substantial quantity at prices that generally yielded good profits; it was a staple crop that had a high price elasticity of demand. Sugar required a warm climate, plenty of land, access to water, and a large workforce capable of undertaking the arduous tasks associated with planting and harvesting this crop. It was essential that a full working complement was available to carry out these tasks. It was also vital that this workforce was disciplined and productive. African slaves proved the most cost-effective way of providing such a large workforce to toil in the cane fields.

Portugal's involvement with slavery became entangled with similar interests on the part of the Netherlands and Spain. Rivalry between the Dutch and the Portuguese had a significant effect on the slave trade to Brazil and slaveholding there. In 1630 the Dutch seized control of the area around Pernambuco. Fifteen years later they captured Angola, the main Portuguese slave exporting region in Africa. The Portuguese therefore shifted their acquisition of slaves to Mozambique. It was not until 1654 that the Portuguese drove the Dutch out of Brazil and reclaimed it as their own. Slavery in Brazil expanded from its initial base in sugar production to encompass a wide range of agricultural activities. Accordingly, slaves in Brazil were found in tobacco, cattle, coffee, and cotton production and as domestic and retail workers in ports and towns.

During the sixteenth century Spanish investors grew sugar in the Canary Islands but, more important, Spanish America became a major destination for disembarkation of African slaves. At the end of the fifteenth century the Spanish had begun to use Arawaks—one of the indigenous peoples of the West Indies—as slaves in the mining industry. But these gradually died out through contact with diseases spread from other continents and immunological zones—notably measles, smallpox, and various fevers. Arawak numbers had been decimated by the end of the sixteenth century. Other indigenous groups in the Caribbean, notably the Caribs, proved adept at resisting Spanish authority or they converted to Christianity, which excluded them from enslavement. The Spanish therefore increasingly turned to enslaved Africans to operate their mining and plantation enterprises in the New World. Slaves were used, just as indigenous workers had been, in silver, mercury, and gold mines and on sugar and cacao plantations. By 1550 sugar production in Hispanic America was located in three areas of Cuba—around Havana, Bayamo and Santiago de Cuba; on the southern shores of Hispaniola; and in Puerto Rico.

The first African slaves taken to Spanish America arrived on a Portuguese vessel in 1502. To promote the slave trade, the Emperor Charles V of Spain instigated the system of the *asiento* in 1521. This legalized the shipment of slaves to Spanish America under a royal licence. After the union of the Portuguese and Spanish crowns in 1580 the Portuguese dominated this system until they revolted against Spanish rule in 1640. The pull of sugar cultivation, the mining of gold, and the operation of the *asiento* enabled slavery to flourish in Spanish America. Between 1551 and 1650 the Spanish colonies received about 190,000 slaves and thousands of additional smuggled slaves. The main ports of slave disembarkation in Spanish America were Cartagena, Veracruz, and Buenos Aires. Cartagena supplied slaves to Peru, Venezuela, and Colombia. Veracruz channelled Africans into Mexico. Buenos Aires, the main port for slave arrivals in mainland Spanish America, supplied Africans for labour mainly in its own hinterland.

England and France coveted the colonial wealth of Spain, but the English were swifter to exploit the possibilities of slave labour than the French. English privateering vessels engaged in repeated acts of plunder on the Spanish treasure fleets in the late sixteenth and early seventeenth centuries. Such ventures identified weaknesses in the Spanish shipment of precious goods to Europe, and made English venturers acquainted with the lucre attached to the sale of those commodities. It was only a matter of time before colonies were added to trading voyages to consolidate England's position in the Atlantic maritime world. Between the 1580s and the 1630s, but especially after the start of the seventeenth century, England set up colonies in the West Indies and in North America. Some of these possessions lay in the tropics. The English, for example, settled colonies in St Kitts (1624), Barbados (1627), Nevis (1628), and Montserrat and Antigua in the 1630s. These were intended to offer opportunities for white settlers and workers; only several decades later were they dominated, in terms of demography and work, by black slaves. French colonies in the Caribbean also made use of African slave workers in the seventeenth century, though by 1700 they had imported less than two-thirds of the number of Africans arriving in the English colonies by that date.

The reasons why slavery, based on the transatlantic shipment of Africans, then escalated significantly in the English colonies are treated in Chapter 1 below. This introductory discussion has established, however, that slavery, the production of tropical crops on plantations, and a thriving slave trade all had precedents in the Americas, primarily in the Spanish and Portuguese colonies, long before the English and French became involved in these colonial enterprises in a substantial way. The deployment of slave labour in the New World was thus intricately connected to rival ambitions among western maritime powers to exploit the agricultural and mineral resources of the New World. But slavery itself and the existence of slave markets can be traced back even further in history to ancient and medieval times. Slavery and the slave trade, as David Brion Davis has shown, were deeply embedded in western culture for well over a millennium before the transatlantic phase of slavery began in earnest. Thus the developments discussed in this book are later forms of the enforced migration of people across national boundaries over long distances to bondage in a different setting.

# 1

# Slavery and the Slave Trade

Slavery and the slave trade in the British Empire resulted from the English settlement of colonies in the Americas during the seventeenth and eighteenth centuries and the use of the enslaved as the main large-scale labour force in most of those territories. During the sixteenth century, English curiosity about the New World stimulated voyages of exploration by John Cabot, Sir Francis Drake, Sir John Hawkins, and others. Defeat of the Spanish Armada in 1588 paved the way for English colonization of the Americas by destroying Spanish naval dominance. English merchants benefiting from the price rises of the sixteenth century formed joint-stock trading companies in the hope of tapping wealth from overseas, notably from the Atlantic world. A greater degree of geographical mobility in England arising partly from a search for better work opportunities, the lure of new territories as a magnet for those wishing to improve their material standards, and serious religious divisions, mainly within Protestantism, provided motives for English people to migrate to the colonies in the Stuart era. Settlers from the mother country went to North America and the Caribbean in their thousands as colonization underwent decades of experimentation. By the end of the seventeenth century around 350,000 English people had crossed the Atlantic. Most settled in the colonies and forged new lives and communities there; relatively few returned home permanently.

## ENGLISH COLONIES IN THE NEW WORLD AND SLAVERY

Before the Civil War, English colonies were scattered along the eastern seaboard of North America and throughout the Caribbean. The main English West Indian settlements were Barbados and the Leeward Islands of Antigua, Nevis, and St Kitts. The chief North American colonies were Virginia, Maryland, and Massachusetts Bay. In 1655 Oliver Cromwell's expeditionary force captured Jamaica—held by Spain since the early sixteenth century—in a well-planned attack known as the Western Design. Jamaica was easily the largest West Indian island to come into British possession. After the restoration of the Stuart monarchy, England settled proprietary colonies in Carolina, East and West Jersey, and Pennsylvania. Colonies also thrived in New England (Massachusetts, Rhode Island, New Hampshire, Connecticut, Maine) and Newfoundland. Except for Newfoundland, slave labour was eventually used in all of these colonies. The concentration of slaves, however, was much greater in the colonies based on plantation labour throughout the Caribbean and south of Pennsylvania on the North American mainland than in settlements north of the Mason–Dixon line.

A scattering of territories was permanently added to Britain's Atlantic empire in the eighteenth century. On the North American mainland Georgia was chartered in 1732 under trustees who wished to establish a haven for debtors from British prisons and for Protestant refugees from continental Europe. Georgia was originally settled as a free colony but by 1750 it permitted the introduction of slavery. In the Caribbean four islands—Grenada, Dominica, St Vincent, and Tobago—were ceded to the British at the Treaty of Paris that concluded the Seven Years War in 1763. All came to embrace slavery. In the same peace treaty New France was ceded to Britain by France, and Florida was ceded to Britain by Spain; Vermont also became a British possession. By 1776 Britain's Atlantic empire comprised thirteen colonies in North America, the Canadian territories of Newfoundland, Ontario, Quebec, Labrador, and Nova Scotia, the Hudson's Bay territory, Bermuda, and a cluster of Caribbean islands. There was also, of course, another part of the British Empire in the East, primarily in Bengal. During the wars with revolutionary and Napoleonic France Britain acquired more colonies that had slave labour. Trinidad was taken from the Spanish in 1797 and ceded to Britain in the Peace of Amiens in 1802. Demerara-Essequibo and Berbice, on the 'wild' coast of north-west South America, were captured from the Dutch in 1802.

Additional British colonies with slaves were situated in the south Atlantic and Indian oceans. The tiny island outpost of St Helena had a small slave labour force supplied by East India Company vessels. The occupation of the Dutch settlement at the Cape of Good Hope in 1795 brought with it an existing slave labour force of Cape coloured people and servile Khoisan labourers (what used to be termed 'Hottentots').

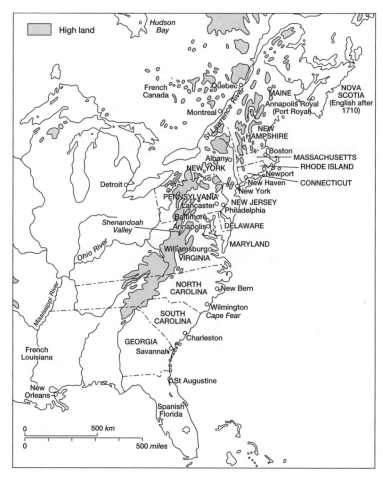

**Map 1.** North America in 1750.

The Cape Colony was returned to the Dutch in 1803, according to terms set down in the Treaty of Amiens, but Britain recaptured it in 1806. Britain's retention of the Cape Colony at the Vienna Settlement after the end of the Napoleonic Wars (1815) absorbed these slaves into the British Empire. The British conquest of the French island of Mauritius in 1810 also meant the acquisition of an existing slave labour force. British annexation of the Seychelles in the same year added to the enslaved people living in the British Empire. Slavery had flourished in

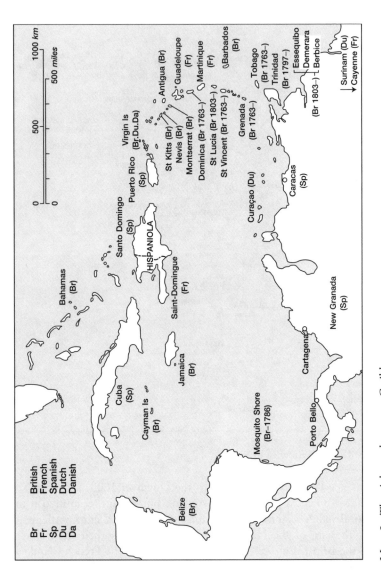

Map 2. The eighteenth-century Caribbean.

Br British
Fr French
Sp Spanish
Du Dutch
Da Danish

Belize (Br)

Bahamas (Br)

Cuba (Sp)

Cayman Is (Br)

Jamaica (Br)

Mosquito Shore (Br–1786)

Porto Bello

Cartagena

New Granada (Sp)

Santo Domingo (Sp)

HISPANIOLA

Saint-Domingue (Fr)

Puerto Rico (Sp)

Virgin Is (Br, Du, Da)

St Kitts (Br)
Nevis (Br)
Montserrat (Br)
Dominica (Br 1763–)
St Lucia (Br 1803–)
St Vincent (Br 1763–)

Antigua (Br)
Guadeloupe (Fr)
Martinique (Fr)

Barbados (Br)

Grenada (Br 1763–)

Curaçao (Du)

Caracas (Sp)

Tobago (Br 1763–)
Trinidad (Br 1797–)

Essequibo (Du)
Demerara (Br 1803–)
Berbice

Surinam (Du)
Cayenne (Fr)

1000 km
500 miles
0    500

India for centuries, though it involved the use of slaves in the military and in trade and administration rather than plantation labour. The British occupation of Bengal therefore included slavery in its midst. When the Nepalese state was formed in the late eighteenth century, slavery was a long-established custom. In the 1780s Lord Cornwallis, writing from Calcutta, stated that 'hardly a man or woman exists in a corner of this populous town who hath not at least one slave child. . . most of them were stolen from their parents or bought for perhaps a measure of rice, in time of scarcity.'[1]

## PLANTATION LABOUR AND THE GROWTH OF THE BRITISH SLAVE TRADE

By the mid-seventeenth century the colonies were regarded as markets for manufactured goods and sources of raw materials for the mother country; they absorbed labour and capital and were a source of profits for Britain. By exploiting available land to produce staple commodities, investors in the colonies sought to make good returns. To do so, they needed to organize agricultural plantations to maximize output: this was the most efficient way of achieving gains from abundant land in the Americas. But a large labour force was needed to work on plantations. Attempts to persuade or coerce Native Americans to carry out the work largely failed: they proved poor workers and either resisted such regimes or died out before 1650 through contact with diseases imported from across the ocean. White workers, mainly in the form of indentured servants, could also form the workforce for plantations. However, they were not a permanent solution to the labour problem. They became independent at the end of their usual term of service (typically, four, five, or seven years). Possession of legal rights enabled them to negotiate their contractual position in local courts. Moreover, their supply dwindled in the late seventeenth century, when the English population underwent a static period and economic conditions improved at home.

The next alternative labour supply proved the solution to planters' needs. This lay with the growth of the transatlantic slave trade. The origins of this traffic stemmed from 1444, when the Portuguese landed a cargo of Africans near Lagos on the Algarve. It lasted until the 1880s

---

[1] Quoted in Marina Carter, 'Slavery and Unfree Labour in the Indian Ocean', *History Compass*, 4 (2006), 802.

when Brazilian and Cuban slavery collapsed. For over four centuries several European trading powers had a flourishing slave trade. The total number of captives shipped via the slave trade is still disputed, but most modern historians suggest that around 12 million enslaved Africans crossed the Atlantic in the entire period of the slave trade. English merchants followed the Spanish, Portuguese, Dutch, and French in shipping large numbers of enslaved Africans across the Atlantic, and put them to work as a captive labour force on plantations. Though it was not essential to have slaves to cultivate staple crops, African captives working on plantations constituted the workforce that sustained colonial trade with large parts of Europe in the early modern period. Indeed, it could be argued that enduring and firm trade links between Europe and the Americas were not forged until slavery was introduced in the New World.

The slave trade operated on a triangular basis, with 'legs' of the voyage stretching from British ports to West Africa, from the African coast to the eastern shores of North America and the West Indies, and from the Americas back to Britain. Chapter 3 analyses the operation of this trade in detail. The trade was extensive, forming part of the largest intercontinental enforced migration known in world history before 1800. Between 1662 and 1807—the main period in which the British slave trade flourished—slave exports from Africa in British and British-colonial ships amounted to nearly 3.3 million people. Down to *c.*1760 there was a significant rise in the annual shipping of slaves in British vessels. Shipments of slaves from Africa were 6,700 per year in the period 1662–70. They multiplied sixfold to reach an annual figure of 42,000 in the 1760s before falling—with marked short-term fluctuations during wartime—thereafter. Bryan Edwards, the planter-historian of the British West Indies, pointed out in the late eighteenth century that the peak years of the British slave trade lay in the quarter century before the American Revolution. During those years more Africans were shipped across the Atlantic by British and British-colonial ships than were taken by any other national carrier. The second largest slave trade of the time was the Portuguese traffic operated by Luso-Brazilians from Angola to Brazil.

The eighteenth century witnessed the heyday of the British slave trade and a rapid upsurge in the number of enslaved Africans in North America and the Caribbean. During that period vessels fitted out primarily in Liverpool, London, Bristol, and Newport, Rhode Island—the major slaving port in North America—took around 3 million slaves from

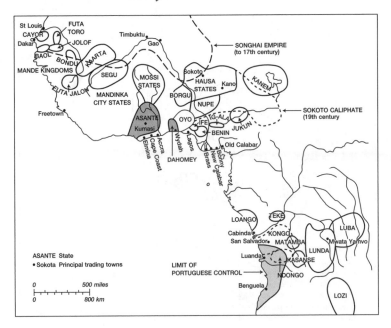

**Map 3.** The major slave-trading regions of Africa.

seven areas: Senegambia, Sierra Leone, the Windward Coast, the Gold Coast, the Bight of Benin, the Bight of Biafra, and West-central Africa. These areas covered between 3,000 and 4,000 miles of the African coast stretching from the River Senegal in the north, flowing into the Atlantic at Saint-Louis, down to Benguela in the south. Slaves were not acquired above Senegambia because the terrain was either the Sahara desert or controlled by Moroccans. Though slaves could be gathered south of Angola as far down as the Cape of Good Hope, this was usually impracticable given the distance and costs from Britain. In any case, sufficient slaves could always be acquired by British slave traders without having to sail that far south in the Atlantic. None of the African areas or polities with which Britain traded were under British sovereignty: there were no British colonies in Africa until the crown colonies of Senegambia (1763–83) and Sierra Leone (1808 onwards) were established. Nor did any other European trading powers own stretches of the African coast. This meant that the West African coast was a 'free' trading zone where European trading powers competed without having to infringe the territorial rights of their white counterparts.

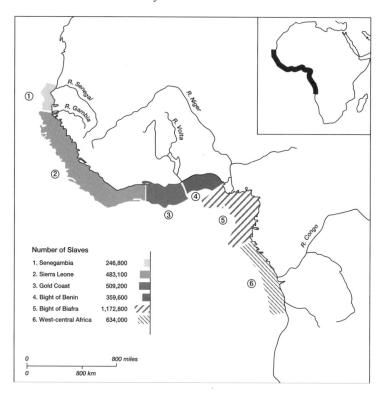

**Map 4.** Shipment of slaves from West Africa in British Empire ships, 1662–1807.

The proportion of slaves taken from each African area varied over time owing to complex patterns of supply and demand, but overall far more slaves were taken from the Bight of Biafra to British America than from any other African region. British vessels took around 1,172,800 slaves—nearly 26 per cent of the total—from that part of Africa between 1662 and 1807. This is remarkable given that the Bight of Biafra was a notoriously unhealthy region for slave mortality. Its ascendancy in the British slave trade owes much to the flourishing internal markets for slaves in the interior of that part of modern Nigeria and the close trading relationships between British merchants, their captains, African middlemen, and other traders in Bonny, Old Calabar, and New Calabar. The second most important area of provenance for enslaved Africans entering the British slave trade was West-central Africa, which provided 634,000 captives between 1662 and 1807. The other main areas for British slave trading in West Africa, in descending order of importance, were the Gold Coast, Sierra Leone, the Windward Coast, the Bight of Benin, and Senegambia.

Most slaves ended up in the Caribbean rather than North America. For instance, in the 1720s only 24,000 (15.8 per cent) out of an estimated total of 152,000 slaves arriving in British America came to the mainland colonies. In the period 1766–75 a similar situation prevailed. Some 36,800 Africans (13.1 per cent) of the 279,000 that came to British American territories entered the southern mainland colonies. South Carolina, Virginia, Maryland, and Georgia, in descending order, were the main destinations for slaves taken by British ships to North America. At all these destinations most slaves were put to work on plantations. These were usually tobacco estates in the Chesapeake and rice plantations in the Lowcountry, though by the middle of the eighteenth century some slaves in Virginia were deployed in grain production and some blacks in South Carolina were employed in cultivating indigo. Before 1700 Barbados claimed most Africans among the British Caribbean islands. But thereafter Jamaica became the single most important destination for slaves taken by British vessels to the West Indies. It was the largest English territory in the Caribbean and its sugar plantation sector expanded considerably during the eighteenth century. After Jamaica became the main disembarkation point for slaves carried by British vessels to the West Indies, Barbados, the Leeward Islands, and the Ceded Islands jostled for second place and shifts occurred over time in their importance as slave markets. Most slaves disembarked in the British Caribbean were bought for work on sugar plantations, though some were deployed on livestock pens, in the retail sector in towns and ports, and, after the Seven Years War, in the newly developed coffee plantations.

The large number of slave arrivals in the Caribbean reflected the backbreaking work, wide range of diseases, and high mortality rate among black workers in that region and the consequent need to replenish the black population regularly through new imports. Depletion rates were such that imports of new Africans always exceeded the growth of the 'seasoned' black population (i.e. those Africans that had survived the Middle Passage for two or three years). The smaller number of slaves taken to North America resulted from a more uneven distribution of regional slave labour than in the West Indies and from lesser demands in the Chesapeake for a large plantation workforce than in the Caribbean.

Smaller imports of Africans into North America compared with the Caribbean also stemmed from an earlier and greater concentration of creole (i.e. American-born) slaves in North America than in the West Indies. Chapter 4 analyses these demographic contrasts between the black population in North America and the West Indies.

## REGIONAL VARIATIONS IN THE DISTRIBUTION OF SLAVES

Slave labour was found in all the British North American colonies from Maine to South Carolina in the late seventeenth century, but it was more important in some than others. Broadly speaking, the proportion of African-Americans in a colony's population increased as one moved from north to south, with most slaves clustered south of the Delaware Valley. In 1750, for instance, 210,400 (86.9 per cent) of the 242,100 slaves in North America lived in the Chesapeake and Lower South. On the eve of the American War of Independence less than 3 per cent of the New England population and less than 8 per cent of the Middle colonies' population was black. On the other hand, by 1740 African-Americans comprised 28 per cent of the Upper South's population and 46 per cent of the Lower South's. By 1780 the black share of the Chesapeake population had increased to 39 per cent, while the African-American element in the Carolinas and Georgia had slightly declined to 41 per cent. From 1710 until *c*.1755 South Carolina was the only British North American colony with a black majority; thereafter Georgia also exhibited this pattern.

These figures nevertheless conceal variations within regions. There were parts of individual colonies where slavery was more significant than in the colony as a whole. In New England more slaves were found in Rhode Island than in any other colony. This was connected to Newport's role in the slave trade and to the mixed economy of the Narragansett region around Newport and Providence: blacks were sometimes brought back via the West Indies on Rhode Island slaving vessels and employed in stock farming and dairying. A Rhode Island census of 1774 indicated that 14 per cent of households in the colony owned slaves. In the Middle Colonies, slaves were mainly clustered in the Hudson River valley, in parts of eastern New Jersey, and the two port cities of Philadelphia and New York, where they were employed in agriculture, at ironworks, in urban trades, and as domestic servants.

By the 1750s about 70 per cent of the wealthier craftsmen in the Quaker city owned slaves. In prosperous, tobacco-growing areas of the Chesapeake more than half the population had slaves by the 1760s. In South Carolina, the black majority was particularly evident in some rural areas in the rice-dominated Lowcountry where blacks could outnumber whites by two to one.

These variations suggest that slavery had a distinctive impact on different areas of North America in the eighteenth century. Most parts of the northern colonies were slaveowning societies while the southern colonies were slave societies. The work, culture and treatment of slaves varied partly on the basis of this concentration of blacks in a colony, town, county, or parish. But the black experience of slavery also changed over time. Ira Berlin has suggested that the seventeenth-century black experience was a 'charter generation' in North America, characterized by the emergence of Atlantic creole communities, where blacks worked reasonably harmoniously alongside whites and were not subject to degradation. This was followed in the period 1700–75 by the 'plantation generation' where racial lines hardened as the staple economies absorbed ever more numbers of enslaved blacks. After 1775 came the 'revolutionary generation' in which slavery and the growth of free black communities took divergent paths in various North American regions.

The British Caribbean was dominated more thoroughly by slaves than the whole of mainland North America. Before 1670 whites exceeded blacks among the people living in the British West Indies but thereafter, once the sugar boom was under way, the boost in Africans imported tilted the balance of the population the other way. By 1700 some 115,000 blacks lived among a British Caribbean population of 148,000. Eighty years later the proportion of blacks in that population had mushroomed: there were then 489,000 slaves and only 48,000 whites. By 1830 the British West Indian population amounted to 684,996 slaves, 102,980 free blacks, and 54,772 white people. Virtually all the sugar islands in the Caribbean comprised populations that were over 90 per cent black. In smaller British territories, where maritime crafts or livestock rearing rather than sugar plantations absorbed most enslaved labour, there were relatively small black populations. The Bahamas, Turks and Caicos Islands, Anguilla, Tortola, and Barbuda are examples of such colonies. The density of population was striking in the smaller West Indian islands dominated by sugar cultivation. By *c.*1834 the number of slaves per square mile amounted to 500 in Barbados, 260 in both Antigua and St Kitts, and 245 in Nevis.

India undoubtedly had the largest number of slaves in British imperial territories. In 1841 Sir Bartle Frere estimated that the slave population of India amounted to between 8 and 9 million. Many of these were agrestic slaves, that is, those who were attached to the land. But there were also many thousands of domestic slaves. The latter were compelled to be chosen from the highest caste of Hindus in order to safeguard their owners' purity. The slaveowning elites, needless to say, came from the highest castes. The number of slaves in islands acquired by Britain in the Indian Ocean were considerably smaller than in India or the Caribbean. The Seychelles had about 7,200 slaves in 1826. The slave population of Mauritius in 1832 amounted to 62,000. In 1830 in the Cape Colony there were nearly 34,000 slaves compared with 59,000 white settlers; but there were also another 42,000 people, mainly Khoisan, who worked in conditions approximating slavery. St Helena, a tiny island outpost mainly visited by East India Company vessels, had only around 2,000 natives (including slaves) in 1812.

## THE FAILURE OF NATIVE AMERICANS AND INDENTURED SERVANTS AS PLANTATION LABOURERS

Indentured servitude and slavery predominated as labour institutions in those parts of seventeenth-century British America dominated by staple crop production on plantations. Though bonded servants and slaves could be found in New England and the Middle Colonies, they were neither so numerous nor so important for labour there as in the southern colonies or the early British Caribbean. But in the Chesapeake region, where tobacco production flourished from the 1620s, and in the Lower South, where rice cultivation predominated from the 1690s, and Barbados, where sugar cultivation began in earnest in the 1640s, both servants and slaves were extensively used. Moreover, in the southern colonies and Barbados a transition occurred from indentured white servants to slaves as the chief type of agricultural labourers. The timing of the transition from one mode of labour to another differed in particular colonies, something that will be discussed below. But throughout the southern mainland and West Indian colonies the evolution of the labour market was closely tied to the need to maintain production levels in staple crops. Planters thereby could make profits and supply European markets with commodities such as sugar, tobacco, and rice that were increasingly in demand there. Tobacco was a luxury product that was processed in Europe into snuff or cut or roll tobacco for pipe-smoking. Rice served as a substitute commodity for basic food requirements when grain harvests were poor in the Iberian peninsula and northern Europe. Sugar consumption catered to the growing demand for sweeteners for tea and cooking purposes.

The initial choices available to English settlers to work the land in the plantation colonies consisted either in using white workers or in engaging or coercing Indian labour. The latter option was explored but proved unsuccessful. This was not because there were few Indians to exploit; quite the opposite in the early seventeenth century. It is possible that nearly a million Native Americans lived east of the Mississippi River on the eve of permanent English settlement. The number in Virginia at this time could have been anything between 14,000 and 170,000, depending on whose estimates one follows. Whatever the numbers, the Indian presence in tidewater Virginia was of long duration by the 1620s; at that time the Powhatan Confederacy in that area embraced about thirty groups of Indians. English settlers and Indians attempted to mediate the cultural gap between themselves by reciprocity over economic matters. But white settlers also tried to co-opt Indian labour for agricultural production. This failed miserably for three main reasons: cultural differences, disease, and conflict.

Native American ways of settlement and land cultivation proved inimical for the sort of agricultural production needed by whites in the Chesapeake. The Indians undertook subsistence agriculture and had their own rules about the use of land and natural resources, but these were different from English conceptions of property in land. Gatherers of beaver, wild turkey, deer, and wampum from forests in hunting territories, and experienced catchers of fish at the water's edge, Native Americans were totally unused to the sort of labour required on plantations. In addition, their knowledge of the terrain meant that it would be difficult to contain them under such a system of land and crop cultivation. There was also a severe demographic problem. Epidemics occurred from time to time in which large numbers of Native Americans were devastated by tuberculosis, pneumonia, influenza, plague, measles, scarlet fever, smallpox, and malaria—diseases that were partly the result of contact with people from a different disease environment. Many English settlers had experienced these ailments as children before crossing the Atlantic Ocean and were thus immune to them; but native communities were swiftly decimated by contact with carriers of these diseases. The spread of disease through contact with Europeans had a similar but even more devastating impact on the native Caribs of the West Indies.

The most important reason why Europeans could not coerce Native Americans to work permanently lay in the white man's view of them as uncivilized savages controlling land that was ripe for the picking. White settlers regarded themselves as culturally superior and saw the land as freely available. Native American resistance to white encroachments spilled over into violent encounters on several occasions in the seventeenth-century Chesapeake. Powhatan risings against the settlers in Virginia were suppressed in 1622 and 1644. A peace treaty was signed in October 1646. The tribes remained weak in Virginia for the next thirty years. In 1676, however, some Native Americans took up arms against the English in Bacon's rebellion. Nathaniel Bacon, the organizer of the uprising, ordered his forces to kill some captured Occaneechees and to murder a group of Susquehannocks. Elsewhere in North America there were similar violent conflicts between Native Americans and white settlers, notably in the Pequot war (1636–7) and King Philip's War (1675–6) in New England. Armed conflict did not stop all trade and exchange between Native Americans and English settlers but it signalled the failure of policies to subjugate Native Americans to the white man's dominance. There were, of course, exceptions. In 1708, for instance, some 1,400 Native Americans were held in bondage by South Carolina planters; they constituted about one-third of the colony's population and had been mainly rounded up from conflicts between Native American groups in the south-east. One can also find occasional Native American workers on Chesapeake tobacco plantations. Nevertheless, Native American slavery declined in the Palmetto province from the early eighteenth century onwards, and few Native Americans could be found on Chesapeake tobacco estates by the same period.

James Axtell has raised some counterfactual speculations about how the development of British North America would have differed if there had been no natives. In particular, he has suggested that black slavery would have spread more quickly in the Chesapeake and would have been more difficult to regulate without the presence of Native Americans. Thus a Colonial America without them would have precipitated an earlier use of black slave labour in the Chesapeake because it took time for white settlers to find that enslaving Native Americans did not work. With virgin land available at cheap prices, this counterfactual scenario implies that settlers would have bought land more easily, enabling them to pay for more enslaved Africans. At the same time, without Native Americans surrounding the border areas of plantations, it would have been more difficult for whites to keep the black population in check, for there would be no Native American slave catchers. These speculations remind us that recourse to black slave labour *en masse* in the seventeenth-century Chesapeake was not the first solution to a labour shortage that settlers looked for or thought feasible.

## ENSLAVING AFRICANS

The first shipment of blacks to British America arrived in Virginia in 1619. 'About the latter end of August, a Dutch man of Warr of the burden of a 160 tuñes' arrived at Point Comfort, on the Virginia capes, and 'brought not any thing but 20 and odd Negroes', which were bought by the governor of Virginia and a Cape merchant.[2] This statement has for long been accepted as indicating the first arrival of blacks in North America, but it is now known that thirty-two Africans were recorded in a census in Virginia five months before the arrival of this cargo, and that these 'founders' of black life in North America were taken from a Portuguese vessel bound from Angola to Vera Cruz. These shipments did not lead quickly to large shipments of Africans to English territories across the Atlantic. Before 1660 the number of Africans in the North American population was relatively small. Indeed, in that period most slaves taken on English vessels were sent to Barbados; the total number shipped was probably about 10,000. After the restoration of the Stuart monarchy, the slave trade grew rapidly. Down to 1698, the trade lay mainly in the hands of the Company of Royal Adventurers Trading into Africa (1660–72) and the Royal African Company (established in 1672), though there were interloping private traders, too. After 1698 an Act of Parliament ended the monopoly of the chartered trading organizations to Africa and opened the slave trade to private merchants. However the trade was conducted, it was regarded, not entirely accurately, as a bonanza. Thus the English writer on trade John Cary, in a classic

---

[2] John Rolfe to Sir Edwin Sandys, ? Jan. 1619, quoted in Susan Myra Kingsbury (ed.), *The Records of the Virginia Company of London*, 4 vols. (Washington DC, 1933), iii. 243.

mercantilist text, waxed enthusiastically about the Guinea traffic as 'a Trade of the most Advantage to this Kingdom of any we drive'.[3]

The large-scale adoption of slave labour owed much to the growth of the English slave trade after 1660. But it was not simply a more regular supply of enslaved Africans that began the racial transformation of the North American and West Indian population. Social and cultural reasons for enslaving Africans also assumed significance. English attitudes towards Africans in the seventeenth century partly reflected a widespread ethnocentrism and xenophobia towards 'others'. Some Englishmen regarded Jews with suspicion and they frequently regarded Irish Catholics and Scottish Highlanders with hostility or downright hatred. And yet none of these groups were enslaved. Thus the other cultural reason for the enslavement of Africans was something more than just ethnocentrism: it consisted of racial prejudice towards black Africans. Blackness, in terms of skin colour, had negative connotations for not just the British but many Europeans in the early modern era (though these associations were probably less marked in Portugal and Spain where there had been a longer tradition of regular contact with African people). Blackness, for Stuart Englishmen, suggested connections with the Devil. A leading English imperialist of the early seventeenth century, intimately involved with the Virginia colony, summarized this view. 'Negroes in Africa', wrote Captain John Smith, 'bee as idle and as devilish people as any in the world.'[4] Africans were also associated with Noah's curse on the son of Ham. George Sandys, an official of the Virginia Company, noted that African slaves were 'descended of Chus, the sonne of the cursed Cam; as are all of that complexion.'[5] Africans were known to be heathens, something that made them seem barbaric to many western Europeans. They were feared for their lust and savagery. Africans were singled out for their sheer difference from Europeans—in their physiognomy, gestures, languages, dress, and behaviour. Together, an amalgam of negative attitudes emerged that constituted racial prejudice towards Africans.

Such attitudes were underpinned by the widespread tolerance of slavery by Europeans in the seventeenth century. European trading

---

[3] John Cary, *Essay on the State of England in relation to its Trade, its Poor and its Taxes, for carrying on the Present war against France* (London, 1695), 74.

[4] Philip L. Barbour (ed.), *The Complete Works of Captain John Smith [1580–1631]*, 3 vols. (Chapel Hill, NC, 1986), iii. 294.

[5] George Sandys, *A Relation of a Journey Begun An: Dom: 1610*, 2nd edn. (London, 1621), 136.

nations with empires knew that slavery had existed in human societies since ancient times; that various passages in Scripture condoned the existence of slave societies; and that the educated classes widely accepted the practice of slavery. Though some dissenting voices were troubled about the moral implications of enslaving other people, notable European jurists such as Hugo Grotius and John Selden did not question the existence of slavery. Thus Grotius declared in *De Iure Belli et Pacis* (1625) that 'it is lawful for any man to engage himself as a Slave to whom he please; as appears in both the Hebrew and Roman Laws.'[6]

Two leading English philosophers of the late seventeenth century also accepted slavery as if it were a normal feature of society. Thomas Hobbes in *Leviathan* viewed slavery as part of the world's system of subordination and authority. For him, a system of law and power had partly replaced the divine order, and, within the new dispensation, slavery was a rational and harmonious component. John Locke, the philosopher of liberty, stressed the nature of contractual obligations between rulers and ruled, and the natural right of the ruled to withdraw their consent when governed in an unjust manner. But slaves were explicitly excluded from this contract theory, which is unsurprising because Locke was a shareholder in the Royal African Company. The reason why advocates of natural rights theories condoned enslavement appears to have lain in their acceptance of slavery as a flourishing African institution. Slaves were a major form of wealth in Africa and a large Islamic slave trade had flourished there for centuries before European merchants participated in the traffic. In other words, European intellectuals could have a clear conscience about slave trading because Africans had already bartered away their liberty before they came into the hands of ship captains on the West African coast.

Negative perceptions of black Africans coupled with a virtually non-existent antislavery posture created the cultural outlook whereby European traders and New World settlers were morally untroubled in enslaving black human beings. But another aspect of the general matrix of white racial superiority should also be added. This was the importance of freedom in English society and the lack of examples of permanent bondage found therein. Englishmen prided themselves on the fact that they were free-born people with legal rights at common law. Even indentured servants, despite their lowly status,

---

[6] Quoted in Robin Blackburn, *The Making of New World Slavery: From the Baroque to the Modern 1492–1800* (London, 1997), 193.

had access to the law courts and hence the means to challenge any treatment of them that they considered unlawful. Evidence from the seventeenth-century Chesapeake indicates that their rights were often upheld in courts when they were in dispute with their masters. There was no tradition of permanent bondage in English society, nothing equivalent to the serfdom that was deeply embedded in Russia and other eastern European societies for centuries. Serfdom, of course, was an enforced labour system like slavery, though it was not so frequently tied to large agricultural holdings. The fact that neither serfdom nor slavery flourished on English soil meant that bonded labour at home avoided chattel status and the concomitant absence of legal rights.

Englishmen's attitudes towards black Africans and slavery underpinned the acceptance of slaveholding in the seventeenth-century Chesapeake, Carolinas, and Caribbean. Merchants and ship captains treated slaves as if they were commodities to sell. Cultural superiority and the heathen nature of many Africans made the enslavement of Africans untroubling for Europeans before the growth of antislavery sentiment during the Enlightenment. During the sixteenth century the Portuguese and the Spanish had given vent to racial prejudice in their use of African labour in Central and South America. There was thus a long-standing discrimination against Africans before the English exploited slave labour. In addition, large European states that entered into trafficking in slaves all had strong centralized administrations and substantial military capacity. They frequently waged war against each in the early modern period, notably in religious wars on the Continent, but state centralization and military threats curtailed individual European powers from capturing and selling each other's subjects. Political factors perhaps were as important as cultural attitudes in explaining why European captives were not the solution to the large-scale labour problems of plantation America.

Whether racial prejudice preceded slavery in North America or whether it escalated when large numbers of Africans were imported regularly has led, however, to disagreement among historians. Some scholars consider that the cultural debasement of blacks explains their large-scale enslavement when the opportunity arose to do so via the English slave trade. In other words, racial prejudice was a sufficiently ingrained trait to justify shipping millions of Africans to the New World. This view supports Winthrop D. Jordan's notion of an 'unthinking decision' in enslaving Africans—something so deeply embedded in the traders that it operated at almost a subconscious level.[7] Other historians are not convinced that socio-cultural attitudes which singled out blacks for degradation are enough to explain the origins of American slavery. They point out that the treatment of blacks and their interaction with whites and Native Americans varied considerably over time. Recently, there has been emphasis on communities of Atlantic creoles, living in the port communities on Atlantic shores, sometimes in Africa, sometimes in the Americas. These black people, many of them Africans by origin, acted as trade and cultural brokers without great interference or debasement from whites. Only some Atlantic creoles ended up as slaves. They could be found along the shores of West Africa as well as in Atlantic ports such as Bridgetown, Kingston, Philadelphia, and Charleston. The social relations between Atlantic creoles and European traders and settlers were more flexible and humane than found in slave societies based on plantation labour.

## THE ORIGINS OF SLAVERY IN VIRGINIA

The origins of slavery in Virginia have long generated discussion. One line of interpretation suggests that racial prejudice was not an important factor in the treatment of slaves in the Chesapeake before 1660. The term 'slave' was used in a fluid fashion before that date to refer to Native Americans, mulattoes, and the servitude of white children as much as to Africans. Therefore it could be argued that slaves were treated as servants before the mid-seventeenth century and that chattel status of slaves, fastening them to hereditary bondage as the property of white people, only came thereafter with the rapid importation of slaves to Virginia and Maryland. A rider to this argument is that the legal status of chattel slaves arose only when tobacco planters attempted to attract voluntary white workers by debasing the condition of involuntary black labour. Only after that occurred was racial prejudice an important factor in treatment of the enslaved. Other historians argue, however, that racism existed from the moment that blacks stepped ashore in Virginia, and that the apparent worsening status of blacks as they became legally defined as chattels codified existing practices. Plenty of evidence shows that blacks were discriminated against in the Chesapeake

[7] Winthrop D. Jordan, *White over Black: American Attitudes toward the Negro, 1550–1812* (Chapel Hill, NC, 1968), ch. 2.

even when the word 'slave' was not used in documents. Others have suggested that the very fact that blacks in the Chesapeake were widely referred to as 'Negroes' set them apart from the white dependent class.

Defects in surviving documentation make it difficult to resolve these opposing viewpoints. From 1619 until about 1640, insufficient documentary material survives to state categorically whether slaves were treated as servants or not. In the twenty years after 1640, however, examples of the central feature of black slavery—hereditary lifetime service—can be found in Virginia. One legal case of 1641 and two official actions of 1656 demonstrated the deterioration of the black's position in the Old Dominion. But it was not until 1661 that perpetual bondage for blacks in Virginia received statutory recognition and not until 1669 that the Negro servant was designated as a chattel rather than as someone whose labour was just the property of his master. Rather than arguing that either chattel slave status increased the propensity for racism among white Virginians or that racial prejudice determined the treatment of Africans from 1619 onwards, it is probably more accurate to demonstrate the changing status of blacks as statutes codified white–black relationships more explicitly. It is hard to believe that racial attitudes did not play a significant part in enslaving Africans, just as it is difficult to accept that such views alone were sufficient to sustain the Atlantic slave trade. But to suggest that a widespread number of those who purchased slaves were necessarily imbued with a deep-seated racial prejudice, and that this was their predominant motive for acquiring enslaved black workers, cannot be proven. One also needs to investigate the economic opportunities and development of plantations in the southern American colonies to understand the widespread adoption of slave labour in British America.

## THE TRANSITION FROM SERVITUDE TO SLAVERY

The transition from servitude to slavery followed different trajectories in the British American colonies. This can be seen in the emergence of slavery in Barbados, Virginia, and South Carolina. The first blacks to reach Barbados came with some of the early settlers in 1627. Their status was determined in 1637 when the Governor and Council of the island ordered that '*Negroes* and *Indians*, that came here to be sold, should serve for life, unless a contract was made before to the contrary.'[8] During the 1630s, when experiments were made to find a viable staple crop for cultivation in Barbados, with tobacco and cotton being tried, English indentured servants mainly carried out the work. As with most British American colonies that later adopted large-scale slavery, therefore, the initial labour force used in Barbados was predominantly white rather than black.

This situation changed abruptly. In the early 1640s the beginnings of sugar cultivation in Barbados was accompanied by a swift changeover to the use of black slave labour for plantation work. This was not because a smaller supply of white indentured servants came to Barbados. Potential servants signed indentures for shorter periods of servitude in Barbados as news of the tough working regimes on Barbadian sugar plantations filtered back to England, but a decline in the supply of servants did not occur until the 1660s. Nor was the transition to black labour in Barbados the result of low slave prices, which rose from £16.5 per slave in 1640 to £27.7 in 1650. The use of slaves as the predominant labour force in Barbados was inextricably bound up with the swift emergence of sugar plantations on the island. Blacks were a majority of the population in Barbados by the 1650s, and accounted for almost 70 per cent of the total by 1680. What factors associated with sugar cultivation account for this rapid transition to slave labour in Barbados? It was not just elasticity of slave supply that was crucial but that the costs of coercing Africans into sugar cane cultivation were lower than attempting to discipline an unwilling white servant labour force to carry out the same tasks. In addition, sugar prices began rising in the early 1640s when tobacco prices stayed low and indigo prices declined drastically. Improved sugar prices, it seems, concentrated white Barbadians on the market production of sugar rather than alternative staple produce in the 1640s. They gave impetus to white Barbadians to secure a large African labour force for plantation work.

The transition from servitude to slavery in the Chesapeake occurred in the four decades between 1680 and 1720. In the 1680s an increased number of slaves became available to Virginia and Maryland, while the supply of indentured servants had already declined. During the 1690s blacks became the majority of arrivals among immigrants to the Chesapeake for the first time. Nevertheless, it still took a couple of decades for slavery to become prominent in that region. If one accepts

---

[8] Quoted in Jordan, *White over Black*, 66.

that slaveowning societies became transformed into slave societies when the black proportion of the population reached 20 per cent, then Virginia only made the transition by 1710 and Maryland by 1720. The regional distribution of slaves varied, however, within each colony. Generally in the tidewater areas, where the best-quality tobacco was produced, between 30 and 40 per cent of the population consisted of slaves at the beginning of the eighteenth century. Once the transition from white servants to slaves had occurred, further African arrivals and strong reproductive rates among the black population meant that the Chesapeake became ever-more committed to slavery: by 1750 some 40 per cent of the African-Americans in the thirteen British mainland colonies lived in that region.

Accounting for the transition from the predominant use of servant labour to the deployment of slave work in Virginia and Maryland during the late seventeenth and early eighteenth centuries is a complex matter. But several notions about how it occurred can be discarded. First, it is important to recognize that slave plantation labour was not vital to tobacco cultivation. Tobacco was a delicate crop that could be grown on small farms or quarters, often with a relatively small workforce of fewer than fifteen or twenty individuals. There were many small white farmers in Virginia cultivating tobacco. It was not necessary to grow the leaf on plantations. Slaves had no prior knowledge of tobacco cultivation from their home communities in Africa. Secondly, the suggestion that fewer workers were needed in the Chesapeake by the 1680s because mortality had declined in that region is also implausible: the drop in mortality levels had already occurred by the 1660s and immigrant workers were as much sought after in the 1680s as they had been earlier.

Some historians have argued that the transition from servitude to slavery in Virginia began just a few years after Bacon's Rebellion rocked the social fabric of white society, and that the demand for greater imports of blacks reflected fears in the Chesapeake about the white underclass. This contention is difficult to prove even though the social dissatisfaction that caused the revolt had hardly withered by the 1680s when tobacco prices were stagnant and economic depression hit the tobacco industry in Virginia and Maryland. A simpler reason for finding this argument unconvincing, however, is that the supply of indentured servants to the Chesapeake had dried up in the years immediately following the disturbance of the 1670s. Even if Virginia farmers and planters had wanted to continue purchasing white servants at that time, the number of indentured migrants was insufficient to meet their needs.

The most convincing explanation of the transition from servitude to slavery in the Chesapeake lies in the changing supply and demand situation for servants at this time and the increased availability of African slaves, obtainable in conditions of nearly perfect elasticity of supply. These related phenomena, it should be noted, did not exactly coincide in time. The availability of new indentured servants had tapered off significantly since 1660. It continued to decline until the late 1670s, when the flow became a trickle. Large importations of slaves to the Chesapeake began only in the 1680s—both directly from Africa and from the West Indies—but it was not until the first decade of the eighteenth century that the supply of Africans to Virginia and Maryland was regular. Thus the rise of slavery in the Chesapeake was a consequence, not a cause, of the decrease in the availability of white bonded labour.

The fall in the supply of white servants partly stemmed from changing social, economic, and demographic conditions in the mother country. English population growth was stagnant in the last half of the seventeenth century. Thus there was not so much pressure on subsistence levels as there had been among the labouring poor before the Stuart Restoration. Wages improved for ordinary workers and there was less geographic mobility among the English population. England produced 100,000 net emigrants in the 1640s, 100,000 in the 1660s, 40,000 in the 1680s, and 50,000 in the 1700s. In addition, pressures existed at home for the government to retain population in the late seventeenth century in order to improve agriculture and manufacturing with the aim of increasing the nation's prosperity. Indentured servants still crossed the ocean in the 1680s and 1690s. But by that period they had a wider choice of destination than had been the case earlier in the century. They could now settle in the Carolinas, East and West Jersey, and Pennsylvania. Their flow was augmented by a large influx of Irish servants and German redemptioners. This trend towards a wider range of American destinations for servants and a more heterogeneous ethnic mix continued after 1700, and was a major difference between the seventeenth- and eighteenth-century indentured migrants to British North America.

During the transition from servitude to slavery in the Chesapeake, comparative prices for both forms of labour played their part in determining planters' decisions to purchase unfree workers. This is not to reduce the switch from one form of labour to another to the level of price determinants only; that would be too reductionist an approach to the complex reasons for enslavement. Even so, purchasers acted in an economically rational manner. A fall in the supply of servants drove their price up. Whereas in Virginia and Maryland probate inventories slaves were valued at three times the price of white servants in the mid-1670s, the ratio fell to less than two to one by 1690. Low tobacco prices in the 1680s and 1690s meant that income for Chesapeake planters to purchase new labourers was tight. Indeed, it might be thought that stagnation in the tobacco industry between 1680 and 1715 would have deterred them from purchasing extra labourers, be they black or white. That this was not the case stemmed from the uneven regional impact of the depression along the tobacco coast: in tidewater localities producing good tobacco for European markets—areas such as the York and James River peninsulas in Virginia and Maryland's lower western shore—buying new slaves offered the prospects of better productivity and higher profits.

By 1690 servant prices were relatively high compared with slave prices (which were low in the 1680s because of a decline in sugar prices and sugar production in the Caribbean). Servants now usually had contracts only for four years (rather than seven earlier in the century) while slaves could be purchased for life and their offspring perpetuated through hereditary bondage. Thus it was not surprising that planters increasingly sought the use of slave labour even though there might have been doubts about the readiness of Africans to assimilate to new work routines and to prove, through work productivity, that they were in fact the better investment. The widespread purchase of enslaved Africans, in turn, was undoubtedly bolstered by the racial prejudice towards black people that we have already identified as part of white settlers' ethnocentrism. The shift from servant to slave labour in the Chesapeake involved a reallocation to some degree of tasks so that whites performed more skilled labour, often of a supervisory nature, and blacks did the unskilled work in the tobacco fields.

The transition from servitude to slavery in South Carolina occurred rapidly after rice production began to dominate the colony's economy after 1690. Founded in 1670 as a proprietary province, South Carolina's economy was based initially on grazing cattle and cutting lumber, with a mixed workforce of free white labourers, indentured servants, Native Americans, and some slaves. A fuller use of slave labour could have occurred at the outset of the colony's history: the Proprietors of South Carolina made slavery legal in order to attract settlers; and strong connections were soon struck up, in terms of trade and settlement, between South Carolina and Barbados, where slave plantation labour had been used for several decades before the Carolinas were settled by whites. A quick transition from a mixed economy and labour force to one based on black gang labour in the swampy Lowcountry proceeded rapidly after the successful cultivation of rice as an export staple crop at the turn of the eighteenth century. The shift from servitude to slavery in South Carolina was already evident by 1703. By 1721, when South Carolina became a royal colony, rice production had secured the rise of a class of wealthy planters, and black slaves dominated the colony's labour force. The slave population of South Carolina rose from 2,400 in 1700 to 5,000 in 1710 to 12,000 in 1720 and to 22,700 in 1730—roughly a doubling of numbers in every decade. As a new immigrant to the colony remarked in 1737, South Carolina seemed 'more like a negro country than like a country settled by white people'.[9]

Between the 1670s and the 1690s indentured servants were never as numerous in South Carolina as they had been earlier in Virginia and Maryland. The chief reason lay in the declining supply of such servants in the late seventeenth century as a result of stagnant population growth and better wages and opportunities at home—the same reasons as discussed above for the falling supply of servants to the Chesapeake in the last quarter of the seventeenth century. Probably a third of the servants attracted to South Carolina were migrants from the Caribbean. But free white men also did not supply widespread manual labour at this time because land prices were relatively low in South Carolina and it was not particularly difficult for an industrious white emigrant to acquire land and enter the yeoman class. Once naval stores such as pitch, tar, and turpentine had proved a profitable export and rice had been introduced as a staple crop, there was an incentive for slave traders to send their ships to Charleston, the principal port of South Carolina, in search of profitable sales. Before 1700 many of these vessels came via the West Indies to South Carolina. Thereafter South Carolina planters quickly purchased Africans for their plantations. In doing so, many were undoubtedly influenced by their West Indian experience of slavery. It was not difficult to justify the deployment of African labour in the Lowcountry when coercion, discipline, and legal codes that discriminated against blacks had already been practised by planters who had previously cultivated Caribbean sugar.

---

[9] 'Samuel Dyssli to his Mother, Brother and Friends', 3 Dec. 1737, in R. W. Kelsey, 'Swiss Settlers in South Carolina', *South Carolina Historical and Genealogical Magazine*, 23 (1922), 90.

The growth in planting rice as a staple crop coincided with a regular supply of 'new negroes' or 'saltwater' slaves, as Africans arriving in America were termed, in a situation where the supply of indentured servants was sporadic. Thus the transition to slave labour in South Carolina did not pass through the protracted phase that had occurred earlier in the Chesapeake where a staple crop (tobacco) was cultivated, plenty of indentured servants were initially available, few slaves were imported, and therefore the attempt to use whites as a plantation labour force lasted for some time. In South Carolina a swifter process occurred: servants were difficult to acquire, African slaves were readily available, and, as in the Chesapeake, Native Americans were not enslaved on a large scale. Before 1700 the possibility of using Indians as slaves was potentially viable in South Carolina, but the situation changed thereafter. A sharp demographic decline occurred in the Native American population of the colony, in which several smaller tribes were totally destroyed. The Yamasee War of 1715–17, in which the Yamasees were deserted by their allies and attacked by Cherokees, caused significant loss to life and property. Some tribes also quit South Carolina in the early eighteenth century.

Africans had an additional attraction for Carolina buyers: namely their familiarity with rice cultivation. European immigrants to the American colonies and Native Americans had little familiarity with sowing rice. But rice was a staple crop in the rain forests of the sub-Saharan region of West Africa. The part of the Windward Coast where rice was especially cultivated was known as the Grain Coast. Some slave arrivals were familiar with growing rice in paddies along river banks in Africa, and were experienced in the planting, hoeing, threshing, winnowing, and cooking of the crop. Indeed, parallels have been found between the mortar-and-pestle technique of processing rice in parts of Africa and similar practices followed by slaves in eighteenth-century South Carolina. An additional reason, then, for the adoption of slave labour in that colony may have been African skills in rice cultivation. This would help to explain the joint growth of slavery and rice production in South Carolina between the 1690s and 1720s and the switch by planters from cultivating rice on dry land to using freshwater swamps. Yet there are doubts about this explanation. The African coastal regions that mainly supplied slaves to South Carolina—notably Angola—were not rice-growing areas. Women were the main growers of rice in Africa, whereas men dominated the slave trade to South Carolina. The type of rice grown in West Africa was cultivated in dry, upland areas, yet the

Lowcountry rice plantation was generally situated in low-lying swampy areas requiring irrigation. These caveats suggest that we should be circumspect in according to African practice the chief impetus behind the cultivation of rice in North America, though they do not deny that some Africans possessed prior skills that enabled them to adapt to working in South Carolina.

# 2

# Merchants and Planters

The chief white personnel who sustained slavery and the slave trade in the British Empire were merchants and planters. Merchants in the slave trade and in associated lines of commerce shipping goods to and fro across the Atlantic were found at the ports of London, Liverpool, Bristol, and Glasgow and at some lesser ports such as Lancaster and Whitehaven. They remained in their counting houses as sedentary merchants but conducted trade through the employment of ship captains and overseas factors and through detailed business correspondence, invoices, and accounts. The planters were based either on plantations in British America or they lived as absentees in Britain. Merchants and planters were not entirely separate people, of course. Merchants often graduated, with the accumulation of profits, to the status of planters. Thus Joseph Marryat, a London merchant and West India planter, noted in 1831 that 'the prosperity of the planter and the merchant' were 'completely identified'.[1] Merchants and planters might combine roles and become merchant-planters or planter-merchants, depending on which role predominated; but some merchants left that status behind them after they had acquired the wealth to live as planters.

The overriding motive of merchants and planters in their involvement with slavery and the slave trade was economic. Slaves together with staple products grown on plantations (especially tobacco, rice, and sugar) potentially generated lucrative returns in the early modern British Atlantic trading world. In 1770 tobacco (worth £906,638) was the most valuable export commodity from British North America and rice (worth £340,693) was the fourth most valuable commodity. In 1772–4 British sugar imports were worth £2,360,000, making sugar easily the most valuable commodity imported from anywhere. Each of these staple trades had different geographical foci. The tobacco trade from the Chesapeake mainly operated through British ports, notably

---

[1] Quoted in *Parliamentary Papers*, 1831–2, XX (381), 150.

London and Glasgow, and the crop was largely re-exported to France, the Netherlands, the German states, and other European destinations. The rice trade from the Carolinas and Georgia served markets in the Caribbean, northern Europe, and the Iberian peninsula. In the case of both tobacco and rice, markets outside Britain were more important than home consumption. The sugar trade involved shipping semi-refined sugar to British ports mainly for home consumption, though re-exported sugar was also significant in certain periods.

## ECONOMIC GAINS

Substantial profits could be made from slavery and the slave trade, but they did not necessarily produce the bonanza that many contemporaries thought. Nevertheless, the average rate of return on invested capital in slave-trading voyages in the eighteenth century lay in the range between 8 and 10 per cent. Sugar was the most lucrative import brought into Britain between about 1670 and 1820, when it was exceeded in value by supplies of raw cotton imported for the textile industry. Sugar catered for changing patterns of consumption in Georgian Britain whereby more and more people, including those quite low on the social scale, began to take sugar as part of their diet, either in beverages such as tea or in cooking food. The escalating European demand for sugar, backed by slave labour, generated substantial returns on capital. Great estates, according to Edmund and William Burke, writing in the late 1750s, could be acquired more quickly in the West Indies than in any other part of the world. Adam Smith stated that sugar plantation profits were 'generally much greater than those of any other cultivation that is known either in Europe or America'.[2] Profit levels on plantations, the largest agricultural units in the first British Empire, were generally acceptable. In the British Caribbean, for example, they lay in the range between 7 and 15 per cent in most peacetime years; and they rarely produced an overall loss on individual islands even though some properties fell into debt.

The wealth levels of the plantation colonies in British America exceeded those of the non-plantation colonies. Historians have analysed wealth levels for British America on the eve of the American

[2] R. H. Campbell and A. S. Skinner (eds.), Adam Smith, *An Inquiry into the Nature and Causes of the Wealth of Nations* (1776), 2 vols. (Oxford, 1976), i. 366.

Revolution. These studies are mainly based on evidence taken from probate inventories, which record personal but not real estate (though estimates can be made for the latter and appropriate calculations made to generate total assets). Naturally they refer solely to the wealth of the white population. Two general conclusions emerge from such analyses. One is that the southern American colonies (Virginia, Maryland, North and South Carolina, Georgia) were much wealthier than the northern colonies (those from Pennsylvania up to Maine). The other is that the wealth of the West Indies far exceeded that of British North America. The British Caribbean, notably Jamaica, was the wealthiest area in the first British Empire. In 1774 Jamaica's private physical wealth (with realty weighted at 45 per cent) amounted to £28 million and total probated and non-probated wealth in the British West Indies came to £51 million. In the same year the per capita wealth of free white settlers in the British Caribbean was £1,042.5. This was ten times higher than the per capita wealth of white people in the southern mainland colonies of North America, the next highest region for wealth accumulation in British America. Though similar estimates have not been made for the West Indies in the period between the American Revolution and slave emancipation, it is likely that the wealth of the West Indies increased over time because the number of absentee planters—usually the wealthiest group of planters—grew over time. Impressed by the money generated in the Caribbean, the planter-historian Bryan Edwards stated in the 1790s that the West Indian contribution to British wealth was 'the principal source of national opulence and maritime power'.[3] The correspondence of West India merchant-planters makes it abundantly clear that they regarded the Caribbean plantations as the means to providing a fortune. This word permeates their *mentalité*. In 1750s the Bristol merchant Henry Bright contrasted the prospects of Jamaica compared with those at Bristol: 'Jamaica is the only place to get money as great fortunes are made there and scarce a livelihood can be got here at any business.'[4]

Because of the potential economic returns to be gained through participation in slavery and the slave trade, merchants and planters were attuned to mobility and to establishing genuinely transatlantic connections. Slave and sugar merchants at British ports often spent time

[3] Bryan Edwards, *The History, Civil and Commercial, of the British Colonies in the West Indies*, 5th edn, 5 vols. (London, 1819), i. 3.

[4] University of Melbourne Archives, Henry Bright to Francis Bright, 9 Aug. 1754, Henry Bright letterbook (1749–69), Bright Family Papers.

in the colonies. This was quite common early in their careers. They served as factors and agents of their principals or, more informally, went to the slave colonies to visit family members already trading there. Usually they returned home, but there might be the necessity for making return visits. Many planters were also mobile, dividing their time between the colonies and Britain, though this was more common among West India planters than among their counterparts in North America. The reason for this distinction, explained more fully below, was that planters in the West Indies were often reluctant to live there permanently—for health as well as social reasons—whereas Carolina or Chesapeake planters were a creole elite. Geographic mobility helped to build up commercial and social connections and to give many British businessmen first-hand knowledge of the plantation colonies and the shipping and commerce of the Atlantic trading world.

## SLAVE, SUGAR, AND TOBACCO MERCHANTS

Slave, sugar, and tobacco merchants organized their business in different ways. Slave traders formed ad hoc partnerships for specific voyages, with partners taking various shares. The shares were divided into halves, quarters, eighths, sixteenths, thirty-second and sixty-fourth parts, as was common in British maritime affairs, and they included both the value of the ship and the inset and outset accounts. The leading partner, who might usually hold half a share or more in the voyage, was known as the ship's husband. After a slaving voyage was completed, the proceeds were settled according to the division of shares. The partners might come together for another slave voyage, but equally they might form a different group of associates for their next enterprise. To carry out the varied tasks connected with a successful slaving voyage, merchants aimed to hire captains who were experienced in sailing to the African coast and across the Atlantic. They liaised closely with networks of factors in the colonies, usually dealing with people who they knew had conducted trade with them beforehand in an efficient and trustworthy manner. The ability of captains to follow letters of instruction and use their judgement in selecting the options therein stated for the delivery of slaves, and the factors with whom they should deal, was crucial for the success of a slave-trading voyage. Owing to the changing ad hoc partnerships in the British slave trade, it was unusual for slave-trading dynasties to flourish.

Sugar merchants more commonly traded as individuals or in partnerships of two people, sometimes father and son. In the seventeenth century, when the sugar plantations were being established, West India merchants usually traded on their own account. Thus they assumed full liability for the financial outcome of voyages. In the late seventeenth century, however, a commission system arose in the London West India trade whereby planters consigned their sugar to metropolitan merchants on the planters' account, with the merchants earning a $2\frac{1}{2}$ per cent commission for their services. Under this system, the planters retained financial control of their sugar. West India merchants were thereby relieved of the risks that faced slave merchants. Sugar planters and slave merchants corresponded regularly and, as in the slave trade, captains received detailed written instructions about the timing, ports of call, and loading requirements of their voyage. The sugar merchants often owned their own vessels and sent them on regular bilateral transatlantic voyages. There was much more continuity of personnel among West India merchants than among slave traders. Family dynasties were founded in which trade passed from father to son over the generations. This happened partly because such merchants had shares in plantations and therefore had a permanent or semi-permanent stake in the Caribbean that could be left as legacies.

Tobacco merchants had several different ways of transacting business, but two basic methods prevailed: the consignment system and the direct purchase system. The former largely gave way to the latter during the course of the eighteenth century. This change was closely related to the expansion of tobacco cultivation in the Chesapeake away from exhausted tidewater land, beyond the fall lines of the major rivers, and into the piedmont interior. The chief differences in the two modes of conducting business lay in the use of employees and ownership of tobacco. In the consignment system ship captains—occasionally supercargoes—were authorized by their British principals to solicit tobacco for shipment from planters, who retained ownership of the leaf until it arrived in Britain and was sold on commission by tobacco merchants there. But in the direct purchase system British merchants bought and immediately assumed ownership of tobacco in the Chesapeake. This was achieved by merchants employing either indigenous merchants or resident salaried factors to do their buying on the spot.

The main characteristics of Bristol's slave merchants and West India merchants in the eighteenth century have been investigated. (Collective portraits of London and Liverpool slave and West India merchants await their historians.) The leading slave merchants at Bristol were a different group of men from the sugar merchants of the port. Leading slave traders at Bristol in the eighteenth century included Sir James Laroche, Isaac Hobhouse, James Jones, John Anderson, James Day, Thomas Deane, Richard Farr senior and junior, and James Rogers. Among the major sugar merchants were Michael Atkins, Mark Davis, Lowbridge and Richard Bright, William Miles, Evan Baillie, John Curtis, and Protheroe & Claxton. In both cases the merchants mainly had origins among the commercial bourgeoisie and artisan classes. Their fathers were predominantly shipowners, merchants, and tradesmen; relatively few were drawn from the ranks of landed gentlemen. They had usually been apprenticed in Bristol but not all were born there. Besides the native Bristolians, young men who later became sugar and slave merchants came from counties in south-west England but also from much farther afield—from Pembrokeshire, Herefordshire, and Scotland, among other places. Early in their careers sugar merchants commonly spent time transacting business in the Caribbean. Those active in the West Indies as young businessmen before setting up in the sugar trade at Bristol included Thomas Daniel, Jr, in Barbados, Evan Baillie in St Kitts and St Vincent, John Pinney in Nevis, Mark Davis, Sr, Lowbridge Bright, and Samuel Delpratt in Jamaica, and Henry Bright in both St Kitts and Jamaica.

## PLANTERS IN NORTH AMERICA

Planters in North America were a distinct group from West India planters: the former created a creole elite that resided in their great houses on plantations, the latter increasingly became absentees. Planters in Lowcountry South Carolina were the wealthiest social group in eighteenth-century North America. Josiah Quincy, Jr, visiting the region from Boston in 1773, referred to them as 'opulent and lordly planters'.[5] They had various antecedents. Some were Anglo-Americans. Others were of Scots or Huguenot stock. Still others were descended from Anglo-Barbadian migrants who had settled in Carolina in the late seventeenth century. But though they were cosmopolitan in background, they looked to English models of refinement and gentility to bolster their

---

[5] Mark De Wolfe Howe (ed.), 'The Journal of Josiah Quincy, Jr', *Proceedings of the Massachusetts Historical Society*, 49 (1916), 454.

social status. They lived as a creole elite, dividing their time between their plantation houses and a social season during the spring in Charleston. Lowcountry plantation homes were often modest in construction and size because they were seasonal dwellings; but large-scale plantation houses were built. The best surviving example of a plantation great house in the Lowcountry is Drayton Hall, a splendid piece of Georgian architecture which the rice planter Thomas Drayton, Jr, built on the west bank of the Ashley River, South Carolina, on the model of his ancestral home in Northamptonshire. Other prominent plantation houses along the Ashley River included Windsor Hill, Chatsworth, and Runnymede, all named obviously after English places.

During the spring planters escaped life on the plantations by repairing to town houses in Charleston and living a life of luxury and social refinement. To some extent this resulted from concern about their health, for the swampy Lowcountry was rife with fever and ague (i.e. malaria) spread by mosquitoes. This was especially the case in areas of rice and indigo cultivation where large amounts of standing water (often stagnant pools) were found. But planters were also drawn to live partly in Charleston for its social amenities. There was a seasonable round of dinner parties, concerts, balls, card games, fine furniture, elegant buildings, and horse races just outside the town. Planters exerted their social power through participation in this annual season in a setting that offered more gentility and diversion than could be found in the port cities of the British West Indies. Lowcountry planters visited Britain and often sent their sons to be educated there. Thus South Carolinians outnumbered students from other colonies by two to one at Oxford between 1761 and 1776. But despite these continuing ties with the mother country, and the assimilation of anglicized cultural models, relatively few Carolinians returned to the metropolis. The Lowcountry plantocracy remained in the Lower South and over the course of time became Americanized.

The Chesapeake was also associated with the rise of wealthy planters in the wake of the successful production of tobacco as a staple crop. By the early eighteenth century Virginia had a self-conscious ruling elite, men who exercised local political and social power, as exemplified by William Byrd the younger, Robert Carter III, Landon Carter, and others. Like their Carolinian counterparts, they too built striking great houses as a display of their wealth and standing. Byrd's family home Westover, on his James River plantation, was a three storey, elegant brick mansion. Robert Carter III presided over a fine Georgian plantation house at Nomini Hall, on the Potomac River. Landon Carter lived at the magisterial Sabine Hall, perched on a ridge on the Rappahannock River about sixty miles north of Williamsburg. The large Chesapeake planters cultivated refined manners, English fashions, and family dynasties. They imported fine silverware, china and furniture from Europe. They congregated at Williamsburg, the capital of Virginia, where amidst the broad streets and ornate baroque buildings they could sit in the House of Burgesses and Council or attend the courthouse, where many important commercial decisions in the colony were made. Like Carolina's planters, they might visit London but they lived as wealthy provincials in Virginia and Maryland. There was not a significant absentee class among them, and that was partly because, unlike in the Caribbean, most planters in North America settled with their families permanently in North America.

## PLANTERS IN THE BRITISH CARIBBEAN

Many West India planters had acquired their interests in the Caribbean during the early years of English colonization and settlement in the seventeenth century. But there were always people who bought plantations later. The acquisition of new colonies, such as St Kitts after the War of the Spanish Succession or the ceded islands after the Seven Years War, opened up investment opportunities for establishing British-owned plantations. Further opportunities for settling plantations occurred with the British acquisition of the Dutch possessions of Demerara, Berbice, and Essequibo in 1797 (later to become British Guiana) and of Spanish Trinidad in 1802. These newly acquired territories expanded the disembarkation points for slaves from British vessels. In each of these cases of newly settled sugar islands, entrepreneurs invested considerably and, in most cases, quickly in order to tap the potential profits in cultivating plantation produce. Thus the Liverpool slave traders Tarleton and Backhouse had property amounting to £200,000 in Demerara by the start of the nineteenth century. Another Liverpudlian merchant, John Bolton, had loans there amounting to the same figure.

Planters came from varied social backgrounds but they acquired real estate in the Caribbean as a means of social and geographic mobility. Some had aristocratic or gentry origins from their landholdings in Britain. Some were aspiring merchants who made sufficient money to purchase real estate 'beyond the line'. Others were parvenus, who expected that money and land would be the path to gentility and social status. Sometimes this geographic and social mobility was associated with particular groups. Thus, for example, Scots entrepreneurs and settlers were notably prominent in acquiring plantations in the ceded islands after those territories became part of the British Empire in 1763. In Tobago, Scots bought over half the land offered for sale under the Land Commission established in 1764. In 1765 Scots acquired over a third of the land allotted on St Vincent. The Campbells and Baillies were among the Scottish families that established a strong presence in Grenada in the last third of the eighteenth century.

Over time the sheer expense of buying and maintaining a plantation increased. Thus the mortgage debt of the Caribbean soared as sugar estates were purchased on credit terms. Creditors of West India property included merchants who had advanced money to obtain consignments or to support links with correspondents; mortgagees, who had advanced money to earn interest; annuitants by purchase, will, or marriage settlement; legatees, many carrying bequests from years ago; consignors of goods to the West Indies on their own account, including captains, mates of ships, and supercargoes; shippers of goods supplying different stores to order; creditors upon simple bonds and notes; and representatives of all these people who were dead or who had assigned their concerns to others. The range of people listed here covers virtually all those who had a regular commercial connection with the West Indies. Thus by the turn of the nineteenth century many West Indian sugar plantations were owned on the basis of complex loans, annuities, and mergers; many were secured through bonds or other legal devices to ensure that the owner's interests were protected. Some merchants and planters bought sugar estates to build up capital; others took out mortgages on plantations to help with debts accumulated.

The West India plantocracy included such notable figures as Christopher Codrington, father and son, Edward Long, Bryan Edwards, 'Monk' Lewis, John Pinney, and William Beckford. These planters were known to contemporaries not just because of their plantation ownership but because of wider accomplishments in military affairs, political life, and the literary world. The Codringtons, a long-established family in Gloucestershire, concentrated their West Indian holdings on three islands—Antigua, Barbados, and Barbuda. Christopher Codrington (1640–98) established one of the richest sugar plantations in Barbados and had (for the time) the largest set of landholdings in Antigua. He also acquired patent rights to Barbuda, a tiny Caribbean island given over mainly to stock rearing. He was successively councillor (1666) and deputy governor of Barbados (1669–72) and later governor-general of the Leeward Islands. He was military commander of an expedition that recaptured St Kitts from the French in 1690, though he failed in a similar attempt to take Guadeloupe and Martinique. His son Christopher Codrington (1668–1710), educated at Christ Church, Oxford, became governor-general of the Leeward Islands and military commander during the war years at the end of the seventeenth century. Though not entirely successful in either capacity, he nevertheless built up a substantial fortune. His wealth at death lay between £80,000 and £100,000. He bequeathed his large library to All Souls College, Oxford, and left his two plantations in Barbados and their slaves to the Society for the Propagation of the Gospel for the setting up of Codrington College. This theological and medical college and school for Barbadian adolescents opened in 1745.

Long (1734–1813) and Edwards (1743–1800) both owned plantations in Jamaica. They became the two most important contemporary historians of the British Caribbean in the eighteenth century. Long wrote a three-volume *History of Jamaica, or, General Survey of the Antient and Modern State of that Island* (1774). This provided a comprehensive account of the history of the island and notably its attachment to sugar and slavery. Edwards published a two-volume *History, Civil and Commercial, of the British Colonies in the West Indies* (1793), later expanded in revised editions. Long came from a family associated with Jamaica since the 1660s. His grandfather Samuel had been Speaker of the Jamaican Assembly and his father Samuel, born in Jamaica, was a member of the Council and owner of Lucky Valley sugar plantation, a rich property in Clarendon Parish. Long married the heiress of Thomas Beckford of Jamaica, and became a member of the Jamaican Assembly for St Ann Parish in 1761, 1765, and 1766. He was briefly speaker of the Assembly in 1768 and left Jamaica the following year to become an absentee planter, dividing his time between his London house in Wimpole Street and his various properties in Berkshire, Surrey, Hampshire, and Sussex. Long's *History of Jamaica* is an invaluable vade mecum to the social, economic, and political life of Britain's largest and wealthiest West Indian colony. Long argued for better schools in Jamaica, improved military defences, a stronger militia, more extensive white immigration, and a solid church foundation. He was a strong proslavery advocate who supported the rights of the plantocracy against the power of the imperial government and defended their cause when faced with humanitarian objections to slavery.

Edwards was sent as a young man to Jamaica to live with his wealthy uncle, Zachary Bayly. Edwards became a member of the Jamaica assembly in 1765, when only 22 and subsequently played an important role in the political life of the island. Apart from a five-year spell in the 1780s, he lived in Jamaica until returning to England permanently as an absentee planter. Zachary Bayly bequeathed him two sugar plantations in Jamaica. He also inherited two further plantations and a cattle pen from a friend, Benjamin Hume. Gaining experience in operating sugar estates, he owned around 1,500 slaves by the time of the American War of Independence. Edwards became a prominent member of the West India Interest after his return home, and defended the plantocracy against the rising tide of anti-slave trade feeling. He settled near Southampton and entered Parliament as MP for Grampound, Cornwall, in 1796. His book on the West Indies is the most comprehensive contemporary account of the customs, politics, and commerce of the British Caribbean by the time of the French Revolution.

John Pinney (1740–1818), a well-known scion of a merchant-planter family with estates in Nevis and land and property in Bristol and Dorset, was born as John Pretor but brought up in Dorset by his Pinney cousins after the death of his parents. He inherited the Pinney estates in Nevis and spent years in that island after 1764 as a successful resident proprietor. During that period he improved his fortune by at least £35,000. He married a white creole woman in Nevis and served in both the Nevis Assembly (1765) and Council (1767). In 1783 he left Nevis to become a West India commission merchant in Bristol, an absentee sugar planter, and a landowner in Somerset and Dorset. 'My greatest pride', he once remarked, 'is to be considered as a private Country Gentleman therefore am resolved to content myself with a little and shall avoid even the name of a West Indian.'[6] Pinney had greater difficulty in controlling his plantations after he returned to Bristol than when he had lived in Nevis, but he kept a tight rein on their management even from a distance, paying meticulous attention to accounts and to profit and loss balances. By the time he died, the Pinneys' West India fortune amounted to around £340,000. The Pinney connection with Nevis continued for another couple of generations, but John Pinney's sons were less successful as businessmen.

---

[6] Quoted in C. M. MacInnes, *Bristol: A Gateway of Empire* (Bristol, 1939), 325.

The best-known of this group was William Thomas Beckford (1760–1844), who was fabulously rich as a result of inheriting several Jamaican plantations from a father who was an MP and twice mayor of London. The father, William Beckford (1709–70) had lived for ten years in Jamaica where he inherited sugar plantations from his father (d. 1735), who himself had been the beneficiary of the sugar fortune amassed by Peter Beckford (1643–1710). William Thomas Beckford lived as an absentee mainly in Bath, where he settled in the fashionable Lansdown Crescent and kept a tower at the top of Lansdown Hill full of artistic decorations, fine furniture, and a sumptuous crimson drawing room. He also presided over Fonthill Abbey in Wiltshire on an estate of 4,000–5,000 acres bought by his father. This famous Gothic folly, designed by the architect James Wyatt, had a tower and a spire, eighteen bedrooms, transepts, galleries, and a mausoleum. By 1801 it had already cost £242,000 even though it was not completed until *c*.1809. William Thomas Beckford was one of the wealthiest men in Britain by that time. His annual income in 1797 was reckoned to be £155,000. He paid little attention to the original source of his wealth—the Caribbean—and lived a high-profile, luxuriant, decadent life centred on his artistic interests and extensive travels on the Continent. He was the author of the gothic novel *Vathek*. By the 1820s, the profits on his Jamaican estates were declining and he started to accrue debts.

Many West India planters were imposing social figures keen to display their largesse and the social status they had achieved through the profits of sugar and slavery. Resident proprietors in the Caribbean built themselves fine great houses on their plantations. Often these were constructed as if they were English country mansions transported to a tropical climate. They copied Palladian designs in their pillars and entablatures. The houses were grandly decorated, with mahogany furniture, the latest fashions in wallpaper and curtains, fine porcelain, and expensive hurricane lamps. The great houses on plantations employed a domestic staff, usually female slaves or elderly male slaves, to cook lavish meals for feasts where neighbouring planters and prestigious visitors would be treated to sumptuous repasts. A great house on a plantation would often have a well-stocked cellar, a livery and stables, and surrounding gardens, sometimes cultivated with botanic specimens.

Planters who lived partly in Britain or retired to live there usually owned Georgian townhouses and one or more country estates. The latter would, once again, be impressive houses designed according to the latest taste, often accompanied by a farm or landscape garden. West India planters lived in style. Conspicuous consumption was their watchword. As participants in the consumer revolution of the eighteenth-century British Atlantic world and as recipients of the profits accruing from sugar and slaves, they displayed to all and sundry that they were men who had made fortunes. Burke's *Landed Gentry* is full of the names and families of men such as these who became wealthy through their West India connections, though the links between those families and slavery and sugar are invariably obscured by the fact that their West Indian interests are deliberately omitted.

Contemporaries were keenly aware of the wealth and social display associated with the West India plantocracy. Jane Austen based the social milieu in several of her novels around the lives of absentee West India planters, notably the figure of Sir Thomas Bertram in *Mansfield Park*. Leading British artists such as Sir Joshua Reynolds painted portraits of West Indian absentee families, including the Lascelles of Harewood House. The wealth of the bachelor sugar tycoon Simon Taylor (1740–1813) was legendary. The fortunes of West India planters were observed by those in the most prestigious positions in the land. In a famous anecdote about the plantocracy, George III, when riding out with his prime minister Pitt while taking the seaside air in Weymouth, saw an impressive stagecoach and horse approaching his own entourage and, recognizing the familiar figure of a West India planter seated in the stagecoach, turned to Pitt and said, 'Sugar, sugar, all that sugar . . . how are the duties, hey Pitt, how are the duties?'[7]

## THE GROWTH OF ABSENTEEISM AND ENGLISH SOCIAL ATTITUDES TOWARDS THE CARIBBEAN

Some planters remained resident in the Caribbean, living in their great houses and occasionally visiting the mother country. Other planters, particularly those also acting as merchants, were genuine transatlantic figures, who divided their time between the West Indies and Britain. Increasingly, however, planters became absentees. By 1775 around 40 per cent of the sugar plantations in Jamaica were owned by absentees and minors. Sixty years later, just after the slaves were emancipated,

---

[7] Quoted in Richard Pares, *Merchants and Planters, Economic History Review*, suppl. 4 (Cambridge, 1960), 38.

the proportion of Jamaica absentee planters came to 80 per cent. What accounts for this growth of absenteeism? The main answer to this question is that absentees were overwhelmingly the wealthier planters who had made sufficient fortunes to enable them to retire home and manage their estates from across the ocean. They employed attorneys (usually responsible for several plantations) or managers (normally controlling one estate) to oversee their West India properties. There were also important social reasons why absenteeism became prominent. Most West India merchants and planters were never fully attached to the Caribbean; they continued to regard Britain as their home. Thus in 1778 John Drummond informed the secretary of state for America that the aim of white subjects in the West Indies was 'only to get Fortunes & return to their native land. Such is the consequence of an Empire over Islands to Britain.'[8] Bryan Edwards observed that it was 'to Britain alone that our West India planters consider themselves as belonging . . . even such of them as have resided in the West Indies from birth.' He added that 'they look on the islands as their temporary abode only, and the fond notion of being able to go home (as they emphatically term a visit to England) year after year animates their industry and alleviates their misfortune.'[9]

The West Indian islands could be exploited for their economic opportunities, but ever since the days of the pirates and buccaneers of the seventeenth century, though less obviously over time, there was a sense in which they were ripe to be ransacked by enterprising white men. Whites were a minority in all of the Caribbean islands; they comprised less than 10 per cent of the population. They were surrounded by a mass of black faces, mainly slaves but including some free coloureds, whom they dominated, controlled, and owned. This social situation generated fear in the hearts of many white people—fear of slave revolts or reprisals against their condition. Social tension was high between blacks and whites and accommodation between the races involved a mixture of concessions and repressive measures—both the carrot and the stick—in order to maintain peaceful relations.

Whites disliked the lack of social amenities in the West Indies. There were few theatres, parks, gardens, assembly rooms, and shops such

---

[8] Quoted in Andrew Jackson O'Shaughnessy, *An Empire Divided: The American Revolution and the British Caribbean* (Philadelphia, 2000), 1.

[9] Bryan Edwards, *Thoughts on the Late Proceedings of Government Respecting the Trade of the West India Islands with the United States of North America*, 2nd edn (London, 1784), 29.

as they would find in cities such as London or Bristol or Bath. The climate was hot and deemed intolerable for those whites who had to endure months in the Caribbean. The insects and mosquitoes were as disagreeable to white settlers as when Alexander Exquemelin had referred to these pesky irritants as white freebooters in his *History of the Buccaneers*. Natural disasters happened more frequently than in the non-tropical world. There was the possibility of earthquakes and each year the hurricane season in late summer and early autumn threatened havoc in settlers' lives. Some Caribbean cities, such as Kingston, were notorious centres of disease, notably yellow fever, and illness. The Caribbean was also a risky place to live during the eighteenth century because it served as the cockpit of international rivalry. Over half of the eighteenth century comprised war years when the French, Spanish, and English navies fought for command of sea lanes to the Caribbean.

Resident Englishmen in the West Indian islands were likely to have their lives disrupted at some point by the demands and effects of war. In the era of the American and French Revolutions, when several West Indian islands were invaded and taken by enemy powers, there was an added volatility to life in the tropics. Thus in September 1778 Dominica was taken by the French, to be followed by St Lucia a few months later. France retook Grenada and St Vincent in 1779, recovering territories lost to Britain after the end of the Seven Years War. France also captured Tobago in 1781. Three Leeward islands—St Kitts, Montserrat, Nevis—fell to the French in 1782 and there were enemy attacks on Antigua, Jamaica, and Barbados. Britain regained all these territories—save for Tobago and St Lucia—at the peace treaty of 1783. During the Anglo-French War in the Caribbean in the 1790s internal dissension broke out in Dominica and St Vincent, Guadeloupe changed hands twice, Martinique and St Lucia were lost for a short period to France, Britain captured Tobago in 1793 and most of the south and west provinces of Saint-Domingue in 1793 and 1794. In 1795 a maroon war by runaway slaves broke out in western Jamaica, and in the following year Grenada witnessed a slave revolt. Given this volatility in West Indian affairs, it is not surprising that many British planters in the Caribbean felt increasingly insecure, both personally and in terms of their property, in the late eighteenth century. Such insecurities added to the flow of absentees back to the mother country.

A skewed sex ratio added to the problems for white settlers in the Caribbean. Many more white men came to the West Indies than white women. Therefore the British Caribbean during the era of slavery was a sphere of demographic failure for whites. The exception to this rule was Barbados, where the sex ratios among the white population were always more balanced than elsewhere in the British West Indian islands during the slavery era. It is no accident that the demographic parity between the sexes among whites in Barbados produced a higher proportion of resident planters there than in Jamaica or the Windward and Leeward islands. Planters took white and black mistresses and concubines, but many of them wanted to see their children return to Britain for an education at Eton or Harrow and then Oxford and Cambridge, or at the inns of court. Many absentees retired to Britain as soon as they could afford to do so. Creole elites did not really form permanently among white settlers in the British Caribbean. Michael Craton has dubbed the white settlers in the British West Indies 'reluctant creoles', which neatly encapsulates the lukewarm attitude of planters towards permanent residence in the Caribbean.[10] By the time of the Napoleonic Wars a successful West Indian planter tended to be an absentee one. 'I do not know one fortune in the Islands,' Henry Senior wrote from Jamaica on 22 February 1815. '*All* the rich landed proprietors are in England, those only come out here who after mortgaging their estates to the last acre run away to escape the King's Bench.'[11]

Whether absenteeism had deleterious effects on the management of the plantations is open to question. Edward Long's view that the growth of an absentee planter class drained Jamaica of men of talent, leaving lesser resident figures to fill their shoes in the island's assembly, has been amplified by some modern historians who claim that, living so far away from the site of their Caribbean properties, and in some cases never visiting them, absentee planters contributed to their own economic problems by neglecting to oversee the work of attorneys and managers effectively. There is also the criticism that absenteeism, by draining the islands of the wealthy, prominent planters, took away the political talent from the Caribbean. These are difficult generalizations to prove, however, and they are more often asserted and repeated rather than analysed with supporting evidence. It is more likely that absentee planters had an important role to play

[10] Michael Craton, 'Reluctant Creoles: The Planters' World in the British West Indies', in Bernard Bailyn and Philip D. Morgan (eds.), *Strangers within the Realm: Cultural Margins of the First British Empire* (Chapel Hill, NC, 1991).
[11] Quoted in Clare Taylor, 'Aspects of Planter Society in the British West Indies before Emancipation', *National Library of Wales Journal*, 20 (1978), 370.

by remaining metropolitan and therefore able to exert pressure on governments to maintain laws and trade regulations that favoured their interest.

## THE WEST INDIA INTEREST

The West India Interest is the name given to the planters, merchants, and lobbyists who protected the right to economic hegemony in the Caribbean. The political pressure exerted by this group came in various forms. To some extent it was filtered through members of Parliament. London, Liverpool, and Bristol all had MPs who were representatives of the West India Interest. Indeed, in Bristol between 1670 and 1750 all of the city's parliamentary members had a strong connection with the Caribbean. The representation of the West India Interest in Parliament was always a minority group, and few of its members rose to national political importance. Thus of the thirty-nine MPs who were connected with Jamaica during the slavery era, one rose to major political office: John Scarlet, who became attorney general in the 1820s. Nevertheless, the West India Interest in Parliament was an articulate group of men prepared to advance firm arguments to support their stake in the Empire. In the middle of the eighteenth century this group was the most influential colonial lobby in London.

The West India Interest was strongly supported by the activities of professional lobbyists who campaigned in and around Westminster in favour of the plantocratic cause. The best-known, and longest-serving, West India agent in the eighteenth century was Stephen Fuller. For thirty years (1764–94) he was the lobbyist for Jamaica, where his family held plantations for half a century. Fuller defended the plantocracy against the rival interests of metropolitan sugar refiners and grocers. He assiduously immersed himself in the social, economic, political, and military interests of Jamaica that needed to be promoted or defended at Whitehall and Westminster. He helped draw up petitions on behalf of the West India planters and consulted them on parliamentary legislation relating to the colonies. In the American War of Independence he liaised with the Jamaica Assembly over military intelligence that could be used to influence ministers in London. After the war was over he published pamphlets in defence of the West India Interest and lobbied the government to oppose restrictions on the trade between the United States and the Caribbean.

West Indian merchants and planters met informally at the Jamaica Coffee House in St Michael's Walk, near the Exchange in London. West India Clubs began to arise in cities such as Bristol, London, Liverpool, and Glasgow after the American Revolution, but usually they were dining and social clubs rather than institutions with political strength. More important was the West India Committee, which met at the London tavern, Bishopsgate Street, London. This served as the formal meeting forum for British West India merchants and planters in seeking to protect their Caribbean investments and properties. Founded in 1775, this was a different body to those that made up the West India clubs or the West India Interest, though it had members who also participated in those groups.

The West India Interest had considerable success in handling matters that did not conflict with the national interest. The safe passage of the Molasses Act through Parliament in 1733 was supported by members of the Commons with Caribbean connections. The act aimed to tax molasses taken to New England from the Caribbean. The money was to be collected from the American colonists and was not a direct burden on the British population. Since the molasses taken to New England ports came mainly from outside the British Empire—mainly, in fact, from the French Caribbean—the legislation suited the mercantilist view of Walpole's government and the protectionist views of the West India merchants and planters. During the era of escalating tension between Britain and North America in the period 1763–75 the West India Interest combined successfully with the Caribbean island assemblies to adopt a posture of loyalty to the Crown. This meant that there was little danger of the West Indian islands wishing to sever the link with Britain, as the North American colonists did after declaring their independence. The American Revolution served as a watershed in the political influence of West India planters. Parliament banned American ships from West Indian ports in the 1780s against the wishes of the planters. And in the 1790s planters attacked the British army's decision to arm slaves in the struggle against revolutionary and Napoleonic France in the Caribbean.

In the 1790s the West India Interest was active in the propaganda battle with abolitionists who wanted to secure an end to the British slave trade. This was the peak period for West India planters and merchants to publicize their political views. They drew up petitions, wrote pamphlets, and lobbied in and out of Parliament to support their case. The planter class repeatedly emphasized their economic importance to the British Empire and countered arguments made by their opponents that free trade and free wage labour should replace protectionism and slavery. Planters believed that slaves were their chattel property and that the British state sanctioned holding enslaved black people in perpetual hereditary bondage by failing to legislate against slavery as an institution. 'That the system of peopling the West India Colonies with Negroes, obtained by purchase in Africa, has long and repeatedly received the national sanction,' a petition of the planters, merchants, mortgagees and annuitants concerned with the Caribbean argued in 1792. The petitioners added that 'a multitude of Acts of Parliament, both ancient and modern . . . as well as treaties of peace, or of commerce, and other national measures and documents, have alike concurred to indicate the system of this country upon the present subject.'[12]

Before the onslaught inflicted by the abolitionist movement from the 1780s onwards, the West India Interest had little difficulty in portraying slaves as racially inferior to Europeans and therefore as suitable candidates for enslavement. They buttressed their case for slaveholding by drawing attention to the poor, dirty conditions in which British industrial workers lived and toiled and argued that material and labouring conditions on the plantations were certainly no worse and in some ways better. They also pointed to the ways in which those involved in slavery and the slave trade sought to take care of their black charges by observing regulations on the slave trade brought in by Dolben's Act (see below) and by private acts of amelioration on the plantations.

Naturally, these views came increasingly under pressure from the rising tide of abolitionism. But it was only after 1820 that the West India Interest came under political threat. This occurred through the revival of the antislavery campaign and by a challenge from the East India Interest, which argued for an equalization of the duties on imported products from the West and East Indies and, in particular, to revamping the sugar duties so that they did not favour Caribbean imports of the cane. The East India Interest could claim not only that it argued for cheaper sugar but that the crop was grown by free labour. Between 1806 and 1827 the West India Interest coped with these pressures because their representation at Westminster underwent steady improvement whereas the East India Interest declined in strength. In 1827 the West India Interest comprised forty-four MPs, its highest ever parliamentary

---

[12] Quoted in David Ryden (ed.), *The British Transatlantic Slave Trade, iv. The Abolitionist Struggle: Promoters of the Slave Trade* (London, 2003), 153–4.

representation. But the economic decline that caused a drop in sugar prices in the late 1820s meant that several members of the West India Interest experienced a rapid fall in their financial credibility. A reduction in the socio-economic status of West India merchants and planters rapidly led to their declining influence at Whitehall and Westminster.

The coming of the Whig Party to power in 1830 dented the political strength of the West India Interest because, for the first time at a British general election, a large number of prospective members stood on an antislavery ticket. This blow to the West India Interest increased after the passing of the Great Reform Act of 1832 because many candidates campaigned for support on the basis that, if successful, they would back the drive to emancipate slaves in the British Empire in the next parliament. In the first reformed parliament held after 1832 sixteen out of thirty-five West Indians lost their seats. All of the losers, unsurprisingly, had voted against parliamentary reform. The West India Interest never recovered its influence after slave emancipation.

# 3

# The Triangular Trade

The ships involved in the slave trade followed a triangular route between Europe, Africa, and the Americas. Generations of historians have therefore referred to transatlantic slaving by its geometrical shape, as a triangular trade. The first leg of the triangle was the outward voyage from the English home port—usually London, Bristol, or Liverpool—to the West African coast. Ships sailed laden with manufactured goods that could be exchanged for slaves in Africa. Sometimes they would stop en route at the Canary Islands or Cape Verde to replenish water and provisions, but often they sailed directly to Africa. A voyage from the vessel's home port to its slaving destination in Africa could take around a month. The second leg of the triangle consisted of the notorious Middle Passage. This was the name given to the Atlantic crossing from Africa, after slaves had embarked on board ship, to the disembarkation point for slaves in the Americas. This was a particularly risky leg of the entire voyage. Ships were buffeted by Atlantic gales and storms, the crew and slaves often became ill through disease, malnutrition, or dehydration, and there was always the threat of slave risings aboard ship. After a month or six weeks sailing across the ocean, slave ships arrived at their destination for the sale of their cargo. This would be one of the British sugar islands in the Caribbean, the Chesapeake colonies, or the Lower South. Slaves were sold at auction; the payments for the sale arranged; and plantation produce loaded to fill the ships' holds. The third and final leg of the slave trade triangle comprised the voyage home from the Americas to the original English port. Ships carried sugar, tobacco, rice, and other staple produce, although these commodities were shipped back to Britain in greater quantities on bilateral vessels established in shuttle trades between Britain and its colonies. The final leg of the triangular slaving voyage took around a month. On arrival vessels discharged their cargoes and crew and the co-owners shared out the proceeds of the voyage. The outfitting of the vessel and the gathering of goods for the next slaving voyage could begin. Altogether, a complete slave-trading voyage took around a calendar year.

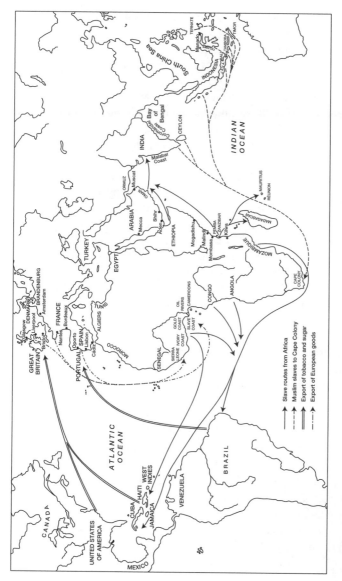

**Map 5.** The slave trade in the Atlantic and Indian Oceans.

The first known example of English slave trading in Africa came in the period 1564–9 when Sir John Hawkins led three slaving raids along the West African coast. These however, were isolated English ventures for slaves at a time when the Iberian powers dominated the transatlantic slave trade. England's maritime explorers were keen to follow in the steps of Spain and Portugal in search of tapping the riches of Africa and the New World. At first, their African voyages were made in search of gold. Between 1618 and 1660 several companies were chartered in England to pursue trade with Africa along these lines. A 'Guinea' Company was established in 1618 and received a revised charter in 1631. Yet there were also private merchants who acted as interlopers in trade. Private merchants already operated a slave trade from London to the West Indies in the 1640s and 1650s, though the records of its size are patchy. Compared with the many thousands of slaves shipped under the flags of Spain, Portugal, and, to a lesser extent, the Netherlands, the early English slave trade was small in scale. In fact, English ships carried fewer than 2,000 slaves per year to the Americas before 1660. Nevertheless, there was recognition that the importation of slaves could be lucrative. Thus, in March 1660, William Brydges wrote from Barbados to his brother Marshall, a London merchant, that 'if you and some other young man would fall into a Guiney trade and so bring negroes hither it would turn to a good Accompt.'[1] The coming of Charles II to the throne led to a revival of the African trade, with the establishment of the Company of Royal Adventurers Trading into Africa. Like the 'Guinea' Company, this was a joint-stock enterprise with royal sanction in which capital could be raised for risky, long-distance trade from numerous investors.

## THE ROYAL AFRICAN COMPANY
## AND THE SOUTH SEA COMPANY

From the restoration of the monarchy until the abolition act of 1807—the peak years of the slave trade—British transatlantic slaving was either conducted by companies or by private traders. The two main companies involved in the British slave trade were the Royal African Company and the South Sea Company. The former was established by a royal charter granted by Charles II in 1672. It succeeded

---

[1] Hereford County Record Office, Hereford, William Brydges to Marshall Brydges, 19 Mar. 1660, Brydges family of Tibberton papers, K 12/15.

the Company of Royal Adventurers Trading into Africa. Many leading figures in that company were members of the Royal African Company which was given, according to its charter, the monopoly right to trade with Africa for a thousand years. The Royal African Company in theory held that monopoly until 1698, when William III and Parliament opened up the slave trade to private merchants in an explicit attack on monopolies held by chartered trading organizations. The company attracted well-heeled city investors, including prominent public figures such as the philosopher John Locke; Sir George Carteret, the Lord Proprietor of Carolina; Sir Edmund Andros, the former governor of New York; and the Bristol philanthropist Edward Colston. The Royal African Company was managed by a Governor, Sub-Governor, Deputy Governor, and twenty-four assistants. Its headquarters was in London. It held two General Courts each year, one for the election of officers and the other for hearing statements about the company's stock. The Court of Assistants, chosen annually by shareholders, dealt with most of the company's business. In West Africa the company usually maintained between fifteen and twenty fortified establishments on the Gold Coast and in Senegambia housing 200 or 300 civilian and military personnel. The company's Agent-General resided at Cape Coast Castle in the middle of the Gold Coast. He could call on the services of sailors, native crew, small craft, and canoes. He received the accounts of the company's factors at factories and dependent lodges such as Anomabu and Accra.

Despite this elaborate organizational structure, throughout its history the Royal African Company struggled to make profits. Its initial capital proved insufficient for its needs. The forts, factories, and lodges in West Africa drained its finances and, even worse, large sums of money were owed to the company from the sales of slaves on credit in the Caribbean. By 1690 planters owed the company £170,000 in Barbados, Jamaica, and the Leewards. Between 1691 and 1708 the company's deteriorating financial position was met by substantial borrowings and calls for more capital. But taking out loans led to further financial difficulties and at the end of 1708 the company had debts at interest of £301,195 and book debts of £11,429. During the War of the League of Augsburg (1689–97) and the War of the Spanish Succession (1702–13) the company lost £300,000 in merchant shipping to foreign privateers. By 1712, such were the financial burdens of the company that it was technically bankrupt.

The Royal African Company's standing gradually declined from the 1710s onwards. But it did not succumb to the pressure of competition without seeking to improve its weak position. It made several attempts to develop commodities for export from Africa. Schemes to this effect were undertaken between 1705 and 1712 by Sir Dalby Thomas, the governor of the company resident on the Gold Coast, who was particularly interested in developing gold and cotton for export. The plans came to nothing because the company's white servants on the coast were usually more committed to their private trade, which they carried out at the expense of the company's business. The Royal African Company also tried to extend its operations in West Africa by erecting a fort on the Loango Coast between 1721 and 1723. The fort was duly constructed overlooking the anchorage of Cabinda Bay. This was the first time that a European trading organization had attempted to establish hegemony on that part of the slaving coast. Unfortunately, the fort soon encountered friction with Portuguese, French, and local Woyo interests in that area. The British garrison at Cabinda Bay surrendered in May 1723 after an attack by a Portuguese expedition sent from Lisbon.

Several propagandists highlighted the financial plight of the Royal African Company and sought extra public funding. A pamphlet entitled *The Case of the Royal African Company of England* (London, 1730) argued for the central role of the slave trade in promoting the plantations, commerce, and wealth of the mother country, and concluded that the African forts should be financially supported by the British public. In the 1740s the mercantilist writer Malachy Postlethwayt wrote a series of pamphlets and tracts seeking to show how the British slave trade should be conducted by a joint-stock organization rather than by private merchants. In *The African Trade, the Great Pillar and Support of the British Plantation Trade in North America* (1745) and *The National and Private Advantages of the African Trade Considered* (1746) he emphasized the strategic role played by the slave trade in generating Britain's commercial opulence. In the latter publication, for example, he declared that 'the Negroe-Trade . . . may be justly esteemed an inexhaustible Fund of Wealth and Naval Power to this Nation.'[2] He also reiterated the case for parliamentary support for the Royal African Company's forts and factories and warned of the danger that France might out-compete Britain in colonial trade and power if these matters were neglected.

---

[2] Postlethwayt, *The National and Private Advantages of the African Trade Considered . . .*, quoted in Kenneth Morgan (ed.), *The British Transatlantic Slave Trade, ii. The Royal African Company* (London, 2003), 202.

This pamphlet came too late to influence Parliament's view on the matter. In 1750 the Royal African Company was reorganized and two years later it was given a new title, the Company of Merchants Trading into Africa. But it never recovered its former prestige and power. The new company was not permitted to trade as a corporate body but was charged with maintaining the English forts and trading factories in Africa. An Act of 1765 divested the Company of Merchants Trading into Africa of its authority over Senegal and Gambia, which became the British crown colony of Senegambia. The other forts remained under company control. In 1783 the Crown restored the forts in Senegambia to the Company of Merchants Trading into Africa. The African Company survived the abolition of the British slave trade in 1807 but was dissolved by parliamentary Act in 1821.

The other main joint-stock enterprise involved in the British slave trade had a shorter existence. This was the South Sea Company, created in 1710. Like the Royal African Company, it had headquarters in London. But its role in the slave trade was more specific than that of the African Company. The South Sea Company chiefly existed to exercise the right of the *asiento* (contract or licence) to deliver slaves in British vessels to the colonies of Spanish America, including New Spain (Mexico), New Granada (modern Colombia), and Cuba. It gained this right at the Treaty of Utrecht in 1713, which concluded the War of the Spanish Succession. Spain had for generations issued various *asientistas* to foreign powers to supply Spanish America with slaves rather than relying on her own rigid *flotillas* that sailed yearly from Seville or Cadiz to do so. The Dutch and the French had held the *asiento* in the decades before 1713; now it was the English turn. The South Sea Company was as much, if not more, a financial organization as it was a trading group. In practice, it made use of Royal African Company ships to deliver slaves to Vera Cruz, Cartagena, Panama, Havana, and various South American ports. The *asiento* trade continued, with brief interruptions, through to 1739, when the outbreak of the War of Jenkins's Ear put a stop to it: this was, after all, a trade war specifically aimed at Spanish depredations on British shipping. The *asiento* finally ceased in 1748, by which time the South Sea Company was defunct. Throughout its existence the South Sea Company found it difficult to make consistent profits.

Why did both companies fare so poorly? In the case of the Royal African Company, there were serious financial and operational problems to overcome. In the case of the South Sea Company, there was a limited market for its operations and a major financial panic to deal with.

In both cases, private traders provided effective competition for a share in American slave markets. The Royal African Company had been established with an initial capital of £110,000 and a wealthy and influential Board of Directors. It had an elaborate and efficient administrative structure in London. But it soon ran into financial difficulties. The main reason lay in the sheer amount of money needed to keep up its fortified establishments in West Africa. From its inception, the Royal African Company had built and maintained trading castles along the Gold Coast and in the Gambia region. Apart from the company's headquarters at Cape Coast Castle on the Gold Coast, there were thirty-odd other forts scattered along the West African coast, including Komenda, Winneba, Tantumquerry, and Accra. Some of these were originally English establishments; others were plundered or acquired from European trading nations such as Holland and France. Originally built to protect stretches of coast from foreign competitors—all of whom had their own fortified castles in West Africa—these large establishments comprised living quarters, barracks, and guns pointing outwards to sea (to withstand enemy assaults). The Royal African Company forts were placed strategically to protect not just the slave trade but also the supply of gold: before 1700 the company was as much concerned with acquiring gold as with gathering slaves. But all this construction was expensive and needed constant upkeep. The Royal African Company found its own resources stretched and regularly requested additional funds from Parliament for the maintenance of its West African forts after the decision had been taken to open up the slave trade in 1698.

The operational difficulties of the Royal African Company lay in its relative inflexibility compared with the situation of private traders. The company relied on chartered ships sent out at set intervals. A syndicate of shareholders invested in these voyages. Private traders, on the other hand, had no such rigid schedule. They took shares in slave vessels when and where they chose; they dispatched vessels to Africa at different intervals to take account of changing supply and demand situations; they were not required to send an annual ship to the same places on the African coast year after year. The Royal African Company depended on the efficiency of its officials in the forts and factories to gather slaves. But whereas the Gold Coast was a prime site for British slave trading in the late seventeenth century, Gambia was never a major supply area of captives for the British slave trade or, indeed, the transatlantic slave trade as a whole. Private traders found during the eighteenth century that they could gather slaves more effectively from areas where there was no Royal African Company presence, namely the Bights of Benin and Biafra and Angola.

The South Sea Company, as already noted, relied upon the Royal African Company to provide the ships necessary to carry out its *asiento* function. This meant that slaves picked up by the company were taken from the same areas as where the Royal African Company forts were situated. The South Sea Company suffered interruptions to its trade in years when Anglo-Spanish diplomatic relations were strained (in 1718–20, 1727–9, and throughout the war years from 1739 until 1748). Thus the South Sea Company could never be an entirely reliable means of handling slave cargoes. Moreover, the company found its credibility seriously challenged after the financial panic known as the 'South Sea Bubble' in 1720, a notorious stock market crash. An overheated stock market saw South Sea Company shares soar to record heights and then the crash came—with serious consequences for the credibility of the company. The South Sea Company, in any case, never delivered the number of slaves it was supposed to vend to Spanish America. It came under increasing competition from private traders supplying slaves to Cuba or mainland Spanish America from Jamaica, often traders that operated in a clandestine fashion. The South Sea Company's factors in the Caribbean also became known for their corruption.

## PRIVATE MERCHANTS AND THE SLAVE TRADE

The challenge by private traders to these companies in the British slave trade was already apparent before the Royal African Company had its monopoly rescinded in 1698. London private merchants and, to a lesser extent, Bristolians had infiltrated the trade by then as interlopers. Before 1700 about half of the slaves delivered to British America came from ships owned by private merchant firms. After the monopoly rights of the Royal African Company were taken away, private merchants increased their role in the trade. Initially, they laboured under a financial disadvantage because they were required to pay a 10 per cent levy on their export cargoes to Africa until 1712. But even in Queen Anne's reign, when this tax was charged, private traders disembarked more slaves in the New World than did company vessels. Thus in the decade after 1698, the first years of free trade in slaves, some 75,000 slaves were brought to Jamaica, Barbados, Antigua, Montserrat, Virginia,

Maryland, and New England combined, but only 18,000 of this total came from Royal African Company vessels. The company fought this situation by campaigning to have its monopoly rights restored. In the period 1708–10, in particular, it amassed much written propaganda to this end at a time when the Board of Trade was conducting an inquiry into the affairs of the company. However, private merchants organized their own counter-propaganda effectively by sending memorials and petitions to Parliament, the Board of Trade, and the Privy Council requesting that an open trade be maintained, which it was.

By the time of the Hanoverian Succession in 1714, private traders from London and Bristol were dominant in the English slave trade. Liverpool merchants had also entered the trade for the first time. Over the ensuing years up to the abolition of the British slave trade in 1807 the conduct of the 'Guinea' traffic lay in the hands of London, Bristol, and Liverpool merchants, for the most part. The relative position of these ports in the slave trade changed over time, however. London retained its ascendancy in the trade until the late 1720s. In 1725, for instance, 87 slave vessels cleared from London and 63 from Bristol. But London was then overtaken by Bristol, which became the leading English slave-trading port until the 1740s. The annual average ship clearances in the slave trade for the 1730s came to 39 for Bristol, 25 for London, and 21 for Liverpool. During the late 1720s and throughout the 1730s Liverpool increased its commitment to the slave trade and by the mid-1740s it had overtaken Bristol to become the nation's leading slave-trading port. From then onwards it never relinquished that position. The annual average number of slave ships clearing from Liverpool numbered 95 in 1772–5, 88 in 1783–92, and 107 in 1793–1804. In each of these sets of years Liverpool easily sent out more slave vessels than Bristol and London combined. In 1807, the last year of the official British slave trade, Liverpool dispatched 101 slave ships; none was sent from any other British port. Small wonder that one contemporary referred to Liverpool as the 'metropolis of slavery'.[3] By the turn of the nineteenth century, Liverpool was not merely the largest slave-trading port in Britain but the largest slaving emporium in the world. It did not lose that position until after the British slave trade ended, after which Rio de Janeiro, in the Luso-Brazilian trade, became the largest slave-trading port around the Atlantic littoral.

[3] *History of the Election for Members of Parliament . . . Liverpool, 1806* (Liverpool, 1806), p. viii.

Why did Bristol overtake London to become England's leading slaving port in the twenty years after 1725, and why did Liverpool then overtake Bristol to assume the ascendancy thereafter? Bristol, of course, was a long-standing provincial port of importance by the early eighteenth century. Favoured with a westward outlook, it was well placed geographically to trade with Africa and the Atlantic world. Bristol had been involved in Atlantic voyages since the days when John Cabot sailed from the city to Newfoundland in the reign of Henry VII. Bristol also had participated in the interloping trade in slaves in West Africa since the restoration of the Stuart monarchy. But a prior track record of trading with the Atlantic world and involvement in the slave trade, when added to a favourable geographical position, do not explain Bristol's rise to prominence in the English slave trade. More important was the fact that Bristol merchants showed enterprise in exploiting opportunities for marketing slaves in colonies such as Virginia and St Kitts and concentrated successfully on supplying slaves to England's largest sugar island, Jamaica.

## THE ASCENDANCY OF LIVERPOOL IN THE BRITISH SLAVE TRADE

Liverpool's rise in the slave trade at the expense of Bristol was linked to several interlocking factors. Bristol lost ground to its north-western rival in the war years of the 1740s. Bristol merchants cut back on their slave voyages during that conflict, converting a good many of their vessels into privateers—armed ships that deliberately set out to capture foreign (usually French or Spanish) vessels and claim their cargoes as prizes. In terms of captured prize vessels, Bristol was more successful at privateering during the War of Jenkins's Ear (1739–42) and the War of the Austrian Succession (1744–8) than any other English provincial port. But Bristol also suffered from its geographical position in wartime, for French *corsaires* and Spanish *guarda costas* could pick off its vessels sailing to Africa in the mouth of the English Channel. Liverpool merchants did not switch their vessels to privateering to the same extent during the war years of the 1740s. They also benefited from being based at a more northerly port, from which ships could sail around the north of Ireland and into the Atlantic, safe from the sea lanes where foreign cruisers predominated and therefore relatively protected from their depredations.

There were many other reasons, however, why Liverpool became ascendant in the slave trade. One lay in the characteristics of its merchant community, which was more flexible in its operation than at Bristol. Whereas Bristol merchants in the eighteenth century were largely separated, in terms of Atlantic trade, into distinct groups of tobacco, sugar, and slave merchants, with only limited movement between the different specializations, Liverpool merchants were much more flexible, moving between the tobacco, sugar, and slave trades as commercial opportunities arose. Liverpool had a much greater commitment to building ships used in the slave trade than Bristol or London. This enabled Liverpool merchants to have quicker access to vessels in the trade built locally. Thus a Bristolian visiting Liverpool in 1773 noted that 'the Liverpool people go on with such spirit', adding that they had a plentiful supply of ships for the slave trade.[4]

Liverpool had particularly strong commercial connections with the Bight of Biafra, the hub of English slave trading in West Africa after 1730. Liverpool's market share, in terms of slave embarkations, was remarkable in the British slave trade by the 1780s. The city's merchants conducted the slave trade with greater efficiency than their counterparts at Bristol and London. This can be demonstrated in terms of total voyage times and voyage times on the Middle Passage during the eighteenth century. Liverpool ships, despite having to cover more distance than either Bristol or London vessels, completed triangular slaving ventures two days more quickly on average than Bristol, the next most efficient port in terms of voyage time. In addition, Liverpool ships saved five days on average over Bristol ships on the Middle Passage and nine days over London vessels.

Liverpool merchants increasingly used the extensive credit connected with bills of exchange to ensure they received payment for the sale of their slave cargoes by extensive use of the 'guarantee' system. This was a system whereby colonial factors selling slaves on behalf of Liverpool merchants remitted their own bills, rather than waiting for planters' bills, and nominated a large, reputable merchant house in London as the guarantee for payment. The bills were submitted in various tranches with different dates specified for payment. Usually, the length of credit allowed on such bills was three, six, nine, or twelve months before

---

[4] University of Melbourne Archives, Lowbridge Bright to Bright, Milward & Duncombe, 5 Nov. 1773, Lowbridge Bright letterbook (1765–73), Bright Family Papers.

payment became due. Since most slaves were sold on credit to meet the financial demands placed on planters, this system was an effective way of ensuring that creditors paid their debts within a time span that was acceptable to Liverpool slave merchants. In the period after the American Revolution, such bills often carried even longer periods of credit, stretching up to eighteen, twenty-one, or twenty-four months. It was not just Liverpudlians who used the 'guarantee' system, for Bristolians and Londoners also participated in this mode of securing payments for slaves. However, Liverpool slave merchants used the system more extensively than their counterparts at other ports and forged close ties with certain London West India sugar houses as their designated sureties, thereby promoting close financial ties between the Mersey port and the metropolis.

## SMALLER PORTS IN THE BRITISH SLAVE TRADE

English ports other than London, Liverpool, and Bristol also participated in the transatlantic slave trade, but on a smaller scale and for lesser periods of time. The two most prominent of the minor English ports in the slave traffic were Whitehaven and Lancaster. Whitehaven's slave trade flourished briefly in the middle of the eighteenth century. Lancaster's slave trade reached a peak in the two decades before the American War of Independence. The demise of slave trading at Whitehaven and Lancaster was probably not so much connected with local capital shortages or lack of access to a burgeoning hinterland with available export goods—though elements of these played their part—but more connected with the lack of well-honed, established commercial contacts throughout the Atlantic world that were essential for successful conduct of the slave trade. Glasgow, curiously, had very little direct role in the British slave trade, though Scots merchants, including Glaswegians, participated in the slave trade of London. In the early eighteenth century, a pioneering slave trade adventure from Glasgow came to grief, with substantial losses incurred for its investors. It may be that, after getting their fingers burned, there was a reluctance to follow through with similar voyages from the Clyde to Africa. But it may have been of greater importance that the assortment of export goods needed for the slave trade was difficult to achieve in Glasgow and its hinterland before the development of industries in and around the city on a large scale after 1750. Altogether, these ports accounted for easily less than 10 per cent of British slave-trading voyages.

Outside England, the slave trade within the British Empire had two centres that dispatched ships to Africa. The less important of the two was Barbados, from which around 190 voyages were sent to Africa to pick up slaves and bring them back in the period before 1740. This was a trade largely carried out in Royal African Company ships. It never revived after the decline of the company, which was fully evident by the 1740s. A more important centre of slave trading in the British Empire was Newport, Rhode Island. This port became the centre of slave trading from the British North American colonies, exceeding quite easily the number of slave voyages trading via bigger ports such as New York and Philadelphia. Newport sent out hundreds of vessels to pick up African captives, who were then sold either in the Caribbean or in South Carolina and Georgia. Newport's advantage over New York and Philadelphia was that it supplied rum as a main export cargo to West Africa and then brought back molasses from the West Indies to fuel its distilleries. Merchants such as Christopher Champlin and Aaron Lopez of Newport made successful slave-trading careers. By the late eighteenth century the ability of the Newport slave traders to trade in rum secured them a trading advantage on some parts of the West African coast over ships sent out from English ports which tended to include alcoholic beverages as only a relatively small part of their cargo.

## THE ORGANIZATION OF THE SLAVE TRADE IN BRITAIN

The transatlantic slave trade was one of the riskiest of eighteenth-century commercial activities, and one subject to losses as well as gains. For success in the trade, care needed to be taken on each leg of the slave-trading triangle. To cope with the capital needs of hiring ships, fitting them out, and paying for cargoes, merchants engaged in slave trading took shares in particular voyages on an ad hoc basis. In other words, a group of English investors combined for a particular voyage to Africa and the Americas; they came together specifically for that venture. They might involve themselves in further slave voyages, but before each venture the arrangements were worked out again from scratch. The leading shareholder was known as the ship's husband. He took care of the final accounting for the voyage. The possibility of holding relatively small shares in ships meant that some investors could be men of modest capital such as shopkeepers, mariners, ship captains, or other retailers; but most investors were merchants. Over time a number of ship captains upgraded their status to that of merchant; and so it sometimes happened that captains of slave vessels graduated to become major investors in such ventures.

Assembling an export cargo normally took several months. The main slaving ports could gather manufactured goods from the production of their own city and hinterland, but they also acquired goods from farther afield. Ironware and metalware often came from south Wales, Birmingham, and the Black Country. For example, Birmingham, the centre of the gunmaking trade in Britain, supplied flintlock muskets, pistols, blunderbusses, gun flints, and gun shot to merchants in the leading British slave-trading ports. Textiles were gathered from south Lancashire, the West Riding of Yorkshire, and the West Country. London merchants in the slave trade could take advantage of regular East India Company sales held at Leadenhall Street, in the City of London, in order to purchase Indian textiles for their voyages to Africa. Liverpool's slaving vessels also drew upon smuggled goods available at the Isle of Man. English slave merchants also gathered brassware from Dutch ports and ironware from Sweden.

## TRADING GOODS FOR SLAVES IN AFRICA

Anglo-African commodity trade comprised less than 1 per cent of total English overseas commerce in the eighteenth century. But though it was much smaller in volume and value than the export trade from England to the Americas, it was nevertheless vital for the conduct of the slave trade. Captains needed to take the right assortment of goods by product category, price, and quality to meet consumer demand on different parts of the African coast. Thus a Liverpool ship captain, embarking on a voyage to the Windward Coast in 1768, was told to be sure during his purchase of slaves to 'keep your cargo well assorted, for shou'd the Traders there learn you are short of any one article commonly carried there, it may detriment your purchase.'[5] Any notion that such demand was simple, unchanging, and geared towards cheaper goods is wide of

---

[5] Liverpool Record Office, James Clemens & Co. to Capt. David Tuohy, 30 June 1768, Papers of the ship *Sally*, Tuohy Papers.

the mark. Africans were discriminating purchasers of trade goods. They were fussy about colour, texture, and prices; their tastes changed over time; and not all of the goods they bought were cheap commodities or gewgaws. In some areas the types of goods favoured by Africans remained reasonably constant; such was the case with English half says and green ells on the Gold Coast and Indian cottons on the Loango Coast during the eighteenth century. In other areas, change occurred. Thus, whereas large cargoes of bar iron but few India textiles were sent in British vessels to Gambia in the late seventeenth century, by the eve of the American Revolution that area absorbed more textiles than iron. English slave traders needed a finely tuned knowledge of the consumer goods of different Africans, and they built up a repertoire of catering for these needs by establishing contact with particular parts of the African coast and with particular traders there.

About two-thirds of the trade goods shipped to Africa to purchase slaves consisted of textiles. In the first three decades of the eighteenth century and again towards the end of the century, East Indian goods dominated textile exports. Many of them were cottons and silks with exotic names—byrampauts, niccanees, romals, chelloes, sastracundies. The colours, designs and finishing of these wares were superior to anything that the textile industry in Africa could produce. African consumers particularly liked the bright colours of Indian textiles. From the 1740s onwards, however, English-produced cottons and linens, many of them manufactured in Lancashire, took an increasingly prominent part in the outward cargoes carried to Africa. These textiles were used for garments such as shirts and dresses. Woollens were also in demand in Africa; they were suited to cool evening temperatures, and could be used as wraps or shawls. Commonly, an assortment of eight or ten different textile goods was included in export cargoes sent to the slave coast. Many other goods apart from textiles were exported to Africa. Copper and brassware, iron products, gunpowder, gunflints, lead shot, muskets, pistols, glass beads, alcoholic beverages—all found their way into the holds of slave-trading vessels. Textiles were generally sold on parts of the West African coast that had little or no textile industry. Similarly, the metals in demand in West Africa were ones where internal supplies could not meet consumer needs.

After cargoes were loaded and ships fitted out, vessels set sail from English ports through the English Channel, down through the Bay of Biscay, around the tip of Portugal, and then usually headed for the Azores or the Canary Islands, where they would often stop to pick up fresh water and provisions. In the period 1713–30, in addition, a significant number of English sailing ships picked up additional goods in the Portuguese Atlantic islands for sale in Africa. The location of trade in West Africa was decided before ships embarked on their voyages. Captains carried letters of instruction from their owners spelling out where they should trade, with whom, and on what terms. English merchants tried, as far as possible, to cultivate trade with certain parts of the African coast, by captains experienced in the rigours of slave trading. Experienced crew who had sailed before on a 'Guinea' voyage were also much prized. Sometimes captains were instructed to pick up slaves at more than one place in West Africa; and sometimes they were requested to trade at one place for gold, redwood, camwood, and ivory, and then to proceed elsewhere to get their slaves. In most instances, however, slaves were gathered at one trading point on the west coast of Africa. The British traded with Senegambia, the Gold Coast, Sierra Leone, the Windward Coast, and the Bight of Benin, which were partly protected by forts, and with the Bight of Biafra and West-central Africa, where trade was conducted without such protection.

Captains of slave vessels had delegated responsibility from their merchant employers in Britain. Much of the success of a slave-trading voyage depended upon the skill, behaviour, and business acumen of captains. Their dealings on the African coast were by no means easy. They had to take account of local supply conditions; they needed to be aware of local political impediments to trade; and they hoped to avoid rainy seasons when diseases spread rapidly and the supply of slaves from the interior was cut off. They had to establish and maintain good relations with African middlemen, who supplied slaves from the interior of the continent to slave vessels, and they needed the acquiescence of local rulers. Thus the success of captains' dealings in West Africa depended on business skill, cultural interaction with suppliers, and knowledge of climatic and seasonal conditions. On certain parts of the coast, such as Old Calabar, some African traders could read and write English. Long-standing friendships and connections between English captains and these African traders considerably aided the British dominance of the slave trade in the Bight of Biafra.

Captains bartered their goods with local middlemen, dealing in local units of account. These units might be copper or iron rods, manillas, or cowries. Manillas were horseshoe-shaped bracelets made from brass and copper, used as a form of currency, notably in the Niger delta. Cowries were shells gathered from the Maldives in the Indian Ocean, shipped to Amsterdam or London, and then sent out on slave vessels to Africa, where they had widespread use. Africans in pre-colonial times did not use numeric currency; rather they calculated the number of goods they received in these units of account. The currency used in certain areas of West Africa, notably by the Akan peoples along the Gold Coast, consisted of gold dust. The use of gold as money involved boxes and bags to hold the gold dust, spoons to transfer the gold dust to weighing scales, and weights and brushes. Gold was linked both to the sale of European goods in Africa and to the supply of slaves. 'The Negro Traders takes goods from us on Slaves,' a trader at Tantumquerry fort informed a Bristol merchant, 'and with the Gold buy slaves; we now give them 8 oz. 8 ac. to 9 oz. Goods for a Man which slave they would sell us from 4 oz. 8 ac. to 5 oz. Gold.'[6] This quotation illustrates in microcosm the way in which European traders in Africa always had to trade on Africans' terms.

Some middlemen with whom captains dealt on the African coast were mulattoes, others were indigenous Africans. There were also European traders resident there. To ensure that slaves were delivered for the goods supplied, captains relied on trust and prior commercial connections. They might need to observe 'comey' and dashes with local rulers as a gesture of goodwill; this meant the offer of gifts as a token of friendly exchange. But in Old Calabar and Bonny, where the English concentrated much of their eighteenth-century slave trade, credit was associated with transactions that exchanged goods for slaves in the form of pawns or pledges. A pawn was a relative of an African trader who was placed temporarily in the custody of ship captains; the pawn was released once the slaves had been delivered to the ship.

English captains and their crew stayed on shipboard in Africa; they did not venture into the interior, nor did they stray far from their vessels while they lay anchored. They erected temporary houses on their ships covered with mats to conduct business. On occasions crew members were sent on canoes upriver over limited distances to gather slaves but this was usually carried out by African middlemen and their helpers. In Bonny in the late eighteenth century, large canoes dispatched to gather slaves could hold around 120 people. But there were also overland routes to inland slave marts. 'Evening is the period chosen for the time of departure,' noted Captain John Adams, 'when they proceed in a

    [6] University of Melbourne Archives, Charles Banville to Thomas Banville, 15 Aug. 1761, loose correspondence, Bright Family Papers.

body, accompanied by the noise of drums, horns, and gongs. At the expiration of the sixth day, they generally return, bringing with them 1,500 or 2,000 slaves, who are sold to Europeans the evening after their arrival, and taken on board the ships.'[7]

The reasons why white men did not penetrate the interior of Africa are not hard to find. Europeans had little knowledge of the geography of Africa beyond fifty or a hundred miles from the coast. It was not until Mungo Park's expeditions of the 1790s that serious attempts to explore the interior occurred. Until then, much of the geography of interior Africa was based on mythical places, people, or polities. Nor did Europeans have the linguistic skills to converse with many African ethnic groups. Even at the peak period of the 'scramble for Africa' (1870–1914) Europeans had reservations about penetrating what the novelist Joseph Conrad termed 'the heart of darkness'. But it was not just European reluctance that determined that the white personnel on slaving voyages remained on or near the coast, for a crucial aspect of the transatlantic slave trade was that African polities and rulers had the power to determine who penetrated inland; and for social and political purposes it suited them to keep the Europeans at bay on the shore.

## THE SUPPLY OF SLAVES TO THE WEST AFRICAN COAST

Slaves were supplied to the ships by various methods. Some were gathered close to coastal areas but others were marched hundreds of miles to the coast. In the eighteenth century the average march of slaves to the coast was about 63 miles in the Bight of Biafra, around 125 miles on the upper Guinea coast and in the Bight of Benin, about 190 miles for the Gold Coast and Senegambia, and around 380 miles in Loango and Angola. Slaves were marched to the coast in coffles (shackled in a line). The men were chained by their ankles to prevent them from escaping. Sometimes these shackles could chain several people together. Yokes could also be used for this purpose. Spiked collars, neck rings, handcuffs, and leg irons were used as devices for restraining and punishing slaves. Equiano's *Autobiography* provides perhaps the most vivid contemporary

---

[7] Captain John Adams, *Remarks on the Country extending from Cape Palmas to the River Congo, including observations on the manners and customs of the inhabitants* (London, 1823), 130.

account of the horror of being captured by Africans and taken to the coast for embarkation in a slaving vessel. It points up the fear, uncertainty, and cruelty of the gathering of black human cargoes. After being captured and taken to the coast, Equiano saw the slave ship at anchor waiting for its cargo. He was filled with astonishment and this

was soon converted into terror when I was carried on board. I was immediately handled and tossed up to see if I were sound by some of the crew, and I was now persuaded that I had gotten into a world of bad spirits and that they were going to kill me . . . Indeed such were the horrors of my views and fears at the moment that, if ten thousand worlds had been my own, I would have freely parted with them all to have exchanged my condition with that of the meanest slave in my own country.[8]

Black Africans were just as culpable in the supply of slaves as white Europeans were in shipping them to the Americas. Sophisticated supply mechanisms existed whereby black Africans became willing accomplices in supplying other Africans to English ship captains. Slavery was an institution with a long history in African societies. For many centuries there had been various slave trades in existence on the African continent. There was a long-standing supply of slaves to Islamic countries and to the Indian Ocean as well as indigenous slavery within Africa. Africans intended for the transatlantic slave trade were largely captured in war or through kidnapping or raids; they might also be taken in lieu of debts. Kidnapping individuals—a practice known as 'panyarring'—was common in some parts of West Africa, notably among the Fante, and this could be a source for the supply of slaves to the coast. The determining factors for the sale of slaves into African slavery or into the Indian Ocean, Mediterranean, or Atlantic trades were relative supply elasticities and the tactics of middlemen. Certain areas, such as the interior of the Gold Coast or the Bight of Benin, had well-known slave marts at which Africans were acquired before their destination was decided.

The demographic balance of slave cargoes assembled for the European slave trades followed a particular pattern. English slave traders preferred to take a ratio of two adult men for each adult woman. This was partly because they considered (rightly) that young adult men in good physical condition would be the easiest to sell in the New

[8] Olaudah Equiano, *Interesting Narrative of the Life of Olaudah Equiano* . . . (1789), quoted in Michael Craton, James Walvin, and David Wright (eds.), *Slavery, Abolition and Emancipation: Black Slaves and the British Empire: A Thematic Documentary* (London, 1976), 39.

World for field labour on plantations. But it was also the case that African societies were often more willing to release men into the transatlantic slave trade than women. Within Africa, women were valued for their work and reproductive role and there was therefore a reluctance to sell them in large numbers into the transatlantic slave trade. Adolescent boys and girls featured regularly among the captives: contemporary documents usually refer to them as 'men-boys' and 'women-girls'. But though babies on the breast were usually taken on board with their mothers, relatively few children aged from 5 to 13 were recruited as slaves. Presumably this reflected the fact that they were too young to sell for independent plantation work. There was a change, however, towards the end of the eighteenth century. In the 1790s the demand for slaves in colonies such as Jamaica was so great that relatively high prices could be charged at sales. This encouraged slave traders to meet the demand by sending more children as slaves from Africa.

## THE MIDDLE PASSAGE

'Quick dispatch' is 'the life of trade' was a phrase frequently used by English merchants and ship captains in relation to trading in coastal Africa. It was imperative to load slaves on shipboard as efficiently as possible: the longer the stay on the coast, the greater the susceptibility of slaves and crew to disease. Provisions such as yams and rice would be loaded to feed the slaves during the Atlantic crossing—Africans were largely vegetarians—and fresh water taken on board. Slaves were chained together beneath deck, side by side, rather in the manner depicted in the famous print of the Liverpool slave ship the *Brookes*. They were allowed up on deck for air and exercise for one or two hours a day, but were otherwise kept confined. A distinction was usually made between male and female slaves. 'When we purchase the Negroes,' William Snelgrave, a slave trade captain and author of an account of the trade explained,

we couple the sturdy Men together with Irons; but we suffer the Women and Children to go freely about: And soon after we have sail'd from the coast, we undo all the Mens Irons. They are fed twice a day, and are allowed in fair weather to come on Deck at seven o clock in the Morning, and to remain there, if they think proper, till sun setting... The Men Negroes lodge separate from the Women and Children; and the places where they all lye are cleaned every day, some white men being appointed to see them do it.[9]

This quotation presents a relatively benign view of the treatment of slaves aboard ships on the Middle Passage. But there were, of course, more unpleasant ways of treating slaves. Misdemeanours by slaves on board ship were often punished by flogging, and sadistic captains in the slave trade gave an even blacker reputation to the trade than it had perforce acquired of its own accord. Barracoons were frequently erected on slave vessels for confining troublesome captives. 'This day fixed 4 swivel blunderbusses in the barricado,' John Newton, a Liverpool slave captain and later a convert to religious antislavery, noted off the coast of Sierra Leone on 7 December 1750, 'which with the carriage guns we put thro' at the Bananoes, make a formidable appearance upon the main deck, and will, I hope, be sufficient to intimidate the Slaves from any thoughts of an insurrection.'[10] On a second voyage to Africa in 1752 and 1753, Newton discovered a slave plot for an insurrection during the Middle Passage and so he put the boys in irons and thumbscrews to extract a full confession, examined six adult male slaves, and punished several of them with collars and neck yokes. A poem entitled 'The Sorrow of Yoruba' (1790) summarized the pain involved in treating the enslaved onboard ship: 'At the savage Captain's beck, | Now like brutes they make us prance: | Smack the Cat about the Deck, | And in scorn they bid us dance.'[11]

The Middle Passage lasted for four, five or six weeks, and was associated with mortality and with slave resistance. In the first half of the eighteenth century around 20 per cent of the slaves taken on board English slaving vessels died en route to the Americas; after 1750, the mortality loss fell to 10 per cent and less. This was a higher loss of life on oceanic shipping voyages than occurred with other long-distance trades such as the shipment of convicts to Australia. 'The closeness of the place, and the heat of the climate,' Equiano wrote in the first major

[9] William Snelgrave, *A New Account of Guinea, and the Slave Trade, containing I. The History of the late conquest of the kingdom of Whidaw by the king of Dahome . . . II. The manner how the negroes become slaves . . . III. A relation of the author's being taken by pirates, and the many dangers he underwent* (London, 1754), 163–4.

[10] Quoted in Bernard Martin and Mark Spurrell (eds.), *The Journal of a Slave Trader (John Newton) 1750–1754* (London, 1962), 22. The Bananoes were small islands off the coast of Sierra Leone.

[11] Quoted in Colin A. Palmer, 'The Middle Passage', in *Captive Passage: The Transatlantic Slave Trade and the Making of the Americas* (Washington DC, 2002), 60.

literary description of the Middle Passage, 'added to the number in the ship, which was so crowded that each had scarcely room to turn himself, almost suffocated us. This produced copious perspirations, so that the air soon became unfit for respiration . . . and brought on a sickness among the slaves, of which many died, thus falling victims to the improvident avarice . . . of their purchasers.'[12]

Though some slaves died from respiratory problems such as inflammation of the lungs, as this contemporary assessment suggests, the mortality on the Middle Passage occurred largely through diseases caught in Africa. The prime cause of death comprised gastroenterital complaints, caused by dirty, unhygienic conditions. Flux, dysentery, and severe diarrhoea were the chief symptoms of gastroenteritis. There were also deaths through dropsy, scarlet and yellow fever, malignant fever, tuberculosis, and a host of other diseases. Dr Alexander Falconbridge, once a surgeon on English slaving vessels, noted that some ships' holds were 'so covered with the blood and mucus which had proceeded from them in consequence of the flux, that it resembled a slaughter house'.[13] The cycle of mortality depended on how long slaves had been stowed on the African coast to await shipment. The longer slaves were kept in compounds, the greater the chance of disease breaking out. In fact, the incidence of disease followed the normal pattern of an epidemic, with deaths rising during the first third of the Middle Passage to reach a peak before falling and levelling off later in the voyage. Apart from diseases, slaves sometimes committed suicide in despair at their captivity, usually throwing themselves overboard into the ocean. Towards the end of the voyage, dehydration sometimes occurred as water supplies became depleted. Crew mortality was also higher on slave-trading voyages than on other oceanic crossings.

Not all slaves accepted their situation with passivity; some staged risings on shipboard to attempt to overthrow their captors. Most of these rebellions occurred fairly soon after ships sailed from Africa; and though most were put down, they nevertheless added to the misery, despair, and riskiness of slaving voyages. There was a regional dimension to the outbreaks against oppression, for more risings occurred on ships

[12] Equiano quoted in Craton, Walvin, and Wright (eds), *Slavery, Abolition and Emancipation*, 41.

[13] Christopher Fyfe (ed.), *Anna Maria Falconbridge, Narrative of two voyages to the River Sierra Leone during the years 1791–1792–1793 and the Journal of Isaac DuBois with Alexander Falconbridge, An Account of the Slave Trade on the Coast of Africa* (Liverpool, 2000), 211.

leaving Senegambia than other West African regions. The prevalence of uprisings on slave ships—and, indeed, the process of enslavement in Africa—reminds us of the violence that characterized the traffic in black human beings. Physical coercion, brutality, injuries, and abuse were everyday occurrences for Africans drawn into the vortex of the transatlantic slave trade.

## SLAVE SALES

Ports of disembarkation for slaves aboard English ships were largely decided by English merchants before ships set sail from their home ports. Letters of instruction to captains advised them of several alternatives where they could sell their slaves. Most ships disembarked their slaves at one pre-arranged port or harbour in the Americas, but if markets for slave sales were slack at particular ports the ships would then sail to another destination, usually within a few days' sail. Specific colonial factors were recommended for the handling of slave sales. The impending arrival of slave vessels in American harbours was not just a matter of sighting a ship sailing towards the shore. The smell of the human bodies kept closely together over such a long ocean passage in cramped, often dirty, conditions meant that the stench of a slave vessel was another way of announcing its arrival.

Slave vessels entering North American and West Indian harbours observed quarantine laws and paid import duties on the slaves they imported. Sales were advertised in local newspapers and a set day and time publicized for the start of the sale. Some slave sales were held on shipboard; others were conducted on shore. Sick slaves (often termed 'refuse' slaves) were usually taken on shore and sold at a tavern by public auction at low prices. For many years, the beginning of a slave sale was marked by a scramble, as Falconbridge vividly described in the early 1790s with regard to the West Indies:

On the day appointed, the negroes were landed, and placed together in a large yard, belonging to the merchants to whom the ship was consigned. As soon as the hour agreed upon arrived, the doors of the yard were suddenly thrown open, and in rushed a considerable number of purchasers, with all the ferocity of brutes. Some instantly seized such of the Negroes as they could lay hold of with their hands. Others, being prepared with several handkerchiefs tied together, encircled with these as many as they were able. While others, by means of a rope, effected the same purpose. It is scarcely possible to describe the confusion of which this mode of selling is productive. It likewise causes much animosity among the purchasers, who, not infrequently on these occasions, fall out and quarrel with each other. The poor astonished negroes were so much terrified by these proceedings, that several of them, through fear, climbed over the walls of the court yard, and ran wild about the town; but were soon hunted down and retaken.[14]

On another occasion, he added, the scramble took place by Africans being brought on deck, the ship darkened with sails suspended over them, and purchasers rushed and seized black captives after the signal was given to start the sale. Scrambles invariably occurred when newly arrived slave vessels were scarce. In Jamaica sales were conducted differently after 1788, when the Consolidated Slave Law passed by the island's Assembly required that slaves be sold in rooms on shore, not on board ship, the intention being to keep families together. Such sales were conducted in a more orderly way than scrambles. They often involved captains marching their slaves through a town or port where they were intended to be sold and placing them in rows where they were examined and purchased. The sales ended with cash auctions to dispose of slaves lingering on hand.

Prospective purchasers were local merchants and planters, for the most part; they either bought slaves singly, in pairs, or in lots. The characteristics of buyers of slaves have been studied for Kingston, Jamaica, the leading slave disembarkation port in the British Empire. In the mid-eighteenth century 65 per cent of the purchasers of slaves at Kingston were from the town, buying 73 per cent of the slaves sold. The remaining buyers came from parishes throughout Jamaica. Wealthy merchants were prominent purchasers of slaves at Kingston, Jamaica. In the mid-eighteenth century they included Zachary Bayly, George Paplay, and Aaron Baruh Lousada, who each left personal estates worth more than £100,000. Nearly a third of the buyers of slaves at Kingston between 1746 and 1782 were seriously wealthy, with personal estates valued at £10,000.

Purchasers eyed up the limbs and muscles of slaves, working along a line of people rather like the hiring of dock workers in Elia Kazan's film *On the Waterfront*. They did not usually buy Africans in lots of uniform size. In the British Caribbean, for instance, the average lot of slaves sold was twenty-seven in the period 1750–1807 for the Leeward and Windward Islands compared with a figure of nine for Jamaica and Barbados. The larger lots sold to purchasers in the smaller islands of the Lesser

---

[14] Quoted ibid. 216–17.

Antilles reflected in part the greater transaction and information costs at smaller harbours. It also stemmed from the fact that a relatively small number of purchasers had to travel only short distances to attend sales. Credit was commonly offered for slave sales except in circumstances where planters were in funds and cash could be demanded. Typically, credit was arranged for the marketing of the healthiest and strongest slaves, which were sold first. Credit sales continued as smaller, less desirable slaves were sold. Often these transactions were effected with bonds or promissory notes to give reasonable assurance that debts would be paid on time. Finally, 'refuse' slaves were sold in a 'vendue' cash auction as sellers found offering credit too risky for slaves with particularly high expected mortality or for those too weak to be of use in the plantation economy. Slaves were either kept in merchants' yards for later resale—such as frequently occurred at Kingston—or transferred to plantations.

Buyers of slaves often expressed preferences for particular African ethnic groups. Thus, for instance, slaves from Old Calabar were invariably in poor repute in colonies such as South Carolina, Antigua, and Jamaica: they were considered poor workers and physically less tough than other Africans. Conversely, in Jamaica and some Leeward islands there was a marked preference for slaves from the Gold Coast and the Bight of Benin. These were thought to be in good physical condition and hard workers. Thus the agents of a Bristol slave-trading partnership in Antigua in 1740 requested that slave vessels should be directed 'to the Gold Coast or Widdaw [i.e. Ouidah], as Negroes from those places, Especially the latter, are in most Esteem here & will always sell at Good Prices, when Bonny Negroes (the men particularly) are held in much Contempt, comparatively with the Others.'[15] A Jamaican planter in the 1790s stated that he had 'ever found that Gold Coast Negroes the Males about 18 & the females about 16 years of age the best calculated for sugar estates. There is always work adapted to them till they come to be seasoned to the country.'[16]

Many attributes accorded to slaves from particular regions of West Africa were based on stereotypes. Europeans commonly used ethnographic labels that grossly oversimplified African identity groups. Moreover, the fact that planters and other buyers desired slaves from

[15] Benjamin King and Robert Arbuthnot to Isaac Hobhouse and Stephen Baugh, 24 Nov. 1740, in Madge Dresser and Sue Giles (eds.), *Bristol & Transatlantic Slavery* (Bristol, 2000), 49.

[16] Derbyshire Record Office, Matlock, John Jaques to W. P. Perrin, 8 Feb. 1794, Fitzherbert Papers, 239M/E17141.

those areas did not mean necessarily that they received them. The slaves on offer for sale at disembarkation points in the Americas were the product of supply conditions; and buyers purchased slaves more on the basis of those supplied by vessels rather than waiting for ships to bring in Africans of the preferred ethnicity and then cherry-picking them. This means that a heterogeneous package of slaves—by age, gender, price, ethnicity—was the norm for slave arrivals in the Americas. Needless to say, during sales families were often split up, if this had not already happened during the process of procuring slaves in Africa.

It was common for the number of crew to be reduced in the Americas: once the control over slaves was no longer required, fewer crew were needed for the homeward-bound voyage. Crew were usually therefore paid the reminder of their wages at American ports. Some decided to jump ship there in any case because they had had their fill of serving on a 'Guinea' vessel. The ships would be scrubbed clean after the black human cargo had been sold, for the stench and grime needed to be cleared away to load plantation produce for the homeward-bound voyage. The payment for slaves sometimes took the form of crops or cash, but a safer and preferred form of remittance was to send home the proceeds in bills of exchange at specified intervals. To ensure bills were honoured, slave merchants at English ports increasingly used merchant houses and financiers that would accept bills at sight and guarantee to pay them.

## COSTS AND PROFITS IN THE SLAVE TRADE

The costs of operating slave-trading voyages were substantial, and they increased as the eighteenth century progressed. British slave merchants sank large amounts of capital into the trade. Bristol merchants invested £50,000–60,000 annually in the slave trade c.1710–11, over £150,000 per annum in the 1730s, and £280,100 on average in the period 1788–92. The annual sums invested in Liverpool's slave trade were c.£200,000 in 1750 and probably more than £1 million in 1800. Such investments were made on the predication that merchants could make a substantial profit from slave trading. Contemporaries certainly thought this was the case. In 1750 Postlethwayt considered that Britain's annual gain from participation in the slave trade amounted to £1,648,600. Henry Bright, a Bristolian resident in Kingston in 1750, had no doubts about the economic importance of the slave trade, for it was 'the chief

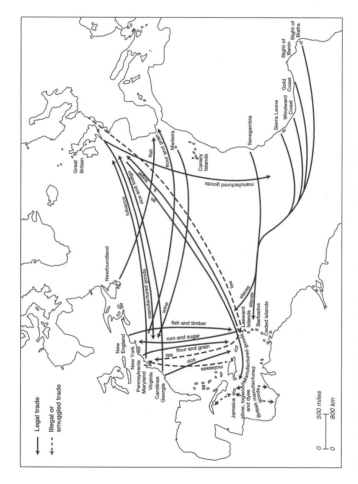

Map 6. The British North Atlantic trading system, c.1768–1772.

motive of people venturing their fortunes abroad'.[17] Just over a decade later a merchant partnership in Virginia noted that the slave trade was 'by farr the most profitable trade that we have in this part of the world'.[18] The merchant, planter, and South Carolina politician Henry Laurens, who himself imported slaves before he got qualms about doing so, was convinced that British slave merchants made considerable booty in the trade.

How far were contemporary predictions correct? What profits were made in the slave trade? And what happened to those profits? It was once argued that the profits of the British slave trade amounted to 30 per cent on capital invested by the 1780s. Analysis of the surviving papers of slave merchants has shown this to be exaggerated, however. Between 1770 and 1792 profits per venture in the Bristol slave trade came to 7.6 per cent. Evidence taken largely from Liverpool shows that, in the second half of the eighteenth century, a rate of return of between 8 and 10 per cent on annual investment in slave-trading voyages was the norm. Any business generating such returns regularly today would consider this a satisfactory return on invested capital. Evidence from other eighteenth-century trades, such as the Levant trade, shows that a 10 per cent return on capital was acceptable. The return on government consols during the eighteenth century, a relatively risk-free form of investment, was usually around the 3.5 per cent mark; and so slave-trading profits were worth the efforts of merchants despite the riskiness and long-drawn-out nature of the voyages.

## THE SLAVE TRADE AND BRITISH ECONOMIC DEVELOPMENT

The contribution of slave-trading profits to the economic development of Britain has been a controversial topic ever since Eric Williams argued in *Capitalism and Slavery* (1944) that the gains were substantial and linked to the origins of industrialization in Britain. He argued that the profits from the slave trade 'provided one of the main streams of accumulation of capital in England which financed the Industrial Revolution',

[17] University of Melbourne Archives, Henry Bright to (?), Sept. 1750, loose business correspondence, Bright Family Papers.
[18] William Allason to Crosbies & Traffords, 4 Aug. 1761, quoted in Darold D. Wax, 'Negro Import Duties in Colonial Virginia: A Study in British Commercial Policy and Local Public Policy', *Virginia Magazine of History and Biography*, 79 (1971), 43.

and that 'the triangular trade made an enormous contribution to Britain's industrial development. The profits from this trade fertilized the entire productive system of the country.'[19] These generalizations have proven highly contentious. Some historians follow their broad thrust in arguing that the slave trade, and by extension overseas demand, made a critical contribution to the origins of British industrialization in the late eighteenth century. Others are more sceptical of the scale of the impact of the slave trade on British economic growth, and emphasize that it did not make much difference 'at the margin'. These latter historians usually offer supply-side explanations of Britain's transition into an industrialized economy.

While accepting that slave trade profits operated at a relatively modest level, one set of estimates shows that the profits of the slave trade could have comprised as much as 39 per cent of commercial and industrial investment in the eighteenth century. According to this interpretation, 'the profits of the slave trade and those derived from the West Indian colonies were quantitatively large compared with total British investment and with commercial and industrial investment, at the beginning of the Industrial Revolution.'[20] This seems an exaggerated claim based on an estimate of profits in the slave trade in relation to total investment in the economy. To look at the contribution of any sector or sub-sector of the economy in relation to national income or GNP is a narrow way of investigating the significance of the slave trade for the development of the British economy. It tells us something useful about a 'one-to-one' economic relationship but can only suggest what could have been the upper limit of the contribution of those gains. Moreover, it is difficult to see how slavery, the slave trade and their main commodity product, sugar, produced an important multiplier effect in Britain during the eighteenth century.

Yet if slave trade profits did not have a significant influence on the British economy, as opposed to the private wealth of individuals, the demand created by the slavery–sugar nexus was a stimulus to British economic performance. In the period 1748–75, in particular, the incomes flowing back to Britain from increased sugar production in the Caribbean and consumption in the mother country led to higher levels of exports and slaves being sent to the West Indies: the exports

---

[19] Eric Williams, *Capitalism and Slavery* (Chapel Hill, NC, 1944), 105.
[20] Barbara L. Solow, 'Caribbean Slavery and British Growth: The Eric Williams Hypothesis', *Journal of Development Economics*, 17 (1985), 106.

were needed to clothe the slaves and to provide equipment for the plantations, and the slaves were necessary to replenish existing slave populations that were subject to heavy mortality as a result of disease, overwork, and poor nutrition. Thus between 1748 and 1776 sugar imports doubled from 900,000 to 1.8 million cwt; sugar consumption doubled to reach a per capita level of 25 lb; and average gross revenues from sugar sales also doubled from £1.6 million to £3.2 million. The annual number of slaves shipped in British vessels rose from around 25,800 between 1749 and 1755 to reach a peak of 43,500 in the period 1763–75. It has been argued that Caribbean-based demand may have accounted for about 35 per cent of the growth of total British exports between 1748 and 1776, and for about 12 per cent of the increase in British industrial output in the quarter-century before the American Revolution. The growth in English exports supplied to the Americas in the mid-eighteenth century helped to expand production in the textile, metal, and hardware industries in Britain. The need to provide such export goods at an accelerating rate may well have aided the diffusion of technical innovation, notably in cotton spinning, to the British textile industry. And so it is likely that the main stimulus of the slave trade to the British economy lay in the channels of increasing demand. It would be incorrect to claim that the wealth flowing home from the slave trade was a major stimulus for industrialization in Britain, but it would not be unfair to claim that the slave–sugar trading complex strengthened the British economy and played a significant, though not decisive part, in its evolution.

# 4

# Slave Demography and Family Life

The demographic composition of the slave population shaped the parameters of slave life in North America and the Caribbean. Sex ratios, age structure, and the relative proportion of African and creole slaves influenced reproductive rates, family formation, and black culture. Though the relative proportion of males and females in the Atlantic slave trade varied over time and by region, generally there was a demographic imbalance. Males outnumbered females, often by a ratio of two to one. This was partly because women were prized in Africa as workers and therefore retained in African societies, and partly because buyers across the Atlantic primarily demanded adult male slaves, especially young, healthy, strong workers. In a nutshell, colonies that depended heavily on an influx of enslaved Africans imported more men than women. Young adult males were thus the backbone of the British transatlantic slave trade. It was not until after that trade was abolished that children became a significant portion of the Africans shipped across the Atlantic.

Apart from the unbalanced sex ratio, several other factors affected the reproductive capacity of Africans taken to America. Many of the enslaved disembarked ship in the Americas already in a debilitated state from the sickness and stresses experienced during the Middle Passage. The epidemiological shock experienced by people entering a new continent and new disease environment tended to produce above average mortality rates. A significant proportion of adult female slaves were already advanced in terms of childbearing years. African women in their prime invariably practised prolonged lactation of up to three years, which acted as a natural contraceptive. These factors meant that fertility among newly arrived African slaves in America tended to be low and mortality relatively high. This naturally created severe problems for family formation. Reproductive rates among the enslaved population of British America were shaped by the proportion of Africans and creoles in a colony. The predominance of creole slaves in a colony produced a more balanced sex ratio than colonies where most slaves were Africans. In the latter case, the greater intake of male rather than female slaves via the Middle Passage created the gender imbalance. Creole slaves had certain other demographic advantages over Africans. Births occurred at an earlier stage of a creole woman's life cycle, adaptation to a new disease environment was not a problem, and consequently fertility increased while mortality waned. Thus African-born slaves in the New World experienced higher age-specific mortality rates and lower fertility rates than creole slaves.

Most slaves disembarked in North America before 1750 were imported Africans but a generation later they were mainly creoles. At the outbreak of the American War of Independence only 20 per cent of the slaves in the thirteen British North American colonies were African-born. The situation was different in the British Caribbean. High mortality rates among imported Africans meant that the slave populations there depended on the continuing influx of newly imported slaves until the abolition of the British slave trade in 1807. It was not until the subsequent period that creoles began to predominate among the slave population in the British West Indies. A creole majority did not appear in Barbados until 1810 and in Jamaica until 1840. These differences led to significant variations in the plantation colonies between the demographic experience of the black population in the Chesapeake, the Lowcountry, and the Caribbean. The chief contrast lay in the more rapid rise of a native-born slave population in the Upper South compared with the Lower South and an even more sluggish shift towards a creole population in the West Indian islands. The demographic difference between the Chesapeake and the Lowcountry was well under way by the second quarter of the eighteenth century. It became an even more notable feature of Chesapeake society in the generation before the Revolution. In the Lower South the proportion of black creoles in the population also rose during the eighteenth century but more slowly. The slave trade continued to South Carolina, with interruptions caused by non-importation policies, until 1808, when Thomas Jefferson's government finally stopped it. Slave importations into Virginia and Maryland, by contrast, effectively stopped in the late 1760s and early 1770s.

## SLAVE DEMOGRAPHY IN THE CHESAPEAKE

The black population in Virginia and Maryland was heavily dependent on an African influx between 1690 and 1740. Africans were imported to the major river systems of the western shore of the Chesapeake Bay where tobacco planting flourished. Thereafter rapid growth among slave families enabled planters to cut back on freshly imported slaves as the black population experienced sustained natural growth and the ratio of births to deaths increased. A contemporary clergyman realized this transformation had begun by the 1720s, for he remarked that 'the Negroes are not only encreased by fresh supplies from Africa and the West India islands; but also are very prolifick among themselves.'[1] In 1728 about half of the adult black slaves in the Chesapeake had arrived within the last decade; by 1750 the proportion was 17 per cent. One-third of enslaved workers in Virginia and Maryland were Africans in the 1750s, by which time the demand for newly imported Africans came mainly from the interior piedmont areas of the region, where tobacco planting was expanding westward to escape soil exhaustion. Two decades later only one tenth of the slave population of the Chesapeake had been born in Africa. This was a remarkable demographic transition within less than a century. Few New World slave populations experienced such good rates of population growth and the rise of a creole-dominated plantation workforce.

In the early eighteenth century several disincentives prevented the early emergence of many creole slaves in the Chesapeake. The 'seasoning' of Africans was a precarious affair. One in four saltwater slaves died during their first year in Virginia and Maryland, mainly from malaria or respiratory illnesses. This, coupled with the scattered nature of slave quarters (often segregated by sex), the low population density of the black population, and the excess of males over females among adult imported slaves, militated against a demographic upsurge. In addition, work routines on the tobacco plantations did not favour slave women. The labour force was not usually divided by sex but by age and physical ability. This meant that pregnant slave women worked alongside men in the tobacco fields, usually with no reduction in work demands because of their condition.

Gradually, these demographic problems receded. As the survivors among the new slaves had children, a better-balanced sex ratio developed. Creole slave women proved more fertile than Africans, largely for the general reasons already mentioned; on average, they bore six children

---

[1] Richard L. Morton (ed.), Hugh Jones, *The Present State of Virginia; from whence is inferred a short view of Maryland and North Carolina* [1724] (Chapel Hill, NC, 1956), 75.

whereas African-born female slaves bore three. Moreover, native-born black women married earlier than African women, often entering wedlock in their late teens. This increased their legitimate childbearing years. Plantation sizes increased in Virginia and Maryland after 1750, and as slave quarters grew in size and black population density followed suit, more opportunities arose for personal liaisons and relationships among male and female slaves. Most slaves in the Chesapeake lived in families by the 1770s and cross-plantation networks among them were common.

## SLAVE DEMOGRAPHY IN SOUTH CAROLINA

South Carolina was heavily dependent on African-born slaves until about 1750. In the first half of the eighteenth century, males exceeded females among the black cargoes entering Charleston, the main port of entry for transatlantic sailing vessels. Between 1720 and 1740 Charleston's slave imports reached their highest levels yet, enabling planters in the province to top up their workforce with new arrivals. Africans in South Carolina escaped some diseases prevalent there. Mosquitoes flourishing in the freshwater marshes of the rice fields frequently spread a dangerous strain of malaria, known as *falciparum*, which caused epidemic outbreaks mainly among the local white population. The spread of yellow fever, again by mosquitoes, was another major killer of white folk in early South Carolina. Yet African slaves in South Carolina often carried a genetic sickle-cell trait that immunized them against the effects of *falciparum*. Many were also naturally immune to yellow fever. African mothers passed antibodies against this virus to their children before they were born, and slave babies then developed their own antibodies to yellow fever.

Yet even if most blacks were spared deaths from malaria and yellow fever, they contracted many other diseases. Epidemics of smallpox, pestilential fevers, pleurisy, and lung diseases occurred from time to time in South Carolina, affecting black people in particular. The living conditions in slave quarters were cramped, unhygienic, and miserable—a breeding ground, in fact, for disease. In this environment, childhood mortality rates in the Lowcountry may have climbed to as high as 50 per cent of births. If so, they probably soared above the usual rates of infant mortality found on West Indian sugar plantations—another demographic killer in the plantation Americas. In addition to epidemiological factors, the hard work of rice cultivation took its toll on adult slaves: a high proportion died while still in their prime as a result of over-exertion and exhaustion. Nutritional deficiency also played its part in the mortality of slaves because the slave diet in South Carolina, though including varied vegetables, was less substantial and provided more sporadically than in the Chesapeake. In addition, protein rations were often inadequate. Lowcountry slaves relied more on self-subsistence than the enslaved in the Chesapeake—through hunting, fishing, and cultivating their own plants—but their overall nutrition suffered.

The aftermath of the Stono rebellion of 1739 curtailed the arrival of Africans for virtually a decade as South Carolinians, shaken up by a slave revolt led by Africans, decided to cut back on 'new negroes'. Native-born blacks therefore had the time to reproduce in the 1740s but a creole majority among slaves had not yet emerged. After 1750, the South Carolina slave population began to reproduce itself. Governor James Glen recognized this demographic growth when he noted that 'importations' of slaves to the colony were 'not to supply the place of Negroes worn out with hard work or lost by Mortality which is the case in our Islands where were it not for an annual accretion they could not keep up their stock, but our number encreases even without such yearly supply.'[2] In fact, this was too sanguine. A surplus of births over deaths was achieved among the South Carolina slave population after 1750 but the reproduction rates were three or four times lower than in the Chesapeake. It is thus unsurprising that South Carolinians continued to take a strong interest in the Anglo-American slave trade until its demise. Native-born blacks in the Palmetto colony comprised 37 per cent of adult slaves in 1730, 44 per cent in 1750, and 56 per cent in 1770.

## EXPLAINING SLAVE DEMOGRAPHIC GROWTH IN NORTH AMERICA

Various explanations can be offered for the demographic growth of the slave population in eighteenth-century North America. The disease environment was less harsh than in the tropical conditions of the Caribbean, though throughout British America epidemic diseases had a

[2] James Glen to the Board of Trade, 26 Aug. 1754, in Elizabeth Donnan (ed.), *Documents Illustrative of the History of the Slave Trade to America*, 4 vols. (Washington DC, 1930–5), iv. 313.

significant impact on the health of enslaved African-American women of childbearing age. In the northern American colonies, slaves caught ailments like measles and whooping cough; they often had poor shelter, ragged clothing, and inadequate nutrients in their diet; and their death rates in Boston and Philadelphia by the 1750s and 1760s were significantly higher than those found among white urban dwellers. The work regimes of the tobacco and rice plantations (discussed in Chapter 5), and even more so of the scattered black communities in the colonies north of Maryland, were less oppressive than the demands of sugar cane cultivation; but overwork and exhaustion, especially at harvest times, helped to maintain the incidence of high morbidity and mortality.

The possibility that black creole slaves in North America adopted European practices of nursing may have aided reproduction among plantation slaves in the Chesapeake and Lowcountry. Such practices encouraged a maximum length of one year for breastfeeding compared with two or three years among African slave women in the British Caribbean. Shorter breastfeeding periods for babies, it is argued, would have aided the resumption of ovulation and contributed to more closely spaced births in North America than in the West Indies. Reproduction was aided by another factor. As the slave population began to reproduce itself in the Chesapeake, the Carolinas, and Georgia by the mid-eighteenth century, slave women tended to form sexual relationships at earlier ages than their African mothers and therefore produced their babies from a younger age. This gave them more childbearing years than African-born women, who tended to begin and end reproduction over a shorter time span.

The nutritional status of slaves in North America appears to have been a crucial factor leading to increasing levels of slave fertility. The southern mainland North American colonies had a plentiful supply of foodstuffs by the early eighteenth century and grains and meats were exported in bulk by 1775. Most slaves in the Chesapeake and the Lowcountry had maize as a staple part of their diet. This was supplemented by vegetables, some meat, water and rum rations, and food foraged by slaves from the fringes of plantations. Chesapeake slaves had better diets on the whole than their counterparts in South Carolina: their grain supplies were more plentiful and more evenly provided. Their meat supplies were also more generous, though they received the heads, ribs and feet of animals rather than their breasts or legs. Though Lowcountry slaves appear to have hunted and fished more than Chesapeake slaves and to have maintained a wider range of plants in their plots and gardens, they probably suffered from greater nutritional deficiency as a result of receiving poorer and slimmer rations from their owners. Contrasts in the diet of Chesapeake and South Carolina slaves made an impact on the different demographic performance of the slave population in both areas during the eighteenth century. The Chesapeake slave population, as already noted, began to reproduce effectively from the 1730s, leading to the growth of more creoles in the black population and consequently a diminishing reliance on new African imports. The South Carolina slave population took longer to reproduce itself; even after the American Revolution, it still relied upon large, if irregular, supplies of newly disembarked Africans until the turn of the nineteenth century.

## SLAVE DEMOGRAPHY IN THE BRITISH CARIBBEAN

The demographic experience of the British Caribbean was a continuous struggle for survival. Throughout the eighteenth century the slave population in those islands was heavily dependent on new imports. This was particularly true for Jamaica and the Ceded Islands. The exception to this rule was Barbados where, from the early eighteenth century, imports of slave women exceeded those of African men. Consequently, it proved easier to establish rates of natural reproduction. This was achieved by the early eighteenth century. By the time of the American Revolution Barbados had a growing creole slave population and had declined as an island for the import of saltwater slaves.

Sugar plantations in the West Indies were in a class of their own in terms of their demographic effects. West Indian slave fertility reached only about 60 per cent of the level of that experienced by slaves in North America. Slaves on sugar plantations experienced a higher mortality rate than slaves, whether Africans or creoles, working in any other type of staple crop production. Thus the death rate on early nineteenth-century Jamaican plantations was 50 per cent higher than on coffee plantations. In Trinidad during the same period nearly three times as many adult males died on sugar as on cotton plantations. It is no accident that high mortality was also common among slaves involved in sugar cultivation in Louisiana and Brazil. Whether the link between sugar cultivation and heavy mortality resulted primarily from the environmental setting for growing sugar—often in low, swampy areas—or whether intensity of labour was a more critical factor is still a debated issue.

Before the abolition of the British slave trade in 1807, buying slaves rather than breeding them was the usual resort of British West Indian slaveowners. This led to problems with maintaining natural increase among the slave population. This was acknowledged by the attorney to Hope plantation, a Jamaican sugar estate, who wrote that a decrease rather than increase in slaves was 'the case with every Estate in the Island, at least with very few exceptions'.[3] Faced with high levels of mortality and poor fertility among their enslaved workforce, planters continually turned to the supply of fresh slaves from Africa to replenish their stock. Thus Jamaica imported 575,000 African captives in the eighteenth century to increase the population by around 250,000. After the slave trade ended, the Jamaican slave population continued to decline. Thus between 1807 and 1834 the Jamaican slave population fell by 43,000, a drop of 12 per cent. Poor reproduction rates were largely responsible for this situation. The fertility rate for selected Jamaican plantations in the period 1754–1832 ranged from 79 to 108 births per 1,000 women aged from 15 to 44. Peak fertility in modern Jamaica, at ages 20 to 24, yields 299 infants per 1,000 woman years. In addition to a low birth rate, the incidence of infant mortality was high. Around 80 per cent of infant deaths in the eighteenth-century British Caribbean occurred in the first two weeks of life; in the nineteenth century, the proportion was 50 per cent.

Slave reproduction was linked closely to the material and working lives of black captives. Slaves were fed on a diet of mainly grain or vegetables, and were required on most West Indian islands to cultivate their own provisions to feed themselves rather than rely on masters' rations. Guinea corn, plaintains, and yams were important crops grown and eaten by Caribbean slaves. Imported foodstuffs added to the diet of slaves but subsistence problems occurred during wartime periods when dry provisions (wheat, flour, other grains) from North America were reduced, notably during the American revolutionary war. Malnutrition was common among the West Indian slave population despite these sources of food. An average daily plantation food allowance amounted to between 1,500 and 2,000 calories and approximately 45 grams of protein. Under average conditions men require roughly 3,200 calories a day and women 2,300, the metabolic rate being slower for women than men. Under conditions of exceptionally heavy labour, both male

[3] National Library of Jamaica, Kingston, E. East to Roger Hope Elletson, 23 Sept. 1778, Roger Hope Elletson letterbook (1773–80).

and female workers need an additional 450 calories. These estimates indicate that Caribbean slaves received less than the energy required for heavy work in the cane fields and around the processing plant on estates. Slave diet was monotonous and deficient in thiamine, calcium, and vitamin A. Slaves lacking supplies of thiamine would have been unable to properly utilize riboflavin and niacin, which would have upset the metabolization of all the B vitamins. Slaves voiced their distress over these nutritional deficiencies. Disputes over food supplies comprised the second largest number of complaints (after brutal punishment) made to the Protectors of slaves in Berbice in the 1820s.

Slave working conditions exacerbated the nutritional problem. The work performed by field slaves was arduous (see Chapter 5). Hard field work took a heavy toll on female slaves in particular because women outnumbered men in the field gangs that carried out the most strenuous work in cane holing, planting, and harvesting sugar cane. In 1800 a Barbadian planter noted that it was the usual practice with planters 'to work all the negroes together, indiscriminately, as the women with men, and the weak with the strong'.[4] Pregnant women working in the cane fields customarily did so until six weeks before delivery; they were often back undertaking field work, accompanied by their infants, three weeks after the baby's birth. In the last decade of slavery, women field workers were often allowed, as a result of ameliorative policies, to be excused from the great gang once they made it known they were pregnant; they were allowed to stop working four months later; and after delivery they were permitted to stay in the second gang while breastfeeding. Despite these concessions, planters were unwilling to excuse women altogether from severely demanding fieldwork.

Pregnant slave women were often subject to brutal physical punishment. Thomas Thistlewood, a white overseer in Westmoreland Parish, Jamaica, regularly flogged slaves of both sexes and hired out pregnant slave women at the full rate of pay for field labourers until they were within two or three months of delivery. 'Monk' Lewis, a prominent absentee planter, stated that 'white overseers and bookkeepers [kicked] black women in the belly from one end of Jamaica to the other'.[5] John Williamson recorded in 1817 that 'prolapses of the uterus

---

[4] J. W. Orderson, *Directions to Young Planters for their Care and Management of a Sugar Plantation in Barbados* (London, 1800), 4.
[5] Matthew Gregory Lewis, *Journal of a Residence among the Negroes of the West Indies* (London, 1845), 174–5.

or womb . . . in consequence of harsh treatment' was common in Jamaica.[6] The early months of pregnancy are those when women are most susceptible to miscarriage, yet the arduous physical labour on plantations, excessive stooping, carrying of heavy weights, and compulsion to work were unceasing during the crop period. Severe beatings would lead to problems in the endocrine system. Poor nutrition, strenuous work demands in the sugar fields, and physical punishment all helped to create conditions for slave women that discouraged reproduction.

These difficulties, it has been suggested, spread anti-breeding attitudes among creole slave women; in other words, such women chose not to reproduce. This argument is impossible to verify given the lack of slave testimony. Contemporaries and some modern historians have also pointed to fluctuations in the menstrual cycle affecting the ability of Caribbean slave women to reproduce. Sometimes this problem was related to the practice of geophagy, the eating of baked clay cakes (called 'aboo') as a natural response to nutritional deficiency. Women, in particular, ate the fine clays, which could be purchased easily in markets. But there are no modern medical findings to support the notion that pica (a vitiated appetite for dirt eating) halts menstruation, though it is related to nutritional deficiencies and amenorrhea (cessation of the menstrual period) directly linked to malnutrition. The psychological basis for interruptions in the menstrual cycle is still not fully understood. Studies carried out on German concentration camp survivors appear to give some weight to the argument that stress has physical repercussions on fertility and can halt the menstrual cycle. Yet one should not push the comparison too far. Material conditions for Caribbean slave women were far from easy or pleasant, but they were not systematically starved or locked up as in the concentration camps. The fact that slave women could undertake physically demanding work suggests that their bodies could withstand a tough regime.

An interesting hypothesis argues that the fertility differentials between slaves in these areas can be explained partly by differences in childspacing, determined partially by lactation practices. African women in the British West Indies practised wider spacing between conceptions as a result of nursing their children for two, sometimes three, years, whereas breastfeeding among North American slave women lasted no longer than a year. As a result, spacing between surviving slave children

---

[6] John Williamson, *Medical and Miscellaneous Observations relative to the West India Islands*, 2 vols. (Edinburgh, 1817), ii. 205.

in the United States in the nineteenth century was less than the three-to-four years found among West Indian slave children. Longer lactation, it is argued, would serve as a means of natural contraception either through the physiological effects of producing breast milk in the mother or through the taboo on sexual intercourse while nursing, which was common in the Caribbean. Whether prolonged breastfeeding reduced the reproductive capacity of slaves is doubtful, however. The contraceptive benefit of lactation generally lasts no longer than a year. This finding undermines the connection between extended lactation and childspacing. For women who were badly nourished, however, the consequence of malnutrition combined with lengthy lactation was significant. Low levels of protein and fat content among slave rations in the Caribbean could have disrupted several reproductive functions of slave women, including a delayed age of menarche, irregular periods, and an early menopause.

Mortality was also an important factor in the demographic problems of the British Caribbean slave population. In particular, fetal, neo-natal, and infant mortality were notably high; not enough slave children survived into adulthood. Evidence gathered in May 1795 on births and miscarriages at Worthy Park plantation, Jamaica, indicates that almost one-fifth of slaves' pregnancies were unsuccessful. At least one of every two youngsters born on Codrington plantation, Barbados, died before the age of 5. Model life tables constructed for the period 1817–32 further show that for infants aged under 5, the death rate in individual West Indian colonies ranged for males from 240 to 580 per 1,000, and for females from 200 to 480 per 1,000. For most of the eastern Caribbean colonies, four out of every ten black children did not live to the age of 5. Slave infant mortality in the British West Indies was significantly higher than in nineteenth-century Britain.

Miscarriage and stillbirth were common in the British Caribbean during the slavery era. These were clearly related to the nutritional deficiencies of slave mothers and the intensity of labour during the sugar harvest. Whether fetal deaths commonly occurred through deliberate abortion by pregnant slave women is unknown. The incidence of infanticide is also unknown. Many serious diseases affected the chances of infant survival. The most common causes of death recorded for slave children under 5 were tetanus, lockjaw, yaws, worms, beri-beri, teething, and whooping cough, whereas deaths from these complaints are unlikely in well-nourished children. Tetanus could possibly have accounted for one-fifth of total slave mortality. Several of these deficiency diseases led to Protein Energy Malnutrition (PEM), which could be life-threatening. PEM gives rise to kwashiorkor, which was often identified in the slavery era as 'teething'. Archaeological investigations into teeth of slave children excavated from a slave cemetery in Barbados have revealed growth arrest lines which show a terrible battle for survival for infants shortly after weaning. This has all the signs of PEM. Children suffering from this condition have a markedly lower capacity to produce specific antibodies. Thus afflicted, they die from the complications of measles, chickenpox, influenza, and even from a common cold.

Disabilities and diseases were also common among adult slaves in the British Caribbean. Many of these complaints could be fatal. Elephantiasis, or swollen legs, was transmitted by mosquitoes and was fairly common in the sugar colonies. It made sufferers appear prematurely aged and unable to continue field work. Many slaves suffered from dysentery, dropsy, fevers, and diseases of the digestive and nervous systems. Yaws, a non-venereal form of syphilis, left its mark on slave bodies in swollen lumps. This was a highly contagious and common disease that planters tried to contain by constructing yaws houses on their estates, usually placing them next to slave hospitals. Dirt-eating was another way in which disease entered the body, in this case through hookworm infestation. In some years epidemic diseases struck the West Indies, such as the widespread outbreak of cholera in Grenada in 1830. European doctors in the Caribbean generally misunderstood the aetiology of these diseases; many, even by the end of slavery, still believed in miasmic theories. The one major disease brought under control in the early nineteenth century Caribbean was smallpox. Empirical knowledge of quarantine, inoculation, and vaccination helped to contain outbreaks of smallpox but only Jamaica (in 1813) and Trinidad (in 1819) among the British sugar colonies set up vaccine establishments before slave emancipation. The sheer range of potentially lethal diseases to which slaves were subject made survival among the enslaved population in the Caribbean a constant struggle. Thus in 1788 Edward Long noted the prevalence of 'epidemic and destructive distempers' in Jamaica among which he singled out smallpox, yaws, dysentery, tetanus, and dirt-eating as causing 'incredible havoc' and leading to an excess of deaths upon estates.[7]

---

[7] National Archives, Kew, Pitt Papers, 30/8/155, fo. 40.

## SLAVE FAMILY LIFE

Besides problems of mortality and fertility, slaves in the British Caribbean struggled to form stable family lives. Many aspects of West Indian slavery were inimical to the creation of families. Africans were not imported in family groups. Many slaves had experienced a sequence of fractures in their personal lives, having been wrested often from families within Africa, sold usually as individuals into slavery on the African coast, and then resold in the West Indies without attention paid by merchants to whether those slaves had prior or current family attachments. The lack of power and capital among plantation slaves, long and hard working conditions, and white brutality must also have made family life difficult to create and sustain. To some extent, of course, there was also a deliberate fracturing of slave families by white estate officials and overseers taking black mistresses, practising miscegenation, and separating households from time to time through hiring out or selling slaves to other plantations.

As if these were not sufficient deterrents, planters seemed more interested in promoting reproduction than in making efforts to assist slave family life. Thus few laws were brought in to assist slaves in family formation. Before amelioration became common in the West Indies—and it was patchy before 1815—some planters regarded slaves as descended from Africans who had lived in a depraved way without a settled family life; others thought that black male slaves were promiscuous and unlikely to stay with their wives and children; still others knew they had no legal responsibility to nurture slave families. When amelioration policies were adopted in the 1820s, many planters promoted Christian marriage ceremonies among their black charges. This was intended to inculcate moral education, ensure social stability, and put pro-natalist policies into practice. Modern sociologists of the West Indies have argued that, faced with these obstacles, nuclear families among slaves were rare, and unstable matrifocal units were the norm.

Evidence on family patterns among slaves in the British Caribbean is widely available at the anecdotal level but systematic data are less easy to find, especially before the American Revolution. The consensus of modern studies, however, is that the nuclear family was the type of household unit most favoured by West Indian slaves. The proportion of slaves living in such a unit varied across individual islands. In 1813, a census for Trinidad showed that 53 per cent of the slaves lived in nuclear families. In 1796, 80 per cent of the slaves on Newton estate, Barbados, lived in nuclear families; so, too, did 70 per cent of the slaves at Montpelier estate, Jamaica, in 1825. In 1821 and 1822, 54 per cent of Bahamian slaves lived in simple nuclear families. The remaining slaves in these and other Caribbean islands lived in a variety of family groups, but relatively few—less than 10 per cent of slaves in Jamaica and Trinidad, for example—lived in extended family households. It may be that several separate households were formed in a polygynous compound and that contiguous houses could form an extended family unit. But, without firm evidence, it is safe to assume that the individual household was equivalent to a family grouping.

These data disprove the modern sociological emphasis on the lack of settled family life among West Indian slaves. They show that the matrifocal unit was not the norm during the slavery era. But by their nature they cannot throw light on the degree of instability in slave family affairs. In the decade before slave emancipation in 1834 half of the married slaves in Barbados and a little over a quarter of slaves married by the Moravians in Jamaica lived separately, presumably on different plantations. This meant that their social and personal relations were fragmented, but it does not necessarily mean that they became the parents of an unstable family group. African traditions predisposed slaves to live in stable, conjugal relationships. Knowledge is lacking, however, about whether specific African family forms survived the Middle Passage to the West Indies and whether, in turn, those adapted forms persisted into the era after the end of the British slave trade when creolization of the black labour force became the norm. Nuclear families among the slaves may have been most common where slaves were living on large plantations; in that situation the family unit was a means of counteracting isolation. They also appear to have flourished where access to slave provision grounds allowed slave families to sell produce at market and enabled children to contribute to family earnings. The predominance of slave women in field work in the Caribbean, with long hours and tough physical tasks, did not deter them from living in family groups. Given the isolation associated with the slave experience—isolation from one's homeland, with no prospect of return, and isolation from the free society of the colony of disembarkation—it is unsurprising that the slave family lay at the centre of emotional and cultural bonds in the enslaved community.

The situation differed on the North American continent where over time slaves formed more settled family lives. But this was not achieved without a struggle. During periods of substantial African migration to the southern colonies, family formation proved difficult to achieve. Most Chesapeake tobacco plantations by the 1720s and 1730s were relatively small units containing only ten or twenty slaves, who were predominantly African males. Slaves were normally housed in outbuildings near to white personnel. Privacy for slaves was thus a rare phenomenon. Male slaves had to find wives away from their plantations. This was made more difficult by the fact that these were scattered rural properties with, at this time, a relatively low density of blacks in the population and few well-developed cross-plantation networks. Moreover, male slaves outnumbered females throughout much of the tidewater area. This led to competition for mates. On larger plantations the unbalanced sex ratios were even more pronounced; although there were more female slaves, they were outnumbered considerably by males, sometimes by two to one. While these circumstances obtained, slave households in the Chesapeake probably contained a number of men living singly but sharing accommodation. This was the situation on the properties of Robert 'King' Carter, the largest Chesapeake slaveholder, when he died in 1732.

These features of early slave family life in the Chesapeake were transformed as creoles became more prominent among the enslaved black population. By 1755 only 15 per cent of Virginia's blacks had arrived in the last decade. Planters in the piedmont interior of the Chesapeake purchased slaves from tidewater areas as well as importing Africans. In the two decades prior to the American Revolution the skewed sex ratios among slaves in the Chesapeake had become a thing of the past: there was now greater parity among the sexes, which aided family formation. Plantation sizes also increased. By 1776 it was more common to find tobacco plantations along the tidewater with thirty to fifty slaves than half a century before; indeed, there were now large estates owned by grandee planters with over a hundred slaves. On larger plantations slaves were often housed in their own villages away from the direct gaze of their owners; they could therefore develop their own communities based on family life. The growing proportion of slaves in the Chesapeake vis-à-vis whites and a greater density of black population in the region both developed in the three decades before the American Revolution. These twin factors contributed to the greater possibilities for family and community life among slaves than in the early eighteenth century, and also served to promote cross-plantation social networks among blacks. Creole slave families in the Chesapeake were predominantly two-parent and extended households; little evidence survives of polygynous practices stemming from African practices. Slave marriages had no legal sanction but slave men and women had partners who were effectively husbands and wives. Their residential patterns were often complex. But living in separate households was not a proxy for emotional or physical separation. Though planters often arranged for slave husbands and teenage children to live separately from wives, mothers, and young children, black families were in regular daily contact with one another.

In South Carolina there was a similar rise in slave family life during the eighteenth century. Before 1750, when the Palmetto colony's slave population mainly comprised newly imported Africans, family formation could be difficult for reasons already emphasized: an excess of males over females, heavy mortality rates, an emphasis by planters on buying 'new' negroes rather than breeding them. Family life among South Carolinian slaves was fragile at the beginning of the eighteenth century. Males and females changed their partners frequently. There was, according to a visiting Anglican minister, a 'constant and promiscuous cohabiting of slaves of different sexes and nations together'.[8] But as the mortality rate declined among South Carolinian slaves and sex ratios became more even from the 1740s onwards, the possibilities for family formation increased. Data in inventories for South Carolina's slave families show that just over half the slaves in the colony lived in families in the 1730s but that the proportion increased to two-thirds by the 1750s and to 69 per cent by the 1770s. Half of these groups comprised two-parent families. Slaves were more likely to form families on larger plantations, as in the Chesapeake. Over time planters seem to have accorded more respect to slave family ties, viewing their preservation as perhaps the most effective way of preserving stability in the slave community. Thus in the mid-eighteenth century Lowcountry owners in their deeds of gift and slave sales tended to bequest slaves in groups. In both the Chesapeake and the Lowcountry slaves had close relations with extended family groups, for kinfolk such as aunts and uncles were an important part of their familial lives.

As yet, little is known about the quality of their family experiences and much remains to be discovered about the patterns of family life over

---

[8] Society for the Propagation of the Gospel (SPG), London, Revd Francis Le Jau to the SPG, 15 Sept. 1708, A4/125.

a life cycle; but no historian can now dismiss the importance of a settled family life for slaves, the obstacles they faced in achieving this goal, and their hardiness in overcoming odds stacked against them. Yet one should not paint too rosy a picture of slave families in North America. Settled family life could be as precarious for slaves in the Chesapeake and South Carolina as it was for slaves elsewhere because white masters ultimately controlled their destiny. The westward movement of tobacco production in the Chesapeake meant that around of a fifth of the slaves in southern Maryland and one-third of slaves on Virginia tobacco plantations left the place of their birth between *c*.1755 and 1780. Some slaves left with their masters for new homes, others were sold and families disrupted as owners adjusted their plantation units for life in another location. The large number of heirs to Chesapeake tobacco plantations also tended to disperse slaves away from their communities at least once during a lifetime. In South Carolina slaves accompanied the spread of rice and indigo production into areas north and south of Charleston and into inland areas. On the eve of the American Revolution slavery in South Carolina was growing most swiftly in backcountry areas. But though this dispersal of slaves increased in the second half of the eighteenth century and sometimes militated against a settled family life, the impact of internal migration on slave communities in North America was never as great as it became with the westward spread of cotton production in the nineteenth century.

# 5

# Work, Law, and Culture

Productive work for white masters was the chief *raison d'être* for importing and employing enslaved Africans in the New World. Most of the waking hours of slaves, on at least six days of the week, were spent toiling for their owners without any wages. Slave work in North America varied over time and according to regional economic demands. In New England and the Middle Colonies there were no staple crops that required a plantation workforce. Moreover, reliance on family labour in many rural households—especially in New England, where good reproduction rates among whites produced sizeable families—meant that recruiting workers from outside the household was a secondary option. Nevertheless, blacks could be found working in a wide range of agricultural and industrial tasks and trades in the northern colonies. In port cities such as New York and Philadelphia, where the reliance on slave labour increased during the first half of the eighteenth century, slaves worked in the maritime trades as sailmakers, coopers and dock workers; they often assisted artisans and tradesmen in shops and workshops; and female slaves found a niche as domestic servants. Middling craftsmen and artisans in New York and Philadelphia increasingly employed one or two slaves after 1750, finding them a useful source of labour when indentured servants were unavailable or wage labourers proved too costly to hire.

Slaves also worked in the rural agriculture of the northern colonies. Northern farmers increasingly replaced servants with slaves in colonies such as Pennsylvania, New Jersey, and New York during the first half of the eighteenth century. They mainly held slaves in ones or twos. In the Narragansett Bay area of Rhode Island slaves could be found in larger numbers, with some stock-rearing farms employing up to twenty slaves. The other extensive rural form of employment for slaves in the northern colonies was in ironworks, situated especially in New Jersey and Pennsylvania. Some of these forges employed between thirty and fifty slaves to work alongside white indentured and free workers. The deployment of African-Americans at ironworks helped entrepreneurs gain control of the pace and costs of charcoal iron production, which required a large number of seasonal tasks throughout a yearly cycle. It also enabled owners to discipline white workers by placing them in a worse bargaining position for their labour because of the presence and availability of slaves as an alternative workforce.

Two chief characteristics of slave work in the northern colonies were that African-Americans' labour was interchangeable with that of various free and unfree white workers, and that work was carried out by individuals or in small groups working together. Supervisory arrangements, as a result, tended to be flexible, especially where blacks were working in masters' households. The situation in the southern colonies was fundamentally different: though domestic slaves were employed and some blacks were assigned artisan tasks, the majority of slaves toiled on plantations producing staple crops for export. The work regimes on plantations were partly determined by the greater agglomeration of blacks within a limited space; but they were equally shaped by the particular seasonal demands of staple crops. This can be illustrated by consideration of the different rhythms and organization of slave work on Chesapeake tobacco estates and on rice plantations in South Carolina and Georgia.

## SLAVE WORK ON TOBACCO PLANTATIONS

Slaves working on tobacco plantations were subject to long hours of work. A contemporary observer, William Tatham, noted that they laboured 'from daylight until the dusk of the evening, and some part of the night, by moon or candlelight, during the winter'.[1] Work filled up six days of the week. Holidays were usually restricted to just three days a year at Christmas, Easter, and Whitsun. Midday lunch breaks were pared back to the minimum time needed to bolt down food. Cultivating tobacco was nowhere near as backbreaking for slaves as sugar cultivation, but it involved regular, monotonous work over a seasonal cycle that lasted from the beginning of the year until the autumn. Slaves prepared land for planting tobacco in January or February. The seed was sown in

---

[1] Quoted in G. Melvin Herndon, *William Tatham and the Culture of Tobacco* (Coral Gables, Fla., 1969), 102.

February and March in newly cleared mulch beds. April saw extensive hoeing and weeding. The ground needed to be tilled regularly until August, when the tobacco harvest began. Slaves cut the tobacco leaves, let them lie in fields for half a day, and then took the leaves to a tobacco house, where they hung them. They stripped the leaves from the stalk before rolling the tobacco and prising it into hogsheads. These activities required close supervision; any slackness or mistreatment of the tobacco leaves could ruin a planter's annual crop.

Gang labour characterized most of the work done on Chesapeake tobacco plantations in this seasonal crop cycle. Under this system, slaves worked in units of commonly nine to twelve workers. Their pace of work was determined by the leader of the gang, a black foreman, under the watchful eye of a white overseer; sometimes the managers of plantations also turned up in the tobacco fields to oversee the work routines. Since managers and overseers tended to place fit, young, male slaves in the position of foreman, the pace of the work—at its most intense during the hoeing and weeding during the spring—could exhaust other members of the gang who were required to work in lines and keep up with the foreman. Thus a certain amount of regimentation occurred (though not as much as in the larger gangs on Caribbean sugar estates). Individuals were closely monitored. Disagreements frequently occurred between the overseers and the gang labourers. The patriarchal Virginia tobacco planter Landon Carter typified the attitude of owners to their gangs when he once threatened a foreman at his Sabine Hall estate with 'a sound correction' unless he 'mended his pace'.[2] William Byrd II echoed this comment in a remark on controlling slaves: 'Foul means must do, what fair will not.'[3] Men, women, and children all laboured in the tobacco fields. As the eighteenth century progressed, women comprised a higher proportion of field workers tending this crop than men. Boys and girls were usually working in the fields by the age of 9.

Gang labour maximized productivity for planters. There was little relief for black workers because tobacco required constant attention and the leaf could mature at any time in August or September. Long hours of work gave slaves only limited opportunities to cultivate their

[2] Jack P. Greene (ed.), *The Diary of Colonel Landon Carter of Sabine Hall, 1752–1778*, 2 vols. (Charlottesville, Va., 1965), i. 430.

[3] William Byrd II to the Earl of Egmont, 12 July 1736, in Marion Tinling (ed.), *The Correspondence of the Three William Byrds of Westover, Virginia, 1684–1776*, 3 vols. (Charlottesville, Va., 1977), ii. 488.

own provisions or to engage, like their West Indian counterparts, in huckstering or private subsistence activities. In their spare time on Sundays slaves usually confined manual labour to tending their own garden plots within the estate. The hard work of slaves on tobacco plantations was exacerbated by two factors. Tobacco was a crop that regularly exhausted the soil. Usually it could not be grown productively on the same land for more than three years in a row. The need to clear new land added to the work burdens of slaves. And since tobacco exhausted the soil, planters started to acquire land away from the original tidewater settlements and expand into the interior of the Virginia and Maryland, setting up new plantations in the hilly, piedmont country beyond the fall lines of the great Chesapeake river systems. By the mid-eighteenth century this process intensified slave work on tobacco estates because, in addition to cultivating new land, much of the piedmont area was heavily forested and slaves had to clear the woods, hoe the land and plant fresh crops rapidly.

## SLAVE WORK ON RICE PLANTATIONS

The general pattern of slave work on the Lowcountry rice plantations in South Carolina and Georgia followed a different pattern. The seasonal cycle was longer, lasting from twelve to fourteen months, and the work much more arduous and unhealthy. Tough manual labour characterized most stages of the production process. It was carried out in swampy areas inhabited by insects, especially mosquitoes, and reptiles. Rice plantations were situated on an inland coastal plain or on the Sea Islands off the Carolinian coast. Hot and humid subtropical conditions, with searing sunshine and plentiful rainfall, made South Carolina's climate oppressive in the summer. Mosquito nets, Jesuit bark, and the inherited sickle-cell trait gave many Africans heightened resistance against mosquitoes and malaria, but disease and physical danger were part and parcel of the work routine. As Alexander Hewatt observed in 1779, 'no work can be imagined more pernicious to health than for men to stand in water mid-leg high, and often above it, planting and weeding rice.'[4] There was no equivalent to the rigours of rice production among the staple economies of North America, for tobacco, as explained above,

---

[4] Alexander Hewatt, *An Historical Account of the Rise and Progress of the Colonies of South Carolina and Georgia*, 2 vols. (1779; repr. Spartanburg, SC, 1971), i. 159.

was not so difficult a crop to cultivate. The nearest equivalent to rice cultivation in British America was sugar production in the Caribbean, which took a similar toll on energy and health.

The cycle of rice production began in January and February when slaves cleared land and trees with axes. The rice was sown between April and June. Workers pressed seed into waterlogged ground, often using their heels to cover the plant with mud. Fields were flooded over the summer to encourage the seed to sprout. After the rice began to germinate, fields were hoed to eliminate weeds and a process of alternate flooding and draining of fields was necessary to provide sufficient moisture for the rice to grow. Substantial irrigation works were often needed to reclaim river swamp. Slaves exerted great effort in constructing dams, building embankments, clearing ditches, and constructing canalized links between rivers and swamps. Often they stood knee-deep in swamp and mud to carry out these tasks. Middleburg estate, a notable rice plantation, contained more than fifty-five miles of bank covering 6 million cubic feet of earth. If one were to calculate the amount of earth included in all the rice plantations in colonial South Carolina and Georgia, they would rank as one of the largest hand-built earthworks found anywhere in the world.

In August, during the peak heat and intense humidity of summer, black workers carried guns to ward off birds from raiding rice in the fields. The rice harvest began in mid-September and a further sequence of complex tasks followed: stacking the rice into large ricks; threshing and winnowing; pounding the rice to remove the grain's outer husk and inner film; storing the rice in warehouses. As winter approached, many post-harvest tasks were combined with preparing land for the next season's planting. Virtually all of these tasks were carried out by hand, though some threshing machinery had appeared in South Carolina by the 1760s and 1770s. Tasks varied at different stages of the production cycle but they were nearly all potentially exhausting and, because of the disease environment, sometimes debilitating. Rice itself, when harvested, was abrasive to the hand. One of the most unpleasant manual tasks consisted of pounding the rice with mortars and pestles—a tiring process that could take hours and leave aching muscles and sore palms. The demanding nature of pounding by hand was relieved somewhat in the generation before the American Revolution with the introduction on some estates of pounding machines driven by livestock.

Rice plantations covered a large acreage. They usually had more slaves attached to them than Chesapeake tobacco plantations. By 1750 one third of South Carolina's slaves lived on plantations with more than fifty black labourers; some rice estates had a slave force in excess of 100 people. Rice was a more straightforward crop to grow than tobacco; it did not require the same degree of close supervisory attention during the production cycle. For this reason, along with the expanse of many rice plantations, the normal method of work on South Carolina and Georgia estates consisted of task work supervised by either a white overseer or a black foreman, known as a driver, or both. Unlike Chesapeake tobacco plantations, where owners tended to live year-round in a great house within the estate's grounds, planters in the Lower South often spent part of the year as urban grandees in towns such as Charleston and Savannah, leaving supervision on the spot to the overseers and drivers. Task work was followed at each stage of rice production. The basic unit in the fields in the mid-eighteenth century was a quarter of an acre per day. But tasking was also used for pounding (measured by the number of mortars used) and for fencing (measured by the number of poles put up) and for other aspects of work. As in the Chesapeake, the field labour force was disproportionately made up of women, though adults of both sexes and children often worked together at different stages of the seasonal cycle.

Rice therefore, like tobacco, was a lucrative staple commodity that had work patterns associated partly with the nature of the crop. For slaves, task work had several benefits. They could carry out their allocated daily portion of work at their own pace. Industrious workers could hope to complete their tasks by early afternoon. Slaves were supervised less directly, allowing them to become self-reliant at work and able to adapt their work practices without too much direct interference. Planters were careful not to impinge on the slaves' time off work or the day of rest on the Sabbath. In the extra time they had as a result of efficient tasking, blacks could devote more time and attention to cultivating their own grounds, which were larger than those in Virginia and Maryland. They grew potatoes, pumpkins, melons, peanuts, and corn. They kept some fowl. These food resources were marketed in an internal economy. In these ways, slaves in the Lower South accumulated cash and exercised a fair degree of autonomy over their lives. But the world of tasking in the Lowcountry was hardly a rosy affair. Disputes frequently arose between slaves and their white superiors over the time needed to complete certain tasks. Often these disagreements were based on slaves insisting they had worked sufficiently hard on a given day whereas overseers challenged their output. For instance, in January 1774 three slaves owned by

George Austin absconded in early December 'for being chastis'd on Account of not finishing the Task of Threshing in due time'.[5] This reminds us of the prevalence of runaway slaves in South Carolina and the whippings and beatings of slaves that occurred frequently.


## SLAVE WORK IN THE BRITISH CARIBBEAN

Slaves in the British Caribbean could be found in relatively small numbers in the urban retail sector, as shopkeepers, mariners, street sellers, and domestic servants in port towns such as Kingston in Jamaica and Bridgetown in Barbados. They also found employment on livestock pens and on coffee, pimento, and ginger plantations. But the overwhelming majority of slaves lived and worked on rural sugar plantations. Sugar was the staple crop that dominated the West Indian economy. Sugar plantations in the Caribbean were large agricultural properties that could range from several hundred to several thousand acres in extent. They were usually found on relatively flat land with access to water, but, since many British West Indian islands were small, they could also be found in hillier locations. Most land on a sugar estate was given over to cane cultivation but there were also sugar factory works for initial processing of the sugar. These included a boiling house, a curing house, and sometimes an adjacent rum distillery where the molasses drained off from processing the cane was made. Usually outlying parts of plantations had provision grounds, where slaves cultivated their own food crops during their limited leisure time, and fields given over to guinea grass, which was grown to feed the livestock needed for hauling on plantations. Many sugar estates were, in fact, situated next to livestock pens containing cattle and mules.

The seasonal cycle of work began in the autumn with the planting of new sugar cane. The crop took about fifteen months to grow. The cane was ready to be harvested between January and June. During those six months, a full workforce was needed to deal with the crop so that the cane was gathered, transferred to the sugar factory, and processed for shipment back to Britain. West India vessels sought to load sugar hogsheads on board before 1 August, which marked the beginning of the hurricane season in the Caribbean, so that they could arrive home in

---

[5] Southern Historical Collection, University of North Carolina, Chapel Hill, Josiah Smith to George Austin, 31 Jan. 1774, Josiah Smith, Jr, letterbook (1771–84).

late August or September. Most sugar produced in the Caribbean was coarse brown muscovado but Barbados produced superior white clayed sugar. Owing to British mercantilist restrictions, sugar could only be semi-refined in the West Indies. The final process of refining took place mainly at refineries in London, Liverpool, Bristol, and Glasgow. It was there that further boiling, curing, and cooling of sugar took place before sugar loaves were produced. These were cut into smaller pieces and sold to sugar bakers and grocers for distribution.

Work on the sugar plantations in the Caribbean was mainly organized in terms of gang labour, though a certain amount of task work became available after the British government brought in a policy of slave amelioration after 1823. Usually a sugar estate had three gangs. The first gang (sometimes known as the great gang) undertook the heaviest physical work. Slaves working in this gang dug the cane holes, cut the matured sugar cane, loaded the cane onto carts, and took it to the sugar factory works. By the early nineteenth century slaves could dig about eighty cane holes a day, amounting to between 600 and 1,500 cubic feet of earth. Hoes and bills and sheer muscle power were used to carry out this work. This was physically arduous in a tropical climate. Cutting the cane was also a tiring task. Sugar cane measures between six inches and a foot in diameter when fully grown and can attain a height of six feet. Therefore the harvesting of the cane was no easy task. Besides the tasks mentioned, the great gang also used their strength to build stone walls, cut wood, make lime kilns, and construct roads through an estate. Most workers in the great gang were women. Just as in many African societies, they carried out the tough physical labour. Altogether, the great gang could comprise more than 100 workers. By contrast, in the Cape Colony, where many slaves also worked on agricultural holdings geared towards export, men did most of the manual work and women avoided the extremes of field labour.

The great gang on sugar plantations was complemented by the second gang, which was responsible for lighter tasks such as clearing away the trash from the cane fields, chopping and heaping manure, cleaning young canes and threshing light canes. This was a mixed gang of men and women, but it was common for adolescents to be allocated to this gang. Sometimes elderly slaves would join this gang. Many estates also had a third gang (or weeding gang) comprising mothers with children. The third gang helped to clear up the refuse in the cane fields and to throw dung into the cane holes. The children in the third gang graduated to the second gang at about age 12 and then, if they had sufficient strength, to the first gang at age 18.

The gang system operated with military precision. Slaves worked in parallel rows almost as relentless cogs in a machine. Thomas Roughley, the author of a well-known planter's guide to slave work in the West Indies, described the great gang as an

admirable effective force, composed of the flower of all the field battalions, drafted and recruited from all other gangs, as they come of age to endure severe labour . . . This gang, composed of a mixture of able men and women, sometimes amounting to an hundred, should always be put to the field work, which requires strength and skill in the execution . . . they should be made to work in a parallel line as they are set in. The head-driver, his assistant-driver, and bookkeeper, should visit each row, and see that they do their work well.[6]

Contemporary colour illustrations of the West Indies often illustrate this parallel working, as, for example, in the painting *Digging Cane Holes* from W. Clark's *Ten Views of Antigua* (1823).

The gangs were supervised by a black driver, usually a skilled and trusted slave who had risen up from the ranks. The driver was responsible for ensuring the pace, quantity, and satisfactory performance of the work. He was in turn supervised by a white overseer, who was often present in the cane fields to oversee the work regimen. Overseers were charged with disciplining the field workers. They discharged this duty by chastisement, whippings, placing slaves in stocks, or withdrawal of customary allowances. Based on biblical precedent in the Book of Deuteronomy, they were supposedly restricted to issuing thirty-nine lashes of the whip. But, of course, cruel overseers exceeded this limit. Overseers had to extract maximum productivity from the slaves during the sugar harvest. They deployed slave labour during that time so that a certain number of slaves could work in the sugar factory on estates. Overseers were responsible to managers or attorneys of estates. Managers operated one plantation while attorneys were responsible for several. Plantation owners sometimes lived on their estates in a great house, but over time they were increasingly absentees who remained in England and left the day-to-day running of their Caribbean properties to their managers and attorneys.

---

[6] Thomas Roughley, *The Jamaica Planters' Guide* (London, 1823) quoted in Michael Craton, James Walvin, and David Wright (eds.), *Slavery, Abolition and Emancipation: Black Slaves and the British Empire: A Thematic Documentary* (London, 1976), 82.

Slaves worked long hours on sugar plantations. The working day amounted to between ten and twelve hours for six days of the week. This is more than twice the average hours of modern factory workers. Sunday was normally treated as a day of rest, though some plantation owners infringed this unwritten rule. After the British government introduced its amelioration policies, attempts were made throughout the British West Indies, but especially in the Crown colonies, to introduce task work to give slaves greater incentive to finish their daily work satisfactorily and in good time. The Crown colonies—primarily Trinidad and what later became British Guiana—came under the direct jurisdiction of Westminster. It was therefore easier there to insist on such regulations than in most British West Indian colonies, which were governed by their own legislative assemblies. Task work operated in a similar way to work on rice plantations in South Carolina and Georgia. Slaves who completed their tasks could finish work by early afternoon and then have time to rest or cultivate their own provision grounds. Some plantation owners had anticipated the British government's move by bringing in private schemes of task work. But even where task work was introduced, owners and their managers still reverted to gang labour during crop time.

## SLAVE PUNISHMENTS

The repression involved in relations between masters and slaves led some contemporaries to take a gloomy view of the pattern of control and obedience that lay at the core of chattel slavery. In 1680 the Reverend Morgan Godwyn lambasted Barbadian planters for their cruelty towards slaves which included 'their Emasculating and beheading them, their *croping off their Ears* (which usually cause the Wretches to broyl, and then compel to eat them themselves); their *Amputations of Legs*, and even Dissecting them alive.'[7] A later, more famous commentator also took a gloomy view of the treatment of slaves by masters. 'The whole commerce between master and slave', wrote Thomas Jefferson, was 'a perpetual exercise of the most boisterous passions, the most unremitting despotism on the one part, and degrading submissions on the

[7] Morgan Godwyn, *The Negro & Indians Advocate, Suing for Their Admission into the Church . . .* (1680), quoted in Alden T. Vaughan, *Roots of American Racism: Essays on the Colonial Experience* (Oxford, 1995), 72.

other.'[8] This remark emphasizes the widest polarity in social relations between white owners and their slaves. There were examples, of course, of humane masters and relatively cordial relations between the white personnel on plantations and the enslaved. But even where benevolence appeared to hold sway, it was always a matter of an iron fist lying behind the velvet glove because slavery ultimately rested on physical coercion.

Recalcitrant slaves were subject to a series of physical punishments: branding on the cheek or the shoulder, lashing on the back, placement in stocks, subjection to physical abuse. Slave women and men were both subject to flogging on the bare parts of their body. The diary of Thomas Thistlewood, a brutal white overseer on Egypt plantation, Westmorland Parish, Jamaica, records such punishments in laconic, factual prose. An entry for 15 July 1750 states: 'this afternoon Dick (the Mulattoe) for his many Crimes & Negligencies was bound to an Orange Tree in ye garden, and whip'd to some purpose. (Given Near 300 Lashes.)' Another entry for 8 August 1755 notes that 'today Nero would not work, but threaten'd to Cutt his own throat. Had him stripped, whipp'd, gagg'd & his hands tied behind him, that ye Muskitoes and Sand Flies might torment him to some purpose.'[9] Whipping normally took place in front of a gathering of slaves and white estate officials.

Abolitionists later campaigned against flogging slaves. This had some effect on the more violent practices. Thus, during the period of official government policy on amelioration after 1823, many West Indian legislatures supported the reduction of flogging, especially for female slaves. But there was never total compliance, and much brutality continued beyond the gaze of the authorities. In the 1830s the period of Apprenticeship brought with it the installation of treadmills on Jamaican plantations, where slaves were punished by grinding wooden slats on a cylindrical drum until they were exhausted or their limbs were damaged by broken wood.

## SLAVERY AND THE LAW

Planters, managers, and owners exercised power through the full support of the law. Because slavery had not existed in England for centuries,

---

[8] William Peden (ed.), Thomas Jefferson, *Notes on the State of Virginia* (Chapel Hill, NC, 1955), 162–3.

[9] Citations from Lincolnshire Record Office, Monson MSS, Thomas Thistlewood diaries.

the common law transplanted as an Anglo-Saxon institution from the mother country to her colonies was silent on the status and treatment of slaves. Successive English governments allowed colonists to formulate their own laws and, in permitting this freedom, they allowed assemblies in North America and the Caribbean to establish their own slave codes. These codes proliferated on a colony-by-colony basis from the mid-seventeenth century onwards. Laws on slavery enacted by colonial legislatures after 1660 and the range of punishments that whites could mete out to blacks appear to support a sombre view of master–slave relations. A Virginian law of 1640 forbade slaves the right to bear weapons. This denial of a right set them apart from the white community. Another statute in the Old Dominion, dated 1662, legislated against miscegenation. It declared that 'if any Christian shall commit Fornication with a negro man or woman, hee or shee soe offending'[10] should pay a double fine. Virginia's first major slave code was passed in 1680 and strengthened in 1705. This law confirmed the separate, degraded status of slaves in the colony: 'All servants imported into the Country . . . who were not Christians in their native Country . . . shall be accounted and be slaves. All Negro, mulatto and Indian slaves within this dominion . . . shall be held to be real estate.'[11] The 1705 law gave owners the full value of executed slaves and ordered that any slave striking a white man should be punished by thirty-nine lashes of the whip. Furthermore, it stipulated that slaves found guilty of murder or rape would be hanged and those convicted for robbery or any other major offence would receive sixty lashes, be placed in the stocks, and have their ears cut off. According to this code, there would in future no longer be a court of judgment for disputes between a master and a slave.

The first statute dealing with slavery in South Carolina was a law of 1683 which forbade trading between servants and slaves. This clearly showed the influence of the existing slave code in Barbados. Thereafter South Carolina had a series of slave codes, including detailed legislation enacted in 1712 that was tightened up in 1740 after the Stono Rebellion (discussed in Chapter 6) had alarmed the Lowcountry planter class. The 1740 law, known as the Negro Act, restricted slaves' lives comprehensively and took away many protections afforded by the

[10] William Waller Hening (ed.), *The Statutes at Large: Being a Collection of All the Laws of Virginia*, 13 vols. (Richmond, New York, and Philadelphia, 1809–23), ii. 170.
[11] Ibid. iii. 447.

common law. Slaves in South Carolina now found that they could not travel away from their master's plantation without written permission; they could not sell goods for their own benefit or hire themselves out to labour; and they could not own livestock, boats, or firearms. They were denied the right to testify in court under oath and were subject to summary legal procedures. Thus a slave accused of a crime received a separate trial procedure that involved the convening of a slave court operated by justices of the peace and freeholders who could 'hear and determine the matter brought before them in the most summary and expeditious manner.'[12] This Negro Act of 1740 formed the basis of the first slave law made by the Georgia Assembly in 1755. With additions, it continued to be the basic slave law for South Carolina until slave emancipation in the American Civil War.

A statutory law of race and slavery existed in all thirteen British North American colonies by the middle of the eighteenth century. These acts singled out slaves as a caste. They gave owners virtually complete control over the movements, fraternization, and behaviour of their slave charges. The laws were draconian, allowing for a wide range of physical punishments including branding on the cheek or thumbs, amputation of body limbs, splitting noses, castration, and the death penalty, each one applied according to the nature of wrongdoing by slaves. There were also punishments for slaves congregating together, practising private rituals, possessing guns and weapons, and acting violently against whites. Under these laws, slaves lacked various rights—the right to marry, the right to testify in court, the right to challenge the hereditary nature of slavery. Enslaved Africans effectively had no legal redress against maltreatment by whites. Even the life of slaves was precarious, for the punishments handed out by the courts for killing a slave were milder than those for blacks found guilty of killing a white person.

Slave laws enacted in the British Caribbean stigmatized Africans as racially inferior, as heathens, and as property rather than as persons. The Barbados slave code of 1661 became the model for slave laws passed in the later seventeenth century in Jamaica and the Leeward Islands. A more elaborate Barbados slave code of 1688 became the basis for the legal treatment of slaves in that island until the end of the eighteenth century. It emphasized the wickedness caused by black 'Disorder, Rapines and Inhumanities to which they are naturally prone

---

[12] Thomas Cooper and David J. McCord (eds.), *The Statutes at Large of South Carolina*, 10 vols. (Columbia, SC, 1836–41), vii. 400.

and inclined'.[13] This code, which largely reiterated the language and clauses of the 1661 Barbados slave law, was copied throughout the British Windward Islands acquired at the end of the Seven Years War. Jamaica adopted the Barbados slave code of 1661 in 1664, when the new governor Sir Thomas Modyford brought it with him from Barbados. Several revisions ensued until Jamaica adopted a slave act in 1696 that closely followed the Barbados legislation of 1688. The Jamaican legislation of 1696 expressed concern about the propensity of slaves to rebel. It was also the first legal instance of masters being urged to spread Christianity among slaves in the sugar islands.

In common with the colonial slave laws enacted in North America, the West Indian slave laws made a sharp distinction between the treatment and punishment of white and black people. Thus the Barbados code of 1688 stated that 'Negroes and other slaves' should be punished without the benefit of a jury because they were 'brutish slaves' who deserved no better treatment on account of 'the baseness of their condition'.[14] Fear of slave insurrection lay behind the Jamaica 'Consolidation Act' of 1788 and its stipulation that slaves should be punished for drunkenness, holding arms, drumming, and gathering together in public. These laws, once again as in North America, were devised by individual colonies; there was no metropolitan input into slave laws, such as existed with the systematic *Code Noir* (1685) issued by Louis XIV. Nor was there any influence of Roman law in the British colonies precisely because slaves in Anglophone territories were defined as property rather than as persons. The West Indian slave laws afforded no possibility of blacks acting as legal agents. Several colonies had provisions for slave manumission, but the laws dealing with this only began to become active if masters took the initiative on behalf of slaves. The legal foundations of slavery in the British Caribbean, established in laws of the seventeenth century, continued with only minor amendments down to the end of slavery in the British Empire.

## MASTER–SLAVE RELATIONS

Despite powerful instruments of coercion and compulsion, however, master–slave relations were not as unremittingly bleak or as harsh

[13] Quoted in *Acts of Assembly, Barbadoes, 1648–1718*... (London, 1738), 137.
[14] Quoted ibid. 122.

as the above discussion suggests. One major reason why this was so lay in the spread of patriarchy as the main ideological underpinning of slave control during the eighteenth century. Large planters in the Chesapeake, men such as the Carters of Nomini Hall or the Tayloes of Mount Airy, were imbued with the spirit of patriarchy. A similar situation can be found with the grandee planters of the Lowcountry, such as Henry Laurens. Patriarchy meant acting towards slaves as a father figure, recognizing that black workers were part, as it were, of an extended household. William Byrd of Westover, Virginia, realized that he played this role. 'Like one of the Patriarchs', he wrote to the Earl of Orrery,

I have my Flocks and my Herds, my Bond-men and Bond-women, and every soart of Trade amongst my own Servants, so that I live in a kind of Independence of everyone but Providence. However this soart of life is attended without expense, yet it is attended with a great deal of trouble. I must take care to keep all my people to their Duty, to see all the Springs in motion and make everyone draw his equal Share to carry the Machine forward.[15]

Byrd recognized, as this statement shows, that the role of a patriarch could be difficult.

While a patriarch could act in a stern, cold, distant way, he could take great interest in the everyday lives of slaves and ensured that African-Americans conducted their own family lives on plantations with a reasonable amount of autonomy. Patriarchs rewarded good work and behaviour by slaves with gifts and possibly promotion to skilled tasks or positions in the master's household. But opposition, recalcitrance, and absconding brought down on the slave the punishments a dutiful father felt were appropriate to control his charges. During the eighteenth century, patriarchy on the American plantations modulated into paternalism. This was a complex process, not occurring everywhere at a similar time, but visible by the latter part of the century. The shift from patriarchy to paternalism was influenced by Enlightenment concerns for benevolence towards others and progress in human society, by a greater number of creoles in the slave population who did not have to be broken into slavery, and by a gradual change in attitudes in Western society about inflicting bodily pain. Patriarchal attitudes emphasized order, obedience, hierarchy, and subjection; they displayed few illusions

[15] Quoted in Pierre Marambaud, *William Byrd of Westover, 1674–1744* (Charlottesville, Va., 1971), 146–7.

about the potential rebelliousness of slaves. Paternalistic attitudes, on the other hand, proffered a generous treatment of slaves and expected gratitude in return; they promoted the myth of the happy, contented bonded black worker.

George Washington is a prominent example of a planter whose treatment of slaves reflected this change. His views about his Mount Vernon estate and his black workers were a mixture of commercial, patriarchal, and paternalist attitudes. Sometimes one of these three models dominated his behaviour as a planter, but it would be simplistic to separate them into distinct modes of thought; they intermingled to make up a complex view of slavery. Washington took a commercial view of slavery as a business, wanting to make profits from tobacco and grain cultivation, oversee agricultural improvements, and keep debts to a minimum. This outlook underscored the fact that the Mount Vernon slaves were also his chattels. He had absorbed patriarchal attitudes from the planter culture of his youth in Virginia. These manifested themselves in strict control of slaves after the manner of a father figure looking after dependants; they meant he acted distantly and sometimes rigorously towards his slaves. But paternalistic elements also existed in his mind: these were reflected mainly in his concern for slave families and their personal relationships and in his dislike of splitting up slaves who had established such ties. The beneficent side of Washington's treatment of slaves is depicted in Junius Brutus Stearns' painting *Washington as a Farmer at Mount Vernon*, which shows him paternally overseeing his slaves and his stepgrandchildren. Washington realized his control of African-Americans required mutual obligations even though he did not identify emotionally with their plight. It is not surprising that each of the three models—commercial, patriarchal, paternalist—underpinned Washington's personal dealings with slaves, for all appear to have been in a state of redefinition in North America in the late eighteenth century.

## THE MATERIAL AND CULTURAL LIVES OF SLAVES

The material and cultural life of slaves has received much illuminating attention from historians in recent years. Given the lack of much direct testimony from the slaves themselves, modern archaeological research, sometimes combined with architectural reconstruction, has provided an insight into the material standards and quality of life experienced by blacks in British America. In recent years, such investigations have proliferated. They have been linked with work in museums, where many artefacts found on plantations can be checked and identified against existing samples. Comprising an important aspect of the re-creation of the past for modern visitors to sites associated with slavery, they shed light on the material realities of slave life in a way that is often not possible from written documents because plantation records tend not to include such facets of ordinary slave life and work. They also project the living conditions of slaves to a much wider public than historians, and in so doing help to shape public consciousness of the legacy of slavery.

In the Lower South, perhaps the most fruitful excavations have been undertaken at Middleburg estate, a former rice plantation situated on the Cooper River near Charleston. The slave houses there either rotted or were torn down in the nineteenth century. But since the site has not been worked over and does not suffer from soil erosion, archaeologists have excavated fragments from artefacts and investigated soil colours around the foundation level of the eighteenth-century slave quarters. At Middleburg plantation the slave quarters were erected with mud walls and thatched roofs. They closely resemble huts built in Africa but are laid out according to the European desire for a symmetrical formation of buildings. Substantial evidence of pottery manufacture has been established for the plantation, with designs that emanated from West Africa. The pottery includes cooking jars and eating bowls. Other artefacts gleaned from the Middleburg site indicate that slaves actively hunted and gathered their own food beyond the allocated rations sometimes mentioned in plantation records. Fragments of turtle bone have been found in a rubble pile. Bones excavated indicate that Africans on the estate ate a varied diet, including chicken, pork, beef, deer, catfish, quail, and possum. Samples of bones from other South Carolina plantations show that slaves also ate frogs, squirrels, and raccoons. Fish hooks, fish weights, and gun flints have been found, indicating that slaves were fishing the creeks and rivers that run through the plantation and using guns to hunt.

Equivalent archaeological investigations have taken place in recent years at various plantation sites in Virginia. Many of these are continuing investigations, and it may be that the most interesting conclusions are yet to appear. The entire buildings and estate at Monticello, Jefferson's mountain-top home near Charlottesville, were designed by Jefferson himself over a forty-year period from 1768; but the house, the gardens, and the tobacco farms were all constructed by slaves. Archaeological reconstruction of the slave quarters at Monticello has been aided by a precise plan made by Jefferson in 1796, in which he described every building and gave it a letter. These buildings were situated on Mulberry Row, which originally contained nineteen houses in a 200-yard strip that also included utilitarian structures containing examples of light industry and fenced-in gardens between each building. Work on the slave dwellings with the letters [R], [S], and [T] has proceeded on sites where a number of artefacts have been found. They include examples of English pearl ware, which was an expensive form of ceramics; enough tea cups and other tea-ware to form a tea set; decorative-style wine glasses; gaming pieces such as dominoes; fragments from musical instruments, notably a fiddle bow; a slate with words engraved on it; and fragments from pencils. These artefacts point to a richer slave culture than we would find in written documents. Doubtless some of them were acquired from white personnel at Monticello.

Archaeological work on British Caribbean sugar plantations have been carried out mainly at sites in Jamaica, Barbados, and Nevis. One of the best-documented sites consists of the New Montpelier sugar plantation in St James's Parish, north-west Jamaica. Excavations here suggest that slave houses had various dimensions but commonly measured 18 by 27 feet. The layout of the houses, identified by surviving stone foundations, was similar to West African compounds such as those of the Igbo and Asante communities, with a rectangular base form. The survival of bone fragments and teeth at New Montpelier indicate that the estate had cows, pigs, chickens, horses, and dogs. Hack or cut marks on a large proportion of the cattle and pig bones indicate the use of a cleaver in butchering and suggest that slave workers on the plantation slaughtered their own animals. Archaeological evidence also points to a large rodent population, which would be a threat to sugar cane production. The excavation of three metal rat traps shows that attempts were made to combat the menace posed by rats. Fishbones found during the excavations show that fish from the sea were a significant part of the slaves' diet at the New Montpelier works.

Most of the identifiable tools found while excavating at New Montpelier were imported metal items. These included planters' bills and hoes, both used for specialized plantation work, but also cutlass blades, which had a wider use as domestic tools. Few utensils for preparing and cooking food were found on this estate, though fragments of iron cooking pots were dug up. Knives were found in abundance at the site. The archaeological record at New Montpelier, however, was dominated by finds of ceramic and glassware. Most ceramic remains were from vessels used for the storage or consumption of food and drink, but tobacco smoking pipes—an indulgence granted by planters to slaves—were also unearthed. The excavations at New Montpelier contain few traces of the textiles that comprised the clothing of plantation workers, but sewing tools and metal buttons have been found.

Lest we should think that the material life of slaves was cosy, the dimensions and bare furnishings of slave quarters should be remembered. Slaves in North America usually lived in small, spartan log cabins about 12 feet by 14 feet. The spaces between the logs were filled with mud. Only one original eighteenth-century slave house survives for the Old Dominion, a building from southern Virginia, so attempts to reconstruct slave dwellings from before the Revolution are based on slender architectural evidence. Such a reconstruction, however, is under way at Carter's Grove plantation, on the outskirts of Williamsburg, the former capital of Virginia where half the eighteenth-century population consisted of unfree black workers. This reconstruction is being carried out using eighteenth-century methods and tools, so that it will appear as authentic as possible. At Williamsburg the reconstruction of other houses that originally had eighteenth-century façades has been coupled with craftsmen in period costume and tour guides to emphasize not so much the oppressive nature of slave work but the contribution of slaves to their own survival and the artefacts and dwellings associated with them.

Slave quarters, whether on or off plantations, were near to their place of work. They were commonly nucleated settlements in villages on Caribbean plantations. In North America, however, dispersed rural slave housing patterns were often found. Despite their modest appearance, slave houses usually enabled African-Americans to exercise control over their own domestic arrangements without too much interference from white overseers or managers. Slave quarters afforded little privacy between individual households because they were huddled together and often arranged around a communal yard. Yet that was probably not problematic in the plantation slave community, for personal relationships and kin were often dispersed among several contiguous households. Slave houses, however, usually afforded privacy from white personnel on a plantation. It was unusual for planters, managers, and overseers to enter slave dwellings. John Baillie, the owner of Roehampton estate, near to the Montpelier works in Jamaica, remarked in 1832 that slaves set great store by their privacy and that planters 'held the property of the Negro in his house so sacred' that they would never 'attempt to go into a Negro house without asking permission'.[16]

Slave dwellings and their surrounding yards were the site of a rich community and cultural life. In the eighteenth-century Chesapeake, slave quarters were the scene for social intercourse on large plantations. An itinerant white traveller on the eastern shore of Maryland commented in 1747 that 'a Negro Quarter, is a Number of Huts or Hovels, built at some Distance from the Mansion-House; where the Negros reside with their Wives and Families, and cultivate at vacant Times, the little Spots allow'd them.'[17] No wonder that slaves took such pleasure in the privacy of their household communities and led a shared communal life with their fellow black workers: this was one way of coping with the isolation and separation that were hallmarks of the slave experience. Most Africans arrived alone off shipboard after the end of the Middle Passage. They had been torn from their roots in Africa, often leaving complex family and kinship ties behind them. They entered the Americas as heterogeneous groups with varied ethnic origins. In North America for most of the seventeenth century, when the imbalance in sex ratios saw too many men and too few women, the construction of slave families was not easy. But with the growth of a creole slave population in the eighteenth century slave families became more common, notably in the Chesapeake where, as explained above, fertility among black women was high. By the late eighteenth century, a rich set of family networks was common in North America as African-Americans used the base of family obligations, love, and affection to sustain their spirits and wellbeing.

Slave customs and cultural beliefs testify to a rich blend of African practices and adjustments to life on a new continent. They provided a focal point for black communities. Slaves enjoyed music and dance, playing a wide range of musical instruments ranging from fiddles to horns and percussion. Drums and drummers, with accompanying gourds and rattles, were an integral part of Akan culture on the Gold Coast. These musical traditions were transported especially to Jamaica, which drew heavily on slave imports from that African region in the eighteenth century. The drums often imitated speech rhythms and

---

[16] Quoted in B. W. Higman, *Montpelier, Jamaica: A Plantation Community in Slavery and Freedom 1739–1912* (Kingston, 1998), 145.
[17] Quoted in 'Eighteenth-Century Maryland as Portrayed in the "Itinerant Observations" of Edward Kimber', *Maryland Historical Magazine*, 51 (1956), 327.

tones. They were used as signals to the slave community. Similarly, the West African practice of calling and shouting was widely adopted by slaves throughout North America and the Caribbean. The African dancing ring symbolized the solidarity of the slave community and the ring shout was frequently heard on the plantation, sometimes rendered as a wordless call.

Slaves sang at work to ease the boredom and rigours of the work routine. This was often a matter of call-and-response in which the lines of the caller were punctuated by a chorus after the call line. This could often be a richly textured polyphony in which voices overlapped. Clapping often accompanied the singing. Slave songs expressed spiritual beliefs, the trials of life, the need to overcome adversity, and sometimes memories of an African homeland. In 1774 Nicholas Cresswell, a British visitor to Maryland, described how on Sundays the blacks 'generally meet together and amuse themselves with Dancing to the Banjo'. He added that 'their poetry is like the music—Rude and uncultivated. Their Dancing is most violent exercise, but so irregular and grotesque.'[18] This observation expresses the misunderstanding of the improvisatory nature and irregular rhythms that were essential components of slaves' musical expression. It also missed an essential point about the social meaning of music for slaves, namely that it played an important part in the retention of cultural memory. That it had an enduring impact on the transported black people to Britain's Atlantic Empire is shown by the continued singing today of 150 songs in the Yoruba language by Trinidad elders.

Slaves had a rich oral culture that provided a form of continuity between the cultural legacy brought from African societies and the New World realities of slavery. One device common among slaves was the use of proverbs, poems, and fables to highlight features of the African background of those in bondage. Folk stories were told that linked with memories handed down from African traditions. Among the best-known Afro-Caribbean folk tales are Anansi stories based on a trickster figure whose appearance and gender changed from human to animal (usually a spider, monkey, or rabbit) depending on the story. Anansi in his or her various guises usually tried to deceive others and the stories associated with this figure are associated with cunning and wrongdoing. Usually, Anansi received his come-uppance as a result of wicked deeds. These stories, passed from generation to generation, served to remind

---

[18] Quoted in *The Journal of Nicholas Cresswell 1774–1777* (London, 1925), 18–19.

slaves, especially children, of the need for good behaviour. They showed that wicked deeds would meet with punishment.

Linguistic transfers took place as slaves entering British America from sub-Saharan Africa brought with them their own sounds, language structure, and vocabulary that was adapted to form a creole patois. More than half of the Africanisms identified as part of modern Jamaican vocabulary stemmed from the Twi language spoken by groups found along the Gold Coast during the slavery era—the Fante, Akyem, Akwapin, and Asante. Perhaps the best known of the slave languages was Gullah, a variant of a tongue still spoken in Sierra Leone, that flourished in the sea islands off the coast of South Carolina, Georgia, and Florida. Gullah has its own grammatical structure. It stems from a mixture of Old English and various African languages. It spread among imported slaves from different West African regions and became the principal means of communication in the early Lowcountry. Gullah speech helped to separate the cultural life of black slaves from that of Europeans and to bind together Africans from widely different social and geographical backgrounds and with different languages and dialects.

In their limited leisure time, these facets of musical and oral culture came to the fore, frequently involving entire slave communities. They were accompanied by festivals and parades at Christmas, the New Year, Easter, and after the crop harvest. In the northern American colonies the festivals of Negro Election Day in New England and Pinkster Day in New York and New Jersey (named after the Dutch word for Pentecost) had become widespread by the mid-eighteenth century. Both celebrations included speech, music, and entertainment, ending with the election and inauguration of black governors, kings, and judges. These figures of authority assumed leadership positions in their black communities. They adjudicated in disputes and proudly displayed their elevated status among their own race. Ritual enactment of elections and pride in public display of honoured figures in the black community came together on these occasions.

Spiritual values were an essential part of slave communities. A belief in spirits often seemed mere superstition to white observers; but it was bound up with a commonly held black belief that spirits cast spells that could harm or cure, something that was linked to medicinal treatments for ailments by herbs. Though African beliefs that filtered through to America had many variations, they all acknowledged the existence of a supreme being and invoked the spirits of nature and ancestors. Magic and the supernatural formed an essential core of African beliefs. These guiding elements, it was thought, played a crucial role in promoting the essential features of life, whether it be survival or death, peace or war, plenty or famine. A belief in ancestral spirits was particularly important in providing slaves with a constant reference point to some larger purpose for their worldly existence and as a means of asserting the continuity of their spiritual values in the face of the isolation and disruption caused by the slave trade. Thus it was believed that each released spirit returned as a soul to its ancestors in Africa.

Life's major staging posts—birth, marriage, death—were all steeped in spiritual significance for slaves. Newborn babies were not recognized as fully human, and therefore not named, until the ninth day. This reflected the precariousness of survival and the notion that such babies were 'ghost-childs' until they lived beyond the eighth day after birth. Funerals, in particular, were observed with a high degree of ritual and ceremony because many blacks believed that death marked a return to Africa. In 1657 Richard Ligon stated that in Barbados 'when any of them die, they dig a grave, and at evening they bury him, clapping and wringing their hands and making a doleful sound with their voices.'[19] Rum and food were sometimes thrown into the grave and commemorative feasts held in Jamaica on the ninth and fortieth nights after the funeral, at which the dead were treated as guests. Africans often had their own burial grounds where they observed their own practices to honour the dead. Archaeological finds at the African Burial Ground in Manhattan, which dates back to the colonial period, have found pennies placed on eyelids and seashells among the artefacts, both intended to symbolize the return of the dead back across the ocean to Africa.

## CHRISTIANITY AND SLAVE BELIEFS

Efforts to Christianize North American slaves were carried out from the beginning of the eighteenth century. The Society for the Propagation of the Gospel in Foreign Parts (the SPG), with headquarters in London, was particularly energetic in proselytizing the Christian message. Active especially in South Carolina, the SPG nevertheless found it difficult to convert more than a handful of slaves. They disapproved of slaves

[19] Richard Ligon, *A True & Exact History of the Island of Barbados* (London, 1657), 50.

working on Sundays on their garden plots, which affronted their sense of Sabbatarianism. They also ran into conflict with slaves who openly failed to behave monogamously in their sexual relationships, considering this sinful in the eyes of God. It was not until the 'Great Awakening' of the 1740s and the religious revivalism that swept parts of the South in the 1750s and 1760s that large numbers of slaves were converted to Christianity. These evangelical stirrings of the soul were associated largely with the Presbyterians, Methodists, and Baptists, who favoured itinerancy, extempore preaching, minimizing doctrinal differences, conversion as a result of God's saving grace, open-air gatherings, fervent hymn singing, and the prospect for all who joined the Christian faith and maintained their faith to live in the hope of everlasting peace in the life hereafter. Such evangelical exhortation had a widespread appeal to blacks as well as the ordinary white population. In the 1750s the Presbyterian evangelical preacher Samuel Davies wrote that there were 'multitudes' of Virginia blacks 'who are willing, and even eagerly desirous to be instructed, and to embrace every opportunity for that end'.[20]

Among the preachers who cared about converting slaves to Christianity, no one was more effective than George Whitefield, the Calvinist Methodist whose preaching took America by storm on seven trips between 1738 and 1770. Unlike John Wesley, who condemned slavery on moral grounds, Whitefield did not attack the institution of slavery, but considered that planters should teach the Gospels to their slaves. Planters sometimes disagreed; there was the uncomfortable realization that baptism of slaves and the evangelical message might steer African-Americans towards the legitimization of freedom. But planter qualms were unable to stem the tide of increasing Christian conversion among slaves in the Chesapeake. By 1776 probably a third of Virginia's Baptists were blacks—testimony to the impact of Protestantism on the slave community at the time of Independence. In the Lower South Christianity spread more slowly among a heavily African-born population that had difficulty in understanding the meaning of preachers' words. Hewatt considered that such slaves were 'as great strangers to Christianity, and as much under the influence of Pagan darkness, idolatry and superstition, as they were at their first arrival from Africa'.[21] The

[20] Samuel Davies, *Letters from the Reverend Samuel Davies, Showing the State of Religion in Virginia, Particularly among the Negroes* (London, 1757), 10.
[21] Hewatt, *An Historical Account*, ii. 100.

growth of Christianity among the American black population became more pronounced after the War of Independence, however, as African-Americans, especially in the northern states, began to form their own churches and chapels.

The impact of Christianity on American slaves and the growth of paternalism in master–slave relations by the time of the Revolution might lead one to suggest that a merging of white and black culture was in train. One historian has advocated this view for the Chesapeake, suggesting that a convergence of European and African-American cultures can indeed be found at the time of American independence. This is rather a sanguine view, however, that over-emphasizes the coming together of distinct cultures. Christianity had not spread widely among the whole American black population by 1776. A flourishing, distinct African-American culture was more characteristic of black society than an accommodation between the values of the masters and the slaves. In the Chesapeake after the War of Independence, white attitudes towards slavery hardened, despite the promotion of a diluted antislavery message. In the Lowcountry the tightening up of racial attitudes also occurred but without much of even a watered-down attempt at abolitionism.

In the West Indies slaves retained spiritual and magical beliefs from their African heritage. In particular, there was reliance on obeahism and myalism. Obeah practitioners were usually older men in the slave community imbued with spiritual and healing powers. They cast charms on people, hung objects outside houses to prevent theft, administered herbal ointments to those in need of healing, and acted as elders who were consulted for their wisdom and contact with the spirit world. Foreign travellers noted the presence of Obeah throughout the British Caribbean in the eighteenth and nineteenth centuries. The practice of Obeah had sinister implications for many whites. Obeah men were thought to have too much control over slaves. They were seen as sorcerers who sometimes poisoned white people with their herbal remedies. They were also charged with inciting slaves to take part in several rebellions. Myalism was a form of Obeah which attracted the criticism of Europeans in the Caribbean. Myal men served as leaders in cult ceremonies designed to drive away evil spirits known as duppies. They organized slaves into groups, plied them with narcotic herbs, and led ritual dancing and drumming, seeming to exert a spiritual hold over the slaves. Whites feared these incitements to an ancestral and spirit world beyond their control; they viewed myalism as bad magic that should be extirpated.

Christianity spread among slaves in the British Caribbean from the end of the eighteenth century. But for many decades its impact was limited. The Church of England did not promote a proselytizing role in the West Indian colonies and many African slaves clung to their beliefs such as Obeah and Myal. There were exceptions to the poor penetration of the Anglican Church in the British Caribbean, however. The major one lay in the educational work and preaching undertaken on the Codrington plantations in Barbados by the SPG. This left a durable legacy in the form of Codrington College, established on the island and still flourishing today. But it was the work of nonconformist missionaries that played a greater role in spreading the Christian gospels to slaves. The Moravians were active in missions in Jamaica from 1754 and in a few other islands. The great phase of expansion of missionary activity came after the end of the Napoleonic Wars, when the Baptists, Congregationists, and Methodists rapidly expanded their presence in the Caribbean. By the time of slave emancipation, for example, there were fourteen Wesleyan missions, twelve Baptist, nine Moravian, and six Presbyterian missions in Jamaica. All but four had been established in and after 1815.

Nonconformist missionaries were guided by their parent societies in Britain. In an age of frequent bickering between nonconformist denominations at home, and between Anglicans and Dissenters, it is unsurprising to find that a sectarian element embedded itself in the missionaries' preaching. Dissenting missionaries played an important role, however, in spreading literacy and Christian moral instruction among British Caribbean slaves. They linked up with the non-denominational British and Foreign School Society, with its Lancasterian monitorial principles, and with the Mico Charity, originally a way of aiding the victims of Barbary piracy, to spread the teaching of the three R's in mission schools. Attempts by missionaries to absorb the slaves' spiritual customs stemming from their ancestors were not always successful, but myalism took over some Christian practices such as the practice of baptism by full immersion in water that was favoured by the Baptists. In the years after the end of slavery parts of Christianity and African religious beliefs combined to form a set of hybrid cultural beliefs in the British West Indies, but the fusion was never full enough to overcome the social and racial gulf between blacks and Europeans in the tropics.

# 6

# Slave Resistance and Rebellion

Resistance to bondage by slaves occurred frequently, as one might expect in a situation where unequal power relationships defined the position of masters and unfree labourers. The most obvious and major form of resistance was collective rebellion, but slave resistance ranged far beyond revolt to incorporate other strategies intended to combat bondage. For slaves, unwillingness to perform work adequately, either because their condition stimulated opposition or because they were badly treated, was a common act of resistance. This could be done by working below the levels of expected productivity, arriving at work late, failing to complete tasks, or sabotaging work routines. Slaves could feign ignorance about learning to use axes or wheelbarrows. They could pretend to be careless. When disenchanted or alienated from their lot, slaves downed tools and stopped work. Opportunities existed to damage a master's property, to steal food, and to interrupt seasonal work routines. Thus sometimes slaves picked tobacco leaves too early, flooded rice fields, or stole sugar cane. Resistance to work arrangements and routines was not entirely a separate form of protest to overt rebellion: the latter was just the final link in a chain of protest that started modestly and then escalated because of slaves' lack of rights. Attacks on the customary rights of slaves could lead to concerted resistance. This happened in Antigua in 1831 when thousands of slaves marched to Government House in St John's, the island's capital, and protested against the British government's attempt to abolish the slaves' Sunday markets. Conversely, slaves could resist passively by refusing to eat rations after they had been punished. Obviously opposition to slavery by group action was likely to disrupt the status quo more drastically than individual acts of defiance.

Sabotage and arson were further tactics that lay at slaves' disposal to disrupt plantations and attack owners' properties. Setting fire to houses, torching sugar cane, or burning storehouses could often be carried out anonymously and under cover of nightfall. In 1740 over 300 houses were burned in Charleston, South Carolina just a year after the Stono rebellion, discussed below, occurred. This outbreak of arson was attributed to slaves. South Carolina's lawmakers responded with alacrity to the attack by including in the colony's Negro Act of 1740 execution as the punishment for slaves, free blacks, mulattoes, or Native Americans found guilty of wilfully burning property and crops. In New York in 1741 slaves were accused of starting several fires. Rumours and incidents of arson continued to occur throughout the slave territories of the British Empire, and played a part in the last major slave revolt before slave emancipation, in Jamaica in the early months of 1832. In Mauritius arson seemed to be increasing in the final years of slavery; it was more common on estates where the owner or overseer was greatly disliked.

Resistance did not necessarily have a political content; in fact, usually this was not present in acts of defiance. Nor did resistance always have the ulterior aim of securing full freedom, though that was clearly the intention of many slave rebellions. Pragmatic considerations usually outweighed ideological dispositions in slave revolts. Resistance took the form of negotiation and renegotiation of the parameters of power and compulsion and the racial polarities associated with them. Far from slaves being docile recipients of whatever their masters doled out to them, they determined or affected when and where cooperation should be suspended. This is not to suggest that all slaves, throughout their period of bondage, were actively and continuously impelled by a spirit of opposition to their owners; but it reminds us that, although they left few written statements justifying their actions, we can infer that they reacted to the treatment they received in a robust way.

Besides overt resistance, there were ways of offering silent resistance or gestures which opposed slavery. An offer of potions or herbal remedies from slaves to white drivers, overseers, or managers, could lead to poisoning. This may have been a widespread tactic carried out by slaves. Between 1740 and 1785 in Virginia, for instance, more slaves were charged with poisoning than with any other crime except stealing. Recently, historians have drawn attention to slaves' apparel and hairstyles as distinctive ways of distancing themselves from their owners, thereby offering resistance by deportment. There could also be verbal or oral resistance by hurling abuse at white personnel on estates. This might involve spitting in overseers' faces, threats to strike managers, or swearing at drivers. Such acts of insubordination, for instance, accounted for over

90 per cent of the 'List of Offences committed by slaves in the colony of Demerara and Essequibo' for the first part of 1828.

To oppose white masters was a courageous act, for the penalties could be severe. Some punishments focused on slave entitlements; others were brutally applied to slave bodies. Fines, whippings, confinement in dungeons, placing iron clamps on feet, occasional mutilation, and removal of privileges are just some of the punishments that met determined acts of resistance. Sometimes brave acts of defiance by slaves had unintended consequences. Malingering by a slave, for example, might lead an owner to the decision that that individual was no longer worth keeping in a plantation gang, possibly leading to the sale of the slave and the break-up of black family ties. But though punishments could be severe, masters also dangled the carrot as well as wielding the stick. To deal with acts of resistance it could be more beneficial to allow slaves extra time to cultivate provision grounds or to improve the state of their dwellings rather than resorting to the lash. Masters wanted slaves to accede to their owners' wishes.

## SLAVE RUNAWAYS

The most extreme form of slave resistance took the form of conspiracies and rebellions. If rebellions represented the ultimate act of collective resistance by bonded labourers, other types of resistance were more prevalent, none more so than attempts to escape bondage through stealing away from masters. Runaway slaves were common in North America and the West Indies during the slavery era. To prevent slaves from absconding, one prominent slave master, Robert Carter of Virginia, boasted of 'having cured many a negro of running away' by cutting off their toes.[1] Most slaveowners rarely took such drastic pre-emptive measures, but they had many means of surveillance that helped to round up escapees, as we shall see.

Slave fugitives usually ran off singly or in pairs; they were often disguised; sometimes they took the tools of their trade to aid their flight. Their aims were diverse. Some wished to escape from coastal neighbourhoods, usually by jumping aboard ship. Others slipped away

---

[1] Robert Carter to Robert Jones, 10 Oct. 1727, in Edmund Berkeley, Jr, 'Robert Carter as Agricultural Administrator: His Letters to Robert Jones', *Virginia Magazine of History and Biography*, 101 (1993), 280.

for brief periods of time to visit friends or relatives in rural areas. Still others headed for the relative anonymity of large urban centres such as Philadelphia, New York, or Kingston. Permanent runaway communities among slaves were fairly uncommon. Some could be found in the backwoods of the Carolinas or Virginia, where they would raid plantations for food or forage in wooded areas, but the terrain was not as conducive to such permanent maroon communities as the forests of the interior of Surinam or the mountains of Jamaica. Perhaps the best-known North American maroon hideout was the Great Dismal Swamp, stretching from Norfolk, Virginia, to Edenton in the Albemarle Sound area of North Carolina. A white traveller commented that this area harboured 'prodigious multitudes of every kind of wild beasts peculiar to America, as well as run-away Negroes, who in these horrible swamps are perfectly safe, and with the greatest facility elude the most diligent search of their pursuers.'[2]

American and West Indian newspapers were full of advertisements for absconders. Rewards were offered for those who collaborated with white masters to find them. Runaways who were caught were subjected to a range of punishments. They could be whipped, placed in iron collars and shackles, or sold. Slaveowners repeatedly complained about the existence of runaways. Some thought that runaways could not be returned successfully to bondage once they had tasted temporary freedom. The fugitives described in newspapers were just the tip of an iceberg of bonded workers who took flight in an attempt to secure liberty. Other documents referring to runaway bonded labourers indicate that the number was far larger than those advertised. This is unsurprising, given that owners would probably spend money on an advert only in cases where a runaway had been absent for a period of at least a month, or where the fugitive was worth recapturing. Most slaves, of course, did not escape from servitude; but the advertisements for those who did reveal their main characteristics and motives.

A notice from the *North Carolina Gazette*, dated 27 April 1775, illustrates some of the main details found in runaway slave advertisements:

Eloped from the Subscribers on Wednesday the 26th Inst. Two newly imported Men Slaves, named KAUCHEE and BOOHUM, about 6 feet high, and, perhaps, 30 Years of Age. They absconded in Company with three other Slaves about two Months ago, and were taken up at Bread-Creek, about 10 Miles off,

[2] John Ferdinand Dalziel Smyth, *A Tour of the United States of America*, 2 vols. (Dublin, 1784), ii. 102.

and brought back by William Gailling of that Place, who has since purchased a Wench who was imported with them; from which it is supposed they are lurking about that Neighbourhood. Whoever takes them up and brings them home, shall have Forty Shillings reward from Edward Batchelor & Co.

This is typical in giving the name, height, approximate age, date of flight, suspected destination, and level of reward mentioned in such advertisements, and also in containing wording based on hearsay, inference, and suspicion. It is just one of thousands of such notices that comprise the main source for analysing the motives and characteristics of black escapees as seen through the eyes of white masters. It is difficult to specify the success with which owners recaptured slaves, but some fugitives were undoubtedly tough, hardened characters who did their utmost to resist capture. Thus in 1815 Appea, a 50-year old runaway in Barbados, had a 'surly countenance, has several scars about his head occasioned by fighting, and a piece of one of his ears, bit out by the same cause; he has eluded every vigilant attempt to take him. He is perhaps one of the most notorious villains the Country ever possessed; and a dangerous person to be at large amongst Plantation Negroes.'[3]

Slaves ran away from their owners for innumerable reasons. Social ties with other blacks were one of the prime motives for absconding. Some African-Americans had experienced separation from family and friends and wished to rejoin them. In Pennsylvania, for example, a 14-year-old slave called Hagar with 'a Scar under one of her Breasts, supposed to be got by Whipping and an iron collar about her Neck' was 'supposed to be harboured in some Negroe Quarter, as her Father and Mother encourage her in these elopements, under a pretence that she is ill used at home' (*Pennsylvania Gazette*, 6 November 1766). After the abolition of the British slave trade in 1807, slave runaways in the West Indies frequently had relatives among free people of colour whom they contacted in order to help their escape. When John Charles of Grand Bas estate, Grenada, deserted in 1815, it was believed that free blacks were harbouring him because he had been intimate with a free black woman on the estate. When Jacob, a cooper on Bromefield plantation, Barbados, ran off in 1813, it was assumed he had sought out relatives in Bridgetown because he had many relations there and had previously worked in that town as a hairdresser. Male runaways frequently sought out wives, children, and parents. A much higher proportion of slaves absconded for these reasons

[3] Quoted in Gad Heuman, 'Runaway Slaves in Nineteenth-Century Barbados', *Slavery and Abolition*, 6 (1985), 106.

in the Chesapeake than in the Mid-Atlantic region because family ties among the black community were stronger on Virginia and Maryland plantations—a result of the healthy reproductive rate among creole slaves—than in Pennsylvania, New Jersey, and Delaware, where slaves were generally held in twos or threes in dispersed rural settlements.

Other reasons why slaves fled included unease about being apprehended after stealing an owner's goods; the desire to escape from cruel masters; the influence of outside agitators; disappointment at not being freed by their owners; and opportunities arising from British military recruitment during the American revolutionary war. One such black fugitive was Cuff Dix, who escaped south from Pennsylvania to Virginia only a fortnight after American independence was declared. 'Negroes in general think that Lord Dunmore is contending for their liberty,' his master declared in an advertisement, and 'it is not improbable that said Negroe is on his march to join his Lordship's own black regiment, but it is hoped he will be prevented by some honest Whig from effecting it' (*Pennsylvania Gazette*, 17 July 1776). John Murray, fourth earl of Dunmore, was governor of Virginia on the eve of American independence. His proclamation to free slaves who were willing to flee and join the British army, made on 14 November 1775, was based as much on the desire to disrupt the slave system and destabilize American society, in the furtherance of military objectives, as on any antislavery motive. Dunmore, in fact, recruited around 1,500 blacks through his offer of freedom but they suffered military defeat and were decimated by a severe attack of smallpox in the spring and summer of 1776.

There were various patterns of slave flight. Some slaves absconded from their masters for a few days and then returned voluntarily. Others, however, aimed to flee permanently. Geographical factors affected their chances of success. Fugitive slaves near the eastern seaboard of the North American colonies or in the Caribbean islands often had the option of stealing away by boat. If they had been living by the shore or along rivers and creeks or in ports, they had often picked up skills that might help them to attempt a maritime escape. Thus an advert in the Kingston *Daily Advertiser* (7 June 1790) referred to a slave runaway from John Munro's wharf at Kingston who was 'well acquainted with all the different islands to Windward' and who had come to Jamaica on a sloop from Rhode Island. He could speak English, French, Dutch, Danish, and Portuguese. It was thought 'he may endeavour to pass for a free man, and may thus impose on foreigners and other seafaring gentlemen.'

Ports and towns were another magnet for slave runaways. By the late eighteenth century Philadelphia, New York, Charleston, Kingston, and Bridgetown had slaves and free black workers in their populations. Mingling with the crowds and changing names, runaways stood a better chance of escaping detection in an urban setting than those who remained in and around plantations. In addition, there were always work opportunities in the retail sectors of towns for runaways to support themselves. Skilled slaves, in particular, could find work as carpenters, masons, tailors, cooks, and in the maritime trades. A fair amount of urban concentration of fugitives existed in Jamaica by the end of the slavery era, for the proportion of runaways in Kingston in 1834 was double the number elsewhere in the island. Between 1805 and 1830 in Barbados over a quarter of the runaways whose destinations are known found refuge in the towns of Bridgetown and Speightstown.

Most slave runaways were male. Females usually comprised between one-tenth and one-fifth of absconders in all locales. This ratio can be explained by the greater sense of familial ties found among slave women, notably their reluctance to leave their children. In addition, because more male than female slaves worked as boatmen, ferrymen, and labourers on roads and as hired workers, men had greater knowledge of the terrain and more opportunities to escape. The majority of runaways were in their twenties. They were better able to cope with the difficulties of life on the run than older slaves; moreover, middle-aged slaves were more likely to have forged relationships, which made them reluctant to move in some cases. In most instances taking flight appears to have been a premeditated act rather a last-minute gamble. A marked seasonal distribution of slave runaways supports this supposition. In North Carolina, for example, the most popular time for African-Americans to quit their masters was either during the harvest season from September to November or between February and April, when the slack season ended and spring planting began. In Virginia more slaves ran off in April, when the seasonal pace of tobacco planting increased, than in any other month. In South Carolina the highest incidence of slave absconding occurred in the summer months from May to August, when rice cultivation was particularly rigorous. In Barbados most slaves ran away in July and August. This was just after the sugar harvest ended and when provisions were commonly in short supply. It may be that Barbadian fugitives fled in those months because supervision was more lax than at the height of the sugar harvest, or possibly because hunger drove them to abscond. Innumerable references in runaway advertisements to slaves fleeing with clothes, guns, the tools of their trade, forged passes, and canoes or horses also suggest that plans for freedom were laid before the moment of flight occurred.

In a pioneering study of slave fugitives in Virginia, Gerald W. Mullin argued that acculturated slaves—those with skills—fled in disproportionately large numbers and stood a better chance of remaining at large. His statistics show that between 1736 and 1801 22 per cent of the fugitive slaves in the Old Dominion were either artisans or domestics. But this argument is not persuasive because he does not provide estimates of the proportion of skilled slaves in Virginia's black population as a whole. Contrary to Mullin's view, it may be that the per-centage of skilled runaways matched their proportion in the overall slave population, thus reducing the emphasis on acculturated slaves as more likely fugitives. A more salient feature of slave runaways in the plantation southern colonies and states lay in differences among African and creole patterns of flight. The typical African-born slave runaway in Virginia left with one other African whereas in South Carolina half of the Africans who quit plantations left in groups of three or four. This probably reflected the greater preponderance of Africans in the eighteenth-century population of the Lowcountry than in the Chesapeake. Creoles throughout the southern colonies generally ran away singly. In the Chesapeake three-quarters of the advertised creole slave runaways left alone; in the Lowcountry the proportion was a half. The main reason for the difference seems to lie in the fact that the South Carolina creoles were less acculturated and therefore less able to cope by themselves.

## MAROONS IN THE WEST INDIES

Permanent runaway communities were uncommon in North America apart from the Great Dismal Swamp area mentioned above. But they were a continuing feature of British Caribbean slave society, though their significance diminished over time. The two geographical areas where maroons—taken from the French word *marronage*, meaning run-away—flourished were the rugged interior of Jamaica and the forested areas away from the coastal plantation fringe in Demerara. However, there were smaller maroon communities elsewhere in the British West Indies—for example, in the woods of Grenada and Dominica. The maroons had originally been at the heart of the resistance movement against the whites of Jamaica. They had fought a series of maroon wars in the late seventeenth and early eighteenth centuries. These compelled the Jamaican plantocracy to seek accommodation with them, something achieved through a peace treaty of 1739 between Colonel Guthrie and the maroon leader Cudjoe and another treaty of the same year signed on behalf of Nanny, the female leader of another band of maroons. These treaties gave the maroons rights to hunt freely throughout unsettled areas of Jamaica, allowed them 1,500 acres of land for cultivation, but obliged them to return fugitive slaves they encountered. Most important, it pledged their support to white settlers when slave rebellions broke out. In 1760 maroons joined white forces in putting down the serious slave revolt in western Jamaica begun by Coromantee rebels and killed the leader, Tacky. Planters lived in fear of reprisals during the revolt. 'I praise God none of mine nor Johnson's Negroes were in the rebellion,' one planter wrote, for 'if they had we might been [*sic*] all Destroyed, as my house is so nigh to the Mountains. They often threatned to come down upon me but I praise God they never did.'[4]

The maroons formed permanent communities such as Old Maroon Town, Trelawney Town, Crawford Town, and their headquarters at Accompong Town. These were isolated and self-sufficient communities situated in impenetrable wooded, hilly, and craggy areas in the Cockpit Country, in West-central Jamaica, well away from most plantations. They were not large in numbers: a contemporary estimate suggests that there were 885 Jamaican maroons in 1770. Nevertheless, they stood as symbols of freedom for enslaved blacks. Today remnants of these communities still exist and an annual celebration of maroon independence takes place on 6 January, when the Accompong maroons make their reunion to visit the stone-marked grave site of Cudjoe.

There was always suspicion by white people in Jamaica that the maroons were a potential threat to social stability. Stephen Fuller, the agent for Jamaica, noted in 1778 that the maroons 'have never become properly incorporated with the rest of the inhabitants, nor are they interested in the defence of the Country, and their conduct in the late insurrections of the slaves sufficiently proved that they are not to be depended upon'.[5] Despite these misgivings, peace with the Jamaican maroons lasted until 1795 when the English commissioner

---

[4] University of California, San Diego, Mandeville Special Collections Library, George Ricketts to Thomas Hall, 30 Aug. 1760, Barnett/Hall Collection, flat box 25, MSS 220.

[5] Boston College, Memorial from Stephen Fuller to Lord George Germain, 23 Dec. 1778, Stephen Fuller letterbook (1776–84), Nicholas M. Williams Ethnological Collection.

assigned to Trelawney Town had two maroons flogged for pilfering from plantations. The island's governor feared the maroons and sent troops to capture Trelawney Town. Maroons ambushed the troops but the British army prevailed after laying siege to the maroon towns by surrounding them with military outposts. One hundred Cuban hunting dogs were imported by the British troops and set among the maroons, who were terrified of them. The maroons agreed to surrender in return for amnesty. In the other Jamaican maroon communities peaceful relations were maintained with whites after the 1739 treaty.

In other parts of the British Caribbean the white authorities acted aggressively to curb maroon communities. This seems to have stemmed partly from the perceived greater threat of such permanent runaway settlements in the wake of the Saint-Domingue slave rebellion of the 1790s (discussed below) and also from the need to retain slaves on plantations in more sparsely settled colonies after the British slave trade ended. In Grenada and Dominica groups of paramilitary Colony Rangers were employed to apprehend maroons. 'Bush negroes' in Demerara maroon communities lived in wooded areas beyond the coastal plantation fringe. These maroons were descended from slaves in Surinam who had signed a treaty in the eighteenth century with the Dutch guaranteeing their freedom. At the time of the Demerara slave revolt of 1823 the plantocracy gained the support of Native Indians to curtail the movement of slaves from coastal plantations to the forested maroon settlements of the interior.

## SLAVE REVOLTS

Given the heritable nature of slavery, one might expect to find that many slave revolts occurred in the British Empire in the seventeenth and eighteenth centuries. But there were, in fact, more aborted risings than actual revolts; more conspiracy scares than actual conspiracies; and not a single slave revolt that proved successful. Why were large risings relatively uncommon in British overseas territories? Before 1670 there were too few slaves for an effective revolt to take place. The influx of large numbers of Africans to North America in the late seventeenth century coupled with the growth of plantations and the subsequent codification of statutes discriminating against blacks might lead one to expect, however, a more concerted challenge by bonded labourers to their misery. That this did not occur frequently resulted partly from the low density of African-Americans in an extensive terrain until the mid-eighteenth century—Virginia and South Carolina, for example, being much larger geographically than Great Britain. In such circumstances, slaves were accommodated in scattered quarters, which effectively nullified moves to coordinate revolts. The lack of homogeneity among the saltwater slaves and the residence of slaveowners on their plantations—permanent absentee ownership was rare—caused divisions among the black workforce and subjected slaves to the constant gaze of white personnel with power. Ironically, the reproductive capacity of the eighteenth-century creole slave workforce, especially in Virginia, and the training of slaves for skilled agricultural work, leading to a pecking order of rewards and responsibilities for the most able workers, might also have served to undercut serious uprisings by ameliorating slave conditions and allowing blacks a meaningful role through which they could gain a measure of autonomy over their lives.

Despite these obstacles to slave uprisings, a number of revolts and conspiracies did occur. Two of these were in New York City. In April 1712 a revolt occurred there in which twenty-five Africans and Native Americans burned several buildings in Manhattan and killed nine whites. The rising was quelled. Whites exacted their revenge, capturing the rebels and hanging them in chains. In 1741 New York experienced a 'Great Negro Plot'. Surviving documentation is ambivalent on whether this really was a slave conspiracy but it led to thirty blacks and four whites being executed. Its leader Caesar, who had hoped to burn buildings in Manhattan and escape to Quebec, was burned alive. In 1734 an attempt at a slave rising occurred in Somerset County, New Jersey, but this failed. On the eve of the American War of Independence rumours circulated throughout the southern colonies about increasing slave rebelliousness. In the early 1770s attempted slave plots affected Perth Amboy, New Jersey; Ulster County, New York; Norfolk, Virginia; St Andrews Parish, South Carolina; Dorchester County, Maryland; and the Tar River region of North Carolina. Each of these conspiracies alarmed whites but did not cause major disturbances. Each could be analysed further, but in order to understand the distinctiveness of North American slave uprisings and why they failed it is better to analyse two leading events in detail: Bacon's rebellion in Virginia (1676) and the Stono revolt in South Carolina (1739). These outbreaks occurred when white internal divisions were apparent. But they followed a different course and both ended in failure.

### BACON'S REBELLION (1676)

Bacon's rebellion had a significant impact on the propertied classes in Virginia. Led by a newly arrived planter, Nathaniel Bacon, the rising attempted to secure land in the westward part of Virginia by poorer whites who felt deprived of economic opportunity by the wealthy planters of the tidewater, led by Governor William Berkeley. Bacon was initially favoured by Berkeley, his second cousin, and was given a place on Virginia's Council soon after settling in the colony. During 1676 Bacon and Berkeley fell out, were briefly reconciled, and then parted their ways again over dealings with Native Americans. There had recently been skirmishes between various tribes and white settlers in the Chesapeake over access to land. Blood was spilt on both sides. Bacon, who hated the Native Americans, repeatedly asked for a commission from Berkeley to attack them with military support. But Berkeley, wanting to trade with them and not wishing to antagonize them, did his best to evade the request. He was worried that Bacon planned to attack Native American tribes indiscriminately rather than to focus a raid on those who had been in conflict with white settlers. On 10 May 1676 Berkeley denounced Bacon and removed him from the Council. But Bacon rounded up supporters to invade Native American lands. They ended up massacring a group of Occaneechees.

Over the summer of 1676 further raids against the Native Americans turned into a rebellion that was almost a civil war in Virginia. The rising was brief but bloody. Fighting took place between Bacon's supporters and the Native Americans, leading to casualties. The rebels paraded Native American captives through Jamestown in early September, offering, as they went along, freedom to servants and slaves who would join Bacon. Anyone who offered resistance was attacked. The rebels drove Berkeley out of Jamestown, torched the town, and seized the government for themselves. They plundered property. They devised a political programme and adopted 'Bacon's Laws', which reinstated freemen with the franchise they had lost to freeholders six years before. Not long after this climax to the revolt, Bacon caught a swamp fever and died, probably of dysentery, on 26 October. Without his leadership the rebellion soon petered out. Berkeley, aided by armed vessels arriving from England with a thousand troops, regained control. The rebellion was put down and 'Bacon's Laws' were repealed. Twenty-three of Bacon's supporters were hanged by Berkeley.

This was the largest uprising so far in the history of Britain's colonies in North America. It involved disgruntled ex-servants, other freedmen, and slaves joining together to oppose the status quo. About one in ten of the slaves in Virginia joined in the uprising. In 1677 an investigation of the causes of the revolt by the king's commissioners found that a significant part of the rebel force had been free men who had recently been servants. One of the last batches of rebels to surrender consisted of a mixed band of eighty blacks and twenty English servants, who were highly critical of their officers capitulating before they did. Historians of the rebellion have highlighted the fears aroused in Virginia with regard to social and political stability as a result of this unruly amalgam of lower-class rebels joining together over a potential racial divide. They have shown how the aftermath of the rebellion led to moves to tighten slave codes in Virginia and to prise apart any future armed cooperation between slaves and ex-servants. They have also underscored the anxiety that the 'giddy multitude', as contemporaries called them, could wreck the hard efforts of propertied settlers in the Chesapeake and lead to potential anarchy.

## THE STONO REBELLION (1739)

The Stono rebellion was the largest slave revolt in the history of the British mainland colonies in North America. It began early on a Sunday morning, 9 September 1739, when a group of slave rebels breaking into a store near the Stono River in a coastal parish twelve miles south of Charleston. Led by an Angolan called Jemmy, the rebels beheaded two white men, seized weapons and alcohol, and headed southwards towards Florida. Gathering anything between fifty and 100 recruits along the way, they marched with drums and banners, and destroyed plantation houses and farm houses. By the afternoon they had reached the Edisto River where they paused in an open field, presumably hoping that extra black recruits would flock to their cause and make them invincible. This gave the white militia time to organize an attack on the rebels, to muster quick support from local planters, and to erect pickets at strategic crossroads and ferry crossings. The rebels and the militia came to blows, and according to a contemporary report 'one fought for Liberty and Life, the other for their Country and every thing that was dear to them.'⁶ Some blacks who were not among the rebels supported their planter owners, while others tried to pacify the rebels. By the evening, most of the black resistance had been quelled. However, some slave rebels escaped and the whites who had confronted them in the afternoon skirmish concentrated their efforts on hounding them down. White fears of the rebelliousness stirred up by the uprising were not quelled for a couple of months. Not until 30 November 1739 did a report in the *Boston Weekly Newsletter* note that 'the Rebellious Negros are quite stopt from doing any further Mischief, many of them having been put to the most cruel Death.' During the rising at least twenty white people and forty-four blacks died. The militiamen 'cut off. . . [the] heads' of the rebels they had killed and 'set them up at every Mile Post they came to' as a gory example to other slaves in the region.⁷

The causes of the revolt remain speculative. Harsh conditions probably played a part. South Carolina had suffered from a bout of epidemic disease in the summer of 1739. The tough work routine of planting rice in swampy areas may have fired some of the resistance. That the Spanish garrison of St Augustine had offered freedom to Carolinian slaves shortly before the uprising broke out was perhaps of greater significance, owing to the proximity of South Carolina to the Spanish border and the fact that the Stono rebels headed south in that direction. This happened at a time when Anglo-Spanish hostilities had spilled over into the War of Jenkins's Ear, a largely colonial war caused by tensions over the safety of English and Spanish ships plying the Atlantic Ocean routes. Whatever the rebels' motives, we know for certain that this was a rising shaped by African tactics. Most of the rebels, including the leader, were slaves born in Africa rather than creoles. In fact, many of them had been dispatched from Angola and were of Congolese extraction. Their actions exhibited notable features of resistance associated with ethnic martial traditions in Africa. For instance, the initial decapitation of the two white men at the start of the revolt mirrored the common resort to displaying severed heads in African societies as trophies of military prowess. The use of banners and drums as the Africans marched south from Stono were integral to fighting methods followed in West-central Africa. It may be that some rebels had had experience of war within Africa; this, after

⁶ J. H. Easterby (ed.), *The Journal of the [South Carolina] Commons House of Assembly, 1741–1742* (Columbia, SC, 1953), 83.
⁷ *Boston Weekly Newsletter*, 8 Nov. 1739.

all, was how many slaves had been taken as captives before they were shipped across the Atlantic.

The collapse of the Stono revolt was not surprising: there was no unanimity among the blacks involved about its purpose and the afternoon pause near the Edisto River gave the white forces time to organize and counter-attack. But though it seems an exaggeration to view such a short outbreak of black violence as a defining moment in the history of South Carolina and of race relations in North America, it left long-lasting fears among the white minority in the Lowcountry about the potential for similar revolts in the future. Thus the secretary to the trustees of Georgia wrote in his journal that 'the [white] Inhabitants cannot live without perpetually guarding their own Safety, now become so precarious.'[8] The response of South Carolina's politicians to Stono reveals the importance they attached to dealing effectively with the aftermath of the uprising. South Carolina went to war with the Spanish in St Augustine to try to block an obvious avenue of escape for their slaves. The South Carolina Assembly introduced a prohibitive import duty on slaves, which cut back the introduction of African slaves into the province for most of the next decade. Most important, South Carolina passed a comprehensive slave code in 1740. Drawing on previous statutes, this tightened up the control over slaves and became the basis of the colony's slave law for virtually the next century. The 1740 code laid down larger fines than previously for planters who failed to control their slaves; it took the granting of manumission away from individual planters and placed it under the authority of the legislature; and it included other clauses that led to greater surveillance of black activity in the province.

## SLAVE REVOLTS IN THE CARIBBEAN

Slave revolts occurred from time to time in the British West Indies. Between 1638, when a general slave rebellion broke out on Providence island, and 1837, when a mutiny occurred among the First West India Regiment in Trinidad, there were seventeen slave revolts in the British Caribbean that involved dozens of slaves, thirty-eight acts of collective resistance with hundreds of slaves, fifteen outbreaks of violence with

---

[8] 'The Journal of William Stephens', in Allen D. Candler and Lucien L. Knight (eds.), *The Colonial Records of the State of Georgia*, 26 vols. (Atlanta, 1904–16), iv. 592.

thousands of slaves, and five rebellions that included many thousands of slaves. Most plots, revolts, and wars which broke out before the turn of the nineteenth century, however, were relatively small-scale affairs that were easily contained by the authorities on the Caribbean islands. The one exception to this generalization was Tacky's rebellion, which occurred in western Jamaica in 1760. This was the second largest slave rebellion to occur on the island. Led by disaffected Coromantee (i.e. Akan) rebels, this outbreak shook the complacency of the Jamaican plantocracy. The uprising began on Easter Day 1760 with slaves plundering the fort at Port Maria. Armed with muskets and gunpowder, they marched south, gathered recruits, and engaged in guerrilla warfare. Tacky was captured and executed, and his own band of rebels was dissipated fairly soon. Fighting continued, however, for several months. Firm reprisals were put in place to quell the rebels. Over 400 slaves were killed during the revolt, 100 were executed, and about 500 transported to British Honduras. Some sixty whites and sixty free people of colour lost their lives in the conflict. After the revolt white Jamaicans feared continuing to allow imports of Africans into the island because it was thought they would add potential numbers to the slave rebel cause. Obeahism was suppressed and greater limits placed on slave meetings and slave access to weapons.

Throughout the plantation Americas the only slave rebellion that ever resulted in the overthrow of white power occurred in 1791 in Saint-Domingue (the western half of Hispaniola), where a massive, planned upsurge of 400,000 blacks, led by Toussaint L'Ouverture and inspired by the French Revolution's ideals of liberty, equality, and fraternity, saw the overthrow of French overlords and the creation of a black republic. Whites in Saint-Domingue had failed to apply the French National Assembly's rule of 15 May 1791 that all financially qualified men of colour could be enfranchised and become full citizens. This gave impetus to violence between whites and free people of colour. The confrontation gathered momentum to become a large slave revolt. Over the next few years the slaves won their freedom and the British sent in troops to support the French plantocracy. L'Ouverture—celebrated as a hero in a sonnet by Wordsworth—ruled Saint-Domingue and negotiated the withdrawal of British troops from the island. Black troops occupied Spanish Santo Domingo (the eastern half of Hispaniola) by the end of 1800 and in the following year L'Ouverture was named governor general for life by his supporters. His regime was challenged by a large French expeditionary force which came to restore white planter rule to Saint-Domingue in 1802. L'Ouverture was arrested and sent to France where he died. Guerilla war broke out in Saint-Domingue between freed blacks under his deputy, General Jean-Jacques Dessalines. The French were forced to evacuate the colony before the end of 1803 and on 1 January 1804 Dessalines proclaimed the colony's independence under the name of Haiti. The Saint-Domingue revolt remained an iconic moment of triumph for all subsequent generations of slaves but nothing on the same scale ever occurred in the British Empire.

Curiously, when the ideas and impact of the French Revolution were at their height and the Saint-Domingue slave rebellion was in progress, few slave disturbances happened in Jamaica, which was only a few days' travel by sea from the site of the French rebel slaves' action. This was largely because of the strong British military presence in the Caribbean during the wars with revolutionary and Napoleonic France. British garrisons deterred Jamaican slaves from staging a rebellion during the turbulent 1790s. Libertarian ideas stemming from the French revolutionary call for liberty, equality, and fraternity, and the revolt in Saint-Domingue, probably influenced free coloureds in Jamaica more than the enslaved population. The major outbreak of slave discontent in the British Caribbean during the 1790s occurred in Grenada in Fédon's rebellion in 1795–6. This involved a distinctive francophone mix of planters, slaves, and free coloureds led by the free coloured planter Julien Fédon against anglophone whites, who had settled in the island after it was ceded to Britain at the end of the Seven Years War. Bloody fighting marked this revolt. The acting governor Kenneth McKenzie sounded a note of alarm when he wrote to London, shortly after the rebellion's outbreak, that 'every moment of inactivity must increase the evil within, as the Negroes are daily joining the Insurgents and desolating the Estates; all of which have been plundered, and a number in the neighbourhood of St. George's . . . have been burnt.'[9] By January 1796 Fédon's forces controlled all of Grenada save for the capital, but the British settlers were helped by armed reinforcements who enabled them to prevail in the struggle. Fédon escaped from the clutches of his enemies and his fate is unknown. The British put down the rebellion with executions and deportation of captives to foreign territories along the Bay of Honduras. This was the biggest challenge by slaves and

---

[9] Quoted in Michael Craton, *Testing the Chains: Resistance to Slavery in the British West Indies* (Ithaca, NY, 1982), 187.

their supporters to British authority in the Caribbean in the French revolutionary era. Though it ended in the British retaining control of Grenada, it caused about £2.5 million damage in property and effectively limited the future expansion of sugar cultivation there. Black Caribs in St Vincent rose up against the plantocracy in the wake of Fédon's revolt and controlled the island for six months before General Sir Ralph Abercromby's expeditionary force, sent from England, defeated the insurgents in early June 1796.

In the last phase of slavery in the British Empire, three large revolts broke out in the British Caribbean. They were in Barbados (1816), Demerara (1823), and Jamaica (1831/2). The geographical diversity of these uprisings and their different timing makes it difficult to discern common threads that incited slaves to rebel in each colony. Economic factors may have played some part in two of the rebellions. Barbados in 1816 was subject to falling sugar prices and an economic slump in the immediate aftermath of the Napoleonic Wars. Jamaica in 1831 was similarly in the midst of a downturn in economic fortunes. The maturity of the three settlements and the composition of their slave populations appear not to have been influential factors in stimulating revolt. Barbados became a British territory in 1625 and had witnessed few slave revolts. Jamaica was a British sugar island from the 1650s and had experienced several slave uprisings. Demerara had been acquired by Britain from the Dutch only in 1803. Over 90 per cent of the Barbados slave population consisted of creoles in 1816. Half of the Demerara and Jamaican slaves were creole in 1823 and 1831 respectively. There is scant evidence that any of the revolts broke out specifically as a result of deteriorating relations between blacks and their white masters. On the contrary, each revolt occurred when amelioration of slave life and work was already being put into practice by planters. Interestingly, in the Cape Colony, where amelioration policies were also pursued, there were no slave revolts between 1826 and effective emancipation in 1838.

If several likely explanations for the outbreak of the three late slave rebellions in the British Caribbean appear to be red herrings, what in fact led to the revolts? The spread of information about possibilities for freedom for slaves seems to have been important. Rumours of Wilberforce's attempt to steer a Registry bill through Parliament in 1815 were rife before the Barbados rebellion of 1816. Some slaves thought that such a bill was the first step towards their freedom. The Demerara revolt of 1823 occurred several months after the Anti-Slavery Society in London announced its policy of gradual emancipation and the Bathurst circular ushered in a government policy of amelioration (see Chapter 8). For slaves in the colonies, this seemed the first step towards granting freedom. In Jamaica in 1831–2 it was widely known that the Whig government had pledged itself to legislate in favour of slave emancipation as soon as the Reform Bill was passed. In all these examples, rumours were circulated by word of mouth and by British and colonial newspapers. Slaves eavesdropped on their masters' table talk. Literate creole slaves could digest the newspaper accounts of improvements to slave life and possible moves towards black freedom and pass them on to their fellow slaves.

The role of missionaries and the emergence of a creole leadership also helped to stimulate these revolts. Nonconformist missionaries were not very numerous in Barbados in 1816 but their presence was notable in Demerara and Jamaica in 1823 and 1831 respectively. These missionaries were instructed by their parent bodies not to incite slaves to rebel but to teach them obedience, piety, and temperance. Often, however, the work of missionaries on the spot opened their eyes to the iniquities of slavery and they found considerable tension between what they were instructed to preach and what they privately felt about the institution of slavery. They also had to cope with the hostility of planters. Thus the Reverend John Smith, based in Demerara, informed the London Missionary Society, a Congregational body, that 'the white people will not come to hear us themselves, but stay at home and say we preach mischief, that we are in league with Mr. Wilberforce and that nothing but the total emancipation of the slaves will satisfy us.'[10] Many planters attributed the outbreak of the Jamaican slave revolt of 1831/2 to missionary influence. As one of their number put it, the cause of the revolt was 'generally attributed to the Sectarian preachers, and you will see, from what has passed, that there are ample grounds, at least, for suspicion.'[11] The planters overreacted in their view of missionaries inciting slaves to rebel. Nevertheless, the mission schools established by nonconformist preachers spread the gospels through a network of literate black deacons, who liaised with the mass of black workers. Thus, in the case of Jamaica, the Baptist missionary William Knibb was stirred to condemn slavery as a result of his sojourn in the western parishes of the

---

[10] Quoted in Emilia Viotti da Costa, *Crowns of Glory, Tears of Blood: The Demerara Slave Rebellion of 1823* (New York, 1994), 140.

[11] Surrey History Centre, Woking, Alexander Bayley to Henry Goulburn, 16 Jan. 1832, Goulburn Collection, 304/J/1/21/152.

island. He became intimately involved with the 1831/2 revolt—known as the Baptist War—and was brought to trial for supposedly inciting the slaves to rebel.

Each of the three late slave rebellions in the British West Indies attracted strong black leaders. Bussa, an African-born slave who was head ranger at Bayleys plantation, St Philip Parish, rallied slaves from all over Barbados to join him in a revolt. Though very little is known about him as an individual, he appears to have been a brave military leader who was killed in the final battle in the revolt. Nanny Grigg, a literate domestic slave living on Simmons's plantation near Bayley's, also played an important role in urging slaves to rebel. Before the revolt broke out she had predicted—on the hearsay evidence of Wilberforce's bill—that 'the negroes were to be freed on Easter-Monday, and the only way to get it was to fight for it.'[12] Quamina, senior deacon at Bethel Chapel, assumed the role of figurehead in the Demerara revolt. Though he himself did not bear arms, he was hunted down, shot dead, and his body hung in chains outside Success plantation where the rebellion had begun. Samuel Sharpe, a black deacon in the Baptist church, was the leader of the slaves in the Jamaican Baptist War. He symbolized the literate, creole leadership that informed and organized slaves. He liaised with other literate blacks after prayer meetings; addressed his fellow slaves with impassioned commitment; and showed organizational capacity once the revolt began. He told Henry Bleby that 'he learnt from his Bible, that the whites had no more right to hold black people in slavery, than black people had to make the white people slaves.'[13]

The rebellions in Barbados and Demerara lasted for one and two weeks respectively. They began shortly after slaves had had a rest day to plan their uprising. They involved work stoppages, damage to sugar estates, fighting with the militia, and, after their end, severe reprisals. Around seventy sugar plantations were affected in Barbados and over fifty in Demerara. In both territories around 100 slaves (but only two whites) were killed during the fighting. Captives were tortured. Public executions took place after which heads were displayed on poles; 170 blacks were deported from Barbados. The Jamaican Baptist War was an altogether larger affair. It broke out suddenly on 27 December 1831, after the slaves had had time to rest and plan their activities over Christmas, and it continued until March 1832. Beginning in St James Parish, it spread to five other parishes in the western half of

---

[12] Quoted in Craton, *Testing the Chains*, 261.	[13] Quoted ibid. 321.

the island and involved around 60,000 slaves. The slaves torched sugar estates, engaged in guerrilla warfare, and hid in the rugged terrain of the interior. The British military garrison in Jamaica had been reduced by 30 per cent in the two years leading up to the rebellion. The rebel slaves knew that this was therefore an opportune time to strike back at the plantocracy. Nevertheless, the militia put down the revolt with great brutality. Over 200 slaves were killed and 312 were executed after trials. More than 300 others were imprisoned or transported. Sam Sharpe was captured and hanged at Montego Bay on 23 May 1832.

The three late slave rebellions left varied imprints. Bussa's rebellion made only a small impact on Barbados. Order was restored. No further slave outbreak on the same scale ever occurred in Barbados. The mild result of the revolt was a successful parliamentary petition to the Prince Regent—when George III was incapacitated through porphyria—declaring that slave emancipation was not an immediate object of British policy. The aftermath of the Demerara revolt was more controversial. This was because the Reverend John Smith, the Congregational missionary, was thrown into gaol on the grounds that he incited the slaves to rebel. He died while imprisoned and this provoked a furore in the British press. Public opinion was more inflamed, however, by the maltreatment of a white clergyman than by any supposed unjust acts against slaves. The Jamaican revolt coincided perfectly in its timing with the later stages of the Reform Bill struggle in Britain. That continuing tussle in Parliament and throughout the political nation gave considerable impetus to the slave cause because it was widely known that the Great Reform Act would pave the way for slave emancipation, as the Whig government had pledged to carry this out and could secure majority support in the newly reformed Parliament to do so.

# 7

# The Abolition of the British Slave Trade

When the British slave trade reached its peak in the quarter-century before the American Revolution, few could have predicted that the entire 'Guinea' traffic from Africa would be abolished by parliamentary statute shortly after the turn of the nineteenth century. Slavery and the slave trade appeared to be so much a part of the peopling and maritime strength of the British Empire, and so necessary to maintain sugar plantations in the Caribbean, that to imagine a British imperial world without a regular supply of new black cargoes would have been fanciful. By c.1750 slavery was accepted by most of the educated classes in Britain and a movement to abolish the slave trade on moral grounds had not begun. Slavery, it seemed, was condoned in the Bible, where examples of the acceptance of slavery could be found. Several major philosophers of the late seventeenth century had also implicitly accepted the existence of slavery, as the references to Thomas Hobbes and John Locke in Chapter 1 have shown. In addition, no significant figure in the Church of England, the established church to which 90 per cent of the British people belonged, raised their voices against slavery before the middle of the eighteenth century.

Before 1750 many people accepted the racial nature of black slavery. Blackness was associated with a congeries of negative factors to Europeans and their settlers in the New World: it connoted heathenism, paganism, and connections with the Devil. The difference of enslaved Africans from Europeans in their complexion, skin colour, language, and gestures singled them out as special candidates for degradation. Many Europeans held racist attitudes towards blacks. Commentaries abounded on the lusty promiscuity and aggressive sexuality of black men. Some thought Negroes had inferior brain power and were descended from apes; others thought their dark skin made them suitable for labour in hot climates. Black slaves were regarded as chattel, as an item of property to be owned, rather than as human beings with their own free will. This degraded status for blacks was upheld by legal systems in British colonies which stigmatized slavery in a draconian way (see Chapter 5).

Negative attitudes towards black people nevertheless began to shift significantly in the second half of the eighteenth century. Enlightenment concern for rational solutions to human problems combined with the birth of a humanitarian conscience to alter intellectual and religious views of slavery. This sea change in ideas took several decades to accomplish. There was then the challenge of disseminating those ideas to the British people, changing views so that the intellectual and social climate was right to oppose the slave trade. That attack began, if one has to pinpoint a date, in 1787 when the Quaker-dominated Society for Effecting the Abolition of the Slave Trade was formed. It continued for twenty years, as information was presented to Parliament on the conduct of slaving voyages and successive proposed measures to abolish the slave trade were debated in the House of Commons. Delays occurred in steering this proposed legislation through Parliament for various reasons, including entrenched sources of opposition to the measure and problems in British domestic and foreign politics caused by the extended war with France. The Anglo-French conflict lasted from 1793 until 1801, with a brief truce in the Treaty of Amiens in 1802, and then resumed until the French were beaten at Waterloo in 1815.

Despite obstacles, Britain secured restrictions on the conduct of the slave trade, via legislation mentioned below designed to limit the number of slaves transported on ships. Britain was also the third country to abolish its slave trade. The French revolutionaries temporarily ended their slave trade in 1794 but Napoleon legalized the trade once again in 1802 to help restore the old colonial system in the French Caribbean. In Denmark there was no long-drawn-out struggle to abolish the slave trade, no popular campaign; the trade was ended by royal decree in 1803. In Britain the story was different, for a vociferous struggle by supporters and detractors of the slave trade continued for many years and made a significant impact on Parliament. Historians have long debated the reasons why the British abolished their slave trade, and have also asked why the campaign took twenty years, from 1787 to 1807.

## THE GROWTH OF ANTISLAVERY IDEAS

Abolition needed parliamentary approval because the slave trade had flourished with the tacit acceptance of the state since the middle of the seventeenth century. But the campaign to get rid of the slave trade was not just fought in Parliament; the issue was widely debated in the nation at large. Popular pressure played an important part in signalling to governments, especially those of the younger Pitt, that many British people found the slave trade morally distasteful and something that should be dismantled on humanitarian grounds. How and why did attitudes change with regard to the slave traffic? And how did these changing views filter through to the wider population? Perhaps the first major landmark in the intellectual attack on slavery came not from a British source but from the work of a distinguished *philosophe*. Montesquieu, in *L'Esprit des Lois* (1748), included an oblique attack on slavery and the slave trade that proved very influential in changing the views of other intellectuals on the subject. Montesquieu regarded slavery as an affront to liberty: 'The state of slavery is in its own nature bad. It is neither useful to the master nor to the slave; not to the slave, because he can do nothing through a motive of virtue; nor to the master, because by having an unlimited authority over his slaves he insensibly accustoms himself to the want of all moral virtues.'[1] Montesquieu argued that where slavery existed, laws must be introduced to guard against its nature. Other notable figures of the French Enlightenment attacked slavery on moral grounds; they included Rousseau, Voltaire, and the Abbé Raynal, philosophers with different ideas on various proposals for social reforms. But Montesquieu's discussion had the greatest impact on changing antislavery attitudes.

The attack on slavery was taken up by various philosophers of the Scottish Enlightenment, who argued more directly against slavery and the slave trade. Francis Hutcheson, Adam Ferguson, and Adam Smith were among the Scots thinkers who viewed slavery as an unsatisfactory condition that denied a certain category of people the right to political and civil liberty. They frequently noted that the condition of slavery, and the existence of the slave trade, precluded 'happiness', which in its eighteenth-century sense meant what we would term the common good. Thus Ferguson's *Institutes of Moral Philosophy* (1769) argued that 'no one is born a slave; because everyone is born with all his original rights . . . The supposed property of the master in the slave is therefore a matter of usurpation, not of right.'[2] Smith's *Theory of Moral Sentiments*

---

[1] Quoted in Roger Anstey, *The Atlantic Slave Trade and British Abolition, 1760–1810* (London, 1975), 103.
[2] Quoted ibid. 110.

(1759) took a compassionate view of the plight of enslaved Africans: 'There is not a Negro from the coast of Africa who does not . . . possess a degree of magnanimity which the soul of his sordid master is too often scarce capable of receiving.'[3] Given Smith's repugnance towards black bondage (as illustrated in his book) one wonders whether dislike of chattel slavery influenced his views on the superiority of free enterprise and free wage labour over protectionism and enforced labour in his *Inquiry into the Nature and Causes of the Wealth of Nations* (1776).

Other attacks on slavery can be found in discussions by philosophers in the third quarter of the eighteenth century. They also appear in the writings of leading legal and political figures whom one would normally term 'conservative'. William Blackstone, the leading English jurist of the mid-eighteenth century, was heavily influenced by Montesquieu in writing his four-volume *Commentaries on the Laws of England* (1765–9). Blackstone rejected all the major reasons for the existence of slavery, arguing against hereditary arguments for possessing slaves—that they were property to be willed from one generation to the next—and also rejecting those who justified the captivity or sales of slaves. Blackstone regarded enslavement as an affront to rationality and natural law. His arguments gained wide currency because of his legal standing and the fact that his *Commentaries* went through nineteen editions in the seven years after their publication. In 1792 Edmund Burke, a leading political spokesman and later the sceptical commentator *par excellence* on the impact of the French Revolution, supported a plan for the gradual abolition of the slave trade on the grounds that liberty was important to establish where it did not exist. He was also influenced by the notion that the 'happiness' of the governed was a criterion of good government. On both counts, liberty and happiness, he regarded slavery as an institution strongly in need of reform.

In the three decades after 1750, these changing attitudes towards slavery by philosophers, lawyers, and political figures transformed the intellectual discussion of slavery. The condition of slavery was becoming increasingly regarded as retrogressive, as a sorry stumbling block in the evolution of human progress. Important changes in religious attitudes, especially among evangelical Protestant groups, accompanied the condemnation of slavery. John Wesley, the founder of Methodism, and his colleague George Whitefield, were adamant in their attack on slavery as a morally evil institution, even though they had split in the early

---

[3] Quoted ibid. 118.

1740s over doctrinal issues relating to the former's Arminianism and the latter's Calvinism. Both Wesley and Whitefield had travelled to Georgia in the 1730s and had seen slaves on plantations; both had preached the gospel of Salvation; both were opposed to the inhumane treatment of subjected people; both had an evangelizing mission to the poor and oppressed; both saw slaves as fit candidates for Christian instruction. But Wesley realized the true horror of slavery only when he exchanged correspondence with the Quaker abolitionist Anthony Benezet in the 1770s. Wesley issued a stern warning to traffickers in the slave trade and slaveowners in his pamphlet *Thoughts upon Slavery* (1774), accusing them of being guilty of 'fraud, robbery, and murder'.[4] He also gave a sermon at the New Room, Bristol, on 6 March 1788 in which he attacked slavery and, as he did so, a strange noise echoed throughout the whole building, causing confusion among the congregation, which panicked, broke benches, and jostled each other. After about six minutes the noise stopped and calm was restored. Wesley and the congregation regarded the incident as a sign of God's wrath against a society of sinners who condoned slavery. In his very last letter, Wesley urged Wilberforce to press on with the campaign against the slave trade, which he termed 'the vilest under the sun'.[5] Slavery must have been on his mind at this time. Two days before writing the letter Wesley had had part of Equiano's *Autobiography* read to him.

## QUAKERS AND EVANGELICAL CHRISTIANS

Despite Wesley's anti-slave trade stance, the 'People called Methodists'—as they termed themselves—were not particularly prominent in this early stage of abolitionism. The religious groups that played the major part in publicizing an antislavery creed were the Quakers and the evangelical wing of the Church of England. They based their assault, as Roger Anstey has demonstrated, on three main principles: benevolence, progressive revelation, and the nature of God's providence. Benevolence referred to the basic New Testament injunction to treat one's neighbour

---

[4] Quoted in Michael Craton, James Walvin, and David Wright (eds.), *Slavery, Abolition and Emancipation: Black Slaves and the British Empire: A Thematic Documentary* (London, 1976), 217.
[5] John Wesley to William Wilberforce, 24 Feb. 1791, in John Telford (ed.), *The Letters of John Wesley, A.M.*, 8 vols. (London, 1931), viii. 265.

as one would wish to be treated oneself. God's providence signified the belief that the world was preordained as a result of his omniscient and omnipotent gaze. God's providence would be revealed—hence the notion of progressive revelation—in bringing peace and plenty to nations where moral worth had been demonstrated and war and destruction to those who acted immorally. All three concepts were central parts of the Christian world view of the later eighteenth century and all seemed directly related to the plight of slaves.

Quakers were drawn to these views and their application to slavery, but they also condemned bondage for reasons peculiar to their own beliefs. The Religious Society of Friends believed in pacifism; they therefore opposed the capture of slaves in tribal warfare in West Africa. They believed that all people were equal in the eyes of God, whatever their skin colour and worldly status. Such attitudes had informed their beliefs from the days of George Fox and William Penn. The London Yearly Meeting in 1727 censured participation in the slave trade as 'not a commendable or allowed practice'.[6] This view became firmer at subsequent meetings until a minute of 1761 called for disowning any Friend who remained in the trade. In 1772 a printed epistle from the London Yearly Meeting condemned slavery as an 'oppressive and unnatural bondage',[7] applauded colonial Quakers who acted against it, and advocated total abolition of the slave trade. North American Quakers also disapproved of their members owning slaves, but it was not until 1758 that the Philadelphia Yearly Meeting ruled that local Friends who imported, bought, or sold slaves should be placed 'under discipline'. Quakers enforced discipline at monthly local meetings and yearly meetings; the ultimate sanction was banishment from the Society. Yet even for the Quakers the crusade against slaveholding did not come easily. In the American heartland of eighteenth-century Quakerism—Pennsylvania and New Jersey—Quakers battled for generations until *c*.1770 before their members accepted the ban on slaveholding. If Quakers found it difficult to make concessions about slaveholding, it was to prove more problematic for other groups in society.

The evangelical wing of the Church of England was also drawn to espouse a doctrine of antislavery. As well as belief in benevolence, God's

---

[6] Quoted in Jacob M. Price, 'English Quaker Merchants and the War at Sea, 1689-1783', in Roderick A. McDonald (ed.), *West Indies Accounts: Essays in the History of the British Caribbean and the Atlantic Economy in Honour of Richard Sheridan* (Kingston, 1996), 67.

[7] Quoted ibid.

providence, and progressive revelation, they were deeply committed
to Salvation. How could someone involved in slaveholding be spared
at the Day of Judgement? Among these Christian evangelicals were
several zealous advocates of antislavery, which they regarded as one
of the leading moral crusades in British public life. They included
William Wilberforce, a member of a prosperous trading family in
Hull, county MP for Yorkshire after 1784, and the leader of the
anti-slave trade campaign in Parliament; Thomas Clarkson, friend of
Wilberforce, assiduous collector of data on the slave trade, organizer
of committees on the slave trade, publicist and writer on abolitionism;
John Newton, a former slave trader, now a priest; Henry Thornton, a
London banker; Granville Sharp, born into a family of the established
church but apprenticed to a Quaker draper, self-educated in languages
and jurisprudence, and founder of the colony of Sierra Leone; the
lawyer and MP James Stephen; Hannah More, the author; and Zachary
Macaulay, philanthropist, bookkeeper, and later manager of an estate
in Jamaica, governor of Sierra Leone in 1793, and later editor of
the *Christian Observer*, which sympathized with evangelicalism and
abolitionism.

   Bound together by their antislavery convictions, most of these Anglican evangelicals became known as the Clapham Sect, so called because
they worshipped regularly at Holy Trinity church, on the north side
of Clapham Common, London. They believed in what Wilberforce
called 'vital religion',[8] a drive to activate the established church into
greater evangelical activity and stir the consciences of the privileged,
propertied classes towards various types of moral reform including the
judicial system, the treatment of the poor, and slavery and the slave
trade. The Clapham Sect was also concerned with upholding morals in
public life. By concentrating on social institutions that needed reform,
evangelicals enacted their belief that man's sinfulness could be redeemed
by good works. Christian evangelicals prominent in the early antislavery
movement set aside doctrinal differences in pursuit of their goal; one
finds Arminians and Calvinists, Unitarians and the evangelical wing of
the Church of England at one on this issue. None of the leading abolitionists believed in the intellectual equality of black and white people.
Nevertheless, all antislavery campaigners were sincerely convinced of the

   [8] William Wilberforce, *A Practical View of the Prevailing Religious System of Professed Christians, in the Higher and Middle Classes in the Country, contrasted with Real Christianity* (Dublin, 1797), 280.

need to better the condition of slaves through promoting amelioration policies and, eventually, the abolition of the slave trade and the emancipation of slaves in the British Empire. They were under no illusions that these tasks would prove easy to achieve. Thus they realized that a two-pronged attack was necessary—first, a campaign to eradicate the slave trade, and then an assault on slavery itself. Such a pattern was repeated in the nineteenth century by virtually every nation involved in slave trafficking.

Energetic, disciplined, zealous, single-minded: to these hallmarks of abolitionists the Quakers and the evangelical Anglicans added good organization. The Quakers maintained a strong transatlantic connection throughout the late seventeenth and eighteenth centuries, with ministers and other Friends criss-crossing the Atlantic on regular journeys and missions. Many of these perambulations combined politics, business, and religion with a network of Quaker associates. The Society of Friends was a cohesive and influential group which had an impact on abolitionism far in excess of its actual numbers. In the 1770s and early 1780s several influential American Quakers visited Britain to espouse the antislavery cause, including John Woolman and Anthony Benezet, who collaborated closely. Woolman, a devout Quaker tailor and husbandman, staunchly advocated abolitionism. He once stood barefoot in the snow outside a meeting to draw a parallel with poor slaves who went throughout the winter in that condition. Benezet, from Huguenot stock, was a printer, schoolmaster, and respected campaigner against slavery. The Quakers were prolific publishers of pamphlets and tracts on moral issues. Benezet argued that the slave trade was 'inconsistent with the plainest Precepts of the Gospel, the dictates of Reason, and every common sentiment of humanity'.[9] The London Yearly Meeting of the Society of Friends presented a petition to the House of Commons in June 1783 calling for total abolition of the slave trade on the grounds that it infringed the main tenets of Christianity, natural rights and human justice. In the same year Benezet had 11,000 copies of his pamphlet *The Case of the Oppressed Africans* (1784) printed and distributed to MPs, JPs and other prominent people in British public life. In 1787 English Quakers formed the majority of the newly created Society for the Abolition of the Slave Trade. They had a well-organized

---

[9] Anthony Benezet, *A Caution and Warning to Great Britain and her Colonies, in a Short Representation of the Calamitous State of the Enslaved Negroes in the British Dominions* (Philadelphia, 1766), 5.

group ready to promote abolitionism as the first parliamentary debates over the conduct of the slave trade began in that year. Quakers and nonconformists were also prominent in many provincial anti-slave trade societies that flourished after 1787.

## THE SOMERSET CASE AND THE *ZONG* CASE

The abolitionist campaign was helped by the legal decision made in 1772 by Lord Chief Justice Mansfield with regard to slavery on English soil. This involved the case of the African-born slave James Somerset, who had been brought to London by his owner Charles Stewart from Boston. In 1771 Somerset, who had not been manumitted, ran away from his master. He was captured and placed in irons on a ship in the River Thames intended for Jamaica. The case was brought before Mansfield at the Court of King's Bench through the instigation of the philanthropist Granville Sharp. Mansfield pondered over his decision for seven months but then ruled that English law did not support the keeping of a slave on English soil and so Somerset must be discharged. This was a limited decision: it meant that slaves could not be forcibly returned to masters in England but it did not end slavery in Britain and, in fact, slaves were still sold on British soil thereafter. Nevertheless, it was a blow for the plantocracy and widely publicized by abolitionists. The anti-slave trade movement was also helped by the publicity surrounding a legal case relating to the ship *Zong* in 1783. This Liverpool slaving vessel had embarked from West Africa to Jamaica with 470 slaves in early September 1781. Faced with spiralling outbreaks of disease among the African captives, the captain decided to have 131 Africans thrown overboard into the Atlantic Ocean. In 1783 the owners of the *Zong* applied to their underwriters to claim maritime insurance for the loss of their human cargo. They lost their case in court, but the scandal was well publicized, notably by Sharp, and immediately afterwards the Quakers petitioned Parliament on the slave trade.

David Brion Davis has argued that the early abolitionists reflected the needs and aspirations of an emerging capitalist order in Britain that was prepared to see the slave trade ended because they considered it unnecessary for the new emerging middle-class commercial strength of the nation that could benefit from free trade. This argument is difficult to evaluate, however, because it equates abolitionists with a new capitalist order when evidence is lacking to indicate that anti-slave trade campaigners were anything of the sort. It also implies that contemporaries could foresee changes in the Caribbean economy that could not be anticipated in the 1780s and 1790s. And so to equate abolitionism with the interests of the ideology of a rising interest in British society tends to obfuscate rather than clarify the historical issues raised by consideration of the movement to abolish the British slave trade.

## ANTISLAVERY PROPAGANDA

What occurred to help the plight of slaves in British territories in the Caribbean? In 1787 and 1788, significant advances were made in parliamentary awareness of the abolitionist movement. Members of Abolitionist committees presented more than a hundred petitions to Parliament in 1787 requesting the abolition of the slave trade. This propaganda campaign made extensive use of petitions as a device for expressing extra-parliamentary pressure on a public issue. Originating with the petitions presented in favour of parliamentary reform by the Wilkite agitators of the 1760s and the Yorkshire Association of the early 1780s, the petitioning campaign against the slave trade was a highly successful form of exerting popular pressure on the government of the day. It has been estimated, for example, that between 1787 and 1792 petitions against the slave trade were signed by 1.5 million out of 12 million people in Britain (almost one-sixth of the total population). In the 1791–2 parliamentary session alone, no fewer than 519 abolitionist petitions were presented to the Commons from all over the nation. Exactly why people signed petitions is difficult to analyse because all they provided was a signature; yet in mass petitioning this was a clear sign of their support for a moral reform cause. In fact, abolitionism engaged more sympathy with the public than the advocates of parliamentary reform could then muster, something that can be attributed to the wide humanitarian appeal of antislavery and its popularity among women (who later, in the 1820s and 1830s, organized many ladies' committees against slavery).

The initial discussions in Parliament about the nature of the slave trade took place at virtually the same time that the United States, at the constitutional convention in Philadelphia, decided to prohibit slave imports for twenty-one years after 1787. Certainly, parliamentarians knew of this development; and there may have been a sense that slavery and the slave trade were issues that could no longer be ignored in the anglophone world. But although the Declaration of American Independence (1776) had memorably stated that 'all Men are created equal' and that they were endowed with 'unalienable Rights' among which were 'Life, Liberty and the Pursuit of Happiness', black slaves were excluded from these sentiments. The rhetoric of the American Revolution was confined to white freedom; and some argue that the revolutionary legacy subjugated blacks even more than had been the case when the thirteen colonies were part of the British Empire. In Britain, by contrast, several colonizing efforts of the 1780s saw the foundation of free societies where slavery was banned: these include the penal colony in New South Wales; a short-lived settlement of displaced British settlers from the Mosquito Shore in the Gulf of Honduras; and the free black settlement in Sierra Leone. In India there were abolitionist attempts with regard to slavery that may have influenced the metropolitan campaigns against slavery. On 22 July 1789 the Governor General of Bengal issued a proclamation banning the export of slaves from the Bengal Presidency. Two years later, in 1791, efforts were made in the Madras Presidency to curtail the sale of children into slavery. Whether these developments had a significant impact on the early abolitionist campaign against the slave trade needs further exploration. Certainly, however, they reveal the increased public concern in Britain with humanitarian ways of dealing with black and Asian people within Britain's imperial orbit.

The experimental settlement in Sierra Leone was the most important of these initiatives so far as abolitionism was concerned. The British naval vessel that arrived in Sierra Leone with 411 blacks on 10 May 1787 did so as a result of philanthropic endeavours by Clarkson, Wilberforce, and Sharp. These abolitionists were members of a Committee for the Relief of the Black Poor who were concerned about the plight of black people in London after the end of the American War of Independence. They thought blacks stood a better chance of independence in a free community based on Christian principles in Sierra Leone. There were two further waves of migrants to Sierra Leone: a migration from Nova Scotia in 1792 of free blacks who had escaped there after fighting for the British Army in the American revolutionary war, and a group of maroons exiled from Jamaica after the Maroon War of 1795. But the settlement, though initiated with high ideals, became plagued by recurrent problems of survival, working the land, outbreaks of disease, widespread pilfering, and political and financial failure. The Sierra Leone settlement began with a constitution written by Granville Sharp in which the laws, customs, and traditions of Britain would be upheld; and it banned slavery and the slave trade. But though it eventually became a British Crown colony in 1808, its problems overshadowed the attempt to find black people a satisfactory independent existence in the British Empire.

Besides petitions, abolitionists also deployed other means of propaganda effectively. Leading anti-slave trade activists gave public lectures on the immorality of the slave trade, presenting their case at length in lectures often lasting for two or three hours. In some instances the length of the presentation was equated with the success of the message being addressed. The major abolitionists did not lack stamina or commitment. Added to public lectures, which took place in all sorts of buildings from church halls to hired rooms, wherever an audience could be accommodated, anti-slave trade campaigners also wrote and distributed cheap tracts and pamphlets espousing their cause. Their literary efforts were widely publicized, notably by the Quaker bookseller James Phillips, who distributed thousands of copies of their works. Two leading members of the London black community also helped to publicize the abolitionist creed. These were Olaudah Equiano (or Gustavus Vassa) and Ottabah Cugoano, two literate ex-slaves who drummed up considerable sympathy for the plight of black people and the racial prejudice against them. Equiano wrote a best-selling autobiography and campaigned all over Britain, speaking out against the hardships of the black community in Britain. Cugoano wrote a series of letters to prominent public figures such as Edmund Burke; made contact with royalty; and wrote a tract, *Thoughts and Sentiments* (1787), which presented the case for the afflictions of black people. Both Equiano and Cugoano were friendly with Sharp.

At a popular level, antislavery values could be found in the literature of the day. A stream of popular works upheld the primitivism of Negroes as something to be admired for its simplicity, sincerity, and lack of worldly vices. This was a variation on the theme of the noble savage, which had begun with Native Americans in the sixteenth century and which spread to Pacific islanders in the late eighteenth century. Long-forgotten poems and plays that were popular in their time depicted enslaved Africans in a favourable light. They included Thomas Day's poem *The Dying Negro* (1773), in which the author transmutes himself into an African and praises the exoticism of his natural environment, and Isaac Bickerstaffe's play *The Padlock* (1768), whose depiction of a black servant, Mungo, highlighted the injustices of the master–slave relationship. The abolitionist message seeped into hymns, notably the

Reverend John Newton's 'Amazing Grace', with its words advocating the cleansing necessary for slaves to be freed.

Other art forms propagated the antislavery message. These included tokens, medals, medallets, satirical and serious prints, engravings, and paintings. Most famous of all were Josiah Wedgwood's medallions with their cameo of a kneeling slave, hands clasped, and the inscription 'Am I not a Man and a Brother?' These medallions were very popular and caught the public's imagination. Not far behind in terms of visual impact was the print of the African slave ship the *Brookes*, which showed a slave vessel sliced in half and the tightly packed bodies of a slave cargo beneath deck, lying like sardines in a can, as if viewed from above. The prints that circulated of this large Liverpool slaving vessel have become one of the most enduring symbols of oppression associated with any social reform movement in modern history. The version of the print that was presented to the parliamentary hearings on the slave trade in 1788 and 1789 was one that had been drawn to take into account the restrictions on the number of slaves that could be carried in relation to a ship's tonnage, as exemplified by Dolben's Act (1788).

## DOLBEN'S ACT (1788)

This statute was the first measure that legally restricted the number of slaves that could be carried according to the tonnage of vessels. Named after Sir William Dolben, the elderly MP for Oxford who had sponsored the legislation as a private member's bill, the act was opposed by the proslavery interest. It passed in the Lords after major amendments had been made to the bill and only a few minutes before Parliament was prorogued for the summer on 11 July 1788. Besides restricting the number of slaves that could be carried on British vessels to five slaves for every three tons up to 200 tons and to one slave for each additional ton thereafter, Dolben's Act also required that surgeons should be present on slaving voyages and should keep a log of illnesses and mortality. This was the first significant piece of legislation by any European power to restrict the so-called 'tight-packing' of slaves on board ship, though in 1773 the Marquis of Pombal had outlawed the Portuguese from carrying slaves to Madeira and the Azores. Modern historians have not proved conclusively that Dolben's Act led, as was intended, to a drop in mortality on the Middle Passage. Nonetheless, it was a modest first step in the anti-slave trade campaign.

## ABOLITIONIST TACTICS

Abolitionists used various tactics to promote their cause. Wilberforce became their leading spokesman in the Commons, tirelessly raising the call for a general abolition of the slave trade year after year. Charles James Fox was an eloquent advocate of slave trade abolition in his contribution to Commons debates. Clarkson toured the leading slave trading ports in 1787 and 1788, gathering information on the conduct of the 'Guinea' traffic for parliamentary scrutiny. He travelled over 35,000 miles in seven years (1787–94), gleaning information, writing about abolitionism, and giving public lectures. Visiting Bristol in 1788, he eavesdropped in the inns and quayside haunts of ship captains and sailors who had been involved in the slave trade. Intense, committed, and single-minded in his ambitions, Clarkson gleaned very detailed information from those he interviewed. In Liverpool, he similarly visited the dock area where it is rumoured that he so irritated some Liverpudlians with his investigations that a group of them tried to push him into the harbour.

The fruits of Clarkson's investigations were apparent in 1788 and 1789 as voluminous evidence was presented to a Select Committee of the Privy Council on the operation of the slave trade, often in a question and answer fashion. These parliamentary proceedings presented material on the gathering of slaves in West Africa, the condition of the forts on the African coast, the horrors of the Middle Passage, the extent of crew, and slave mortality. In fact, they provided evidence on virtually all aspects of the slave trade that have been analysed by modern historians. Clarkson outlined some of the findings of his tours in *The Substance of the Evidence of Sundry Persons* . . . (1789). Based on interviews with twenty-two witnesses, this remarkable compilation was effectively the first detailed account of the slave trade in the English language based on first-hand observation. Clarkson qualifies as one of the pioneers of oral history.

## ANTISLAVERY CAMPAIGNERS VERSUS PROSLAVERY DEFENDERS

Wilberforce, speaking in the Commons in an increasingly favourable climate, had sufficient confidence to bring resolutions against the slave trade to Parliament in 1789, 1791, and 1792. Passionately devoted to abolitionism, capable of delivering monumental speeches, and imbued with moral authority and an independent political position, Wilberforce rose to the occasion on innumerable parliamentary occasions to speak out on the evil of slavery and the slave trade. In 1789 his political opponents blocked the discussion. In 1791 the House debated Wilberforce's notion but voted against it by 163 votes to 88. The 1792 discussions were more successful for Wilberforce, and his colleagues secured agreement in the Commons that the supply of slaves to foreign territories should be stopped at once and the rest of the British slave trade abolished by 1796. Yet this decision was not supported in the Lords and the matter was shelved. For a bill for the abolition of the slave trade to be successful it would, as now, need to pass through three readings in the Commons, proceed to a committee stage, and gain approval by the Lords all within a single parliamentary session. Any gains short of this procedure would lead to the bill being reintroduced from scratch in the next parliamentary session. Wilberforce operated in a parliamentary context where party lines were not as clear-cut as today—the prime minister, the younger Pitt, did not regard himself as a party man. Many MPs were independents and there was no whip system to lean on supporters to vote en bloc. It was therefore quite difficult to gain support for reform measures in parliamentary debates.

In the few years between 1787 and 1792 considerable progress had been made in the abolitionist cause, but the end of the trade had still not occurred. Important obstacles stood in the way of slave trade abolition. The West India Interest, comprising mainly planters and merchants, was a powerful presence, bringing influence to bear on the Privy Council, lobbying members of both houses of Parliament, and presenting favourable witnesses before committees. With representation in Parliament and the assiduous lobbying activity of Stephen Fuller, the agent for Jamaica, it organized an effective print campaign to match the abolitionists' propaganda. In *Observations, occasioned by the attempts made in England to effect the abolition of the slave trade . . .* (1789), the slaveholder Gilbert Francklyn, a member of the Society of West India Merchants and Planters, argued that the plantocracy treated their slaves humanely by providing sufficient food, clothing, and shelter. His pamphlet argued that Parliament would be acting unconstitutionally if it attacked the property of planters. A brief pamphlet entitled *Commercial Reasons for the non-abolition of the slave trade, in the West-India islands, by a planter and merchant of many years residence in the West Indies* (1789) defended the slave trade because of its contribution to British wealth. Tampering with the slave trade, so the argument ran, would harm British manufacturing, increase unemployment, and allow foreign powers to benefit from transporting African captives.

In February 1788 the London West India committee of Planters and Merchants established a standing committee to oppose abolition. In *An Appeal to the Candour and Justice of the People of England in Behalf of the West Indian Merchants and Planters* (1792), they argued that there were long-standing national sanctions for slavery and the slave trade. The main points in the argument can be summarized. Parliament had originally permitted the traffic to flourish; slaves were necessary for sugar cultivation in the West Indies; and they needed to be replenished regularly via the Atlantic slave trade. Conditions in shipment on the Middle Passage had improved after the introduction of Dolben's Act. Slaves would regard the abolition of the slave trade as a step towards slave emancipation and would thus become dissatisfied with their lot. Moreover, the sugar colonies were a vital part of the revenue of the British Empire. The petitioners concluded that the issue of the slave trade should be dropped or compensation supplied on the grounds of humanity and justice.

The Jamaican sugar tycoon Simon Taylor expressed succinctly the fears of the West India merchants and planters. Comparing the government's actions over abolitionism with the way that Pharaoh wanted the Israelites to make bricks without straw, he stated that the only difference was that 'they want us to make Sugar without Negroes, and Negroes are as necessary to make sugar as the Straw was to burn the bricks.'[10] He emphasized the continuing economic importance of the slave trade to Britain by arguing against Pitt's and Fox's support for Dolben's Act:

if they lose the African trade and destroy the manufactory of Sugar and Rum so that those Articles shall bring in no revenue how will they find the necessary funds for the support of Government without them. If the price of a Negro is raised by this limitation so high that the Planters cannot buy them the English Adventurer will not send any vessel to the Coast, but the Trade must fall into the Hands of the French, the Spaniards, the Portuguese & the Dutch.[11]

Other opponents of the abolition of the slave trade included George III and many members of both houses of Parliament. The younger Pitt, though no evangelical, was a close friend of Wilberforce, and

---

[10] Cambridge University Library, Simon Taylor to Chaloner Arcedeckne, 5 July 1789, Vanneck MSS.
[11] Ibid., 30 Aug. 1788.

privately sympathized with the abolitionist cause; but he eschewed open support for eradicating the slave trade because of powerful opponents. Moreover, it was characteristic of Pitt to remain lukewarm about a reform cause which, in his view, stood little realistic chance of passing through Parliament. Even so, he was willing to denounce the trade in unequivocal terms. 'There is no nation in Europe that has, on the one hand, plunged so deeply into this guilt as Great Britain,' he told the House of Commons in 1792, 'or that is so likely, on the other, to be looked up to as an example.'[12]

The influence of the West India Interest in Parliament added to these problems. Several cities where the slave trade had made an impact were represented by MPs sympathetic to the West India Interest. This was true, for instance, of Bristol, where Matthew Brickdale and Henry Cruger, the city's two members, opposed Wilberforce and his fellow abolitionists in 1788 and 1789. Altogether, about fifty MPs were tied to the proslavery lobby by the 1790s. In the House of Lords the Duke of Clarence (the future William IV) led the planters' defence of slavery and the slave trade. The loss in the House of Commons of Wilberforce's bill to abolish the slave trade in 1791 was greeted by leading members of the West India Interest as the 'best of all possible events, for all of us concerned with West India property'.[13] But the renewed discussions on the same issue in the next parliamentary year led to fears by West India merchants and planters 'that the Resolution of a Gradual Abolition will be looked upon by them in the light of a new victory gained; the consequences of which perhaps will be fresh dispositions to disturbances & insurrections.'[14]

## THE FRENCH REVOLUTION, WAR, AND THE SLAVE TRADE

General political developments prevented the cause of abolitionism making much progress between 1793 and 1804. In large part this resulted from the backlash to reform causes that accompanied the

---

[12] *The Parliamentary History of England, from the Earliest Period to the Year 1803* (London, 1817), xxix. 1152.

[13] Aberdeen University Archives, Stephen and Rose Fuller to Charles Gordon, 13 May 1791, Papers of the Gordon Family of Buthlaw and Cairness: Estate and Family Papers, MS 1160/4/64.

[14] Ibid., 18 Apr. 1792, MS 1160/4/76.

progress of the French Revolution. The younger Pitt's government was deeply worried about the spread of Jacobinism across the English Channel. The French monarch, Louis XVI, had lost his head in 1789; the Catholic Church had been ransacked; the *ancien régime* had crumbled; the monarchy had been abolished; and the Terror associated with Robespierre and the guillotine had arrived in France by 1793. In that year Britain went to war against France; the political atmosphere at Westminster became more tense; and the government avoided any issue that might detract from the national interest. Slavery was one such issue. General radical developments were another. Any hope for furthering reform causes received a severe jolt as the government concentrated on what were the mainsprings of eighteenth-century parliamentary life—war, finance, and foreign policy.

French revolutionary ideas spread to the Caribbean, where France had an important economic and strategic stake in Cayenne, Martinique, Guadeloupe, and Saint-Domingue. Fear of rebellion occurred after the massive slave revolt on Saint-Domingue, the leading French sugar colony, broke out in 1791 in response to miserable conditions and poor treatment of enslaved blacks. For the first and only time in world history, oppressed blacks rose up en masse to overthrow their French overlords, both planters and mulatto creoles, in a bloody conflict before the outbreak of war between Britain and revolutionary France. Britain sent troops to Saint-Domingue to try to restore French control; 20,000 lost their lives. Internal violence wracked Saint-Domingue for over a decade; the sugar economy, once so vibrant, collapsed. Toussaint L'Ouverture, the leader of the Saint-Domingue revolt, was heralded as a great leader. But the independent black republic that was established in Haiti in 1804 proved short-lived—though the nation still exists today—because Napoleon Bonaparte regained power over the colony. France also regained its other Caribbean islands—notably Martinique, under British control between 1794 and 1802—and brought back slavery. While the Saint-Domingue revolt lasted, however, it sent ripples of fear throughout the Atlantic slaveholding world.

For all these reasons, Pitt's government adopted an increasingly 'conservative' stance during the troubles of the 1790s, which also included a major Irish rebellion in 1798. It introduced repressive legislation on civil rights known as 'Pitt's reign of terror' (which sounds worse than it actually was). In this highly charged political climate, radical groups were viewed with great suspicion and the government developed an intelligence network via the Home Office to monitor potential troublemakers; it was unlikely that the anti-slave trade campaign would make further progress in the short term. Two modest successes were an act of 1797 and the Slave Carrying Bill (1799), which followed up Dolben's Act in specifying the number of slaves that could be carried legally by ships in relation to their carrying capacity.

Nevertheless, Wilberforce's regular motions in the House of Commons for a general abolition of the slave trade fell upon deaf ears. He introduced such measures in 1797, 1798, 1799, and 1802, and on several occasions these came close to success; but Pitt was unable to make abolition of the slave trade a government issue while the nation was still at war. In 1804 Wilberforce lamented the decline in public enthusiasm for abolition, writing to Hannah More that 'the tales of horror, which once caused so many tears to flow, are all forgotten.'[15] But this did not deter him from reviving the matter in Parliament. Wilberforce's motion to abolish the slave trade passed in the Commons on each of its three readings in 1804 but failed in the Lords. Reintroduced in the Commons in 1805, it was narrowly defeated. These were signs that abolitionism was becoming reinvigorated; in fact, it was the first major reform issue to do so after the government's clampdown on radicalism and reform issues in 1795. By 1805 the anti-slave trade campaign was no longer associated with the Jacobinism of a decade earlier, for Napoleon had restored the monarchy in France and recaptured Haiti. The anti-slave trade campaign was therefore ripe for revival as a relatively uncontroversial political issue for the British elite.

By the time the younger Pitt died in 1806, prematurely at the age of 47, the anti-slave trade campaign had been waged inside and outside Parliament for nineteen years. There had been a great deal of pressure exercised on ministers; plenty of abolitionist activity; three laws that restricted the carrying of slaves on shipboard; but the slave trade still existed. It was clear that the subject of transatlantic slaving did not attract the interest of most MPs. If one adds up the number of votes cast each time the Commons debated abolition of the trade, less than half the chamber exercised their right to vote. By 1806, the anti-slave trade cause had failed to win over the majority of independent MPs whose votes were necessary to carry the day.

---

[15] Quoted in Robert I. and Samuel Wilberforce (eds.), *The Correspondence of William Wilberforce*, 2 vols. (London, 1840), i. 299.

## SECURING ABOLITION

Within a year of Pitt's death, however, abolition of the British slave trade had been achieved. How can we account for the rapidity of this development after so many years of delay? One interpretation that proved influential for many years was that provided by Eric Williams in *Capitalism and Slavery* (1944), which, as its title suggests, was influenced by Marx's writings on capital accumulation. Taking issue with the emphasis on abolition of the slave trade put forward by older 'imperial' historians, who regarded it as a victory of 'saints', and of humanitarian campaigners led by Wilberforce, Williams insisted that the British abolished their slave trade for economic rather than moral reasons: economic determinism explained why the abolition of the slave trade occurred in 1807. Building upon the work of Lowell J. Ragatz's *The Fall of the Planter Class in the British Caribbean, 1763–1833: A Study in Social and Economic History* (1928), Williams argued that many Caribbean sugar estates, especially in Jamaica, suffered from soil exhaustion, indebtedness, and over-production after the Seven Years War; that particularly bad times hit West Indian agriculture during the American War of Independence and the early years of the French revolutionary wars; and that, as a result of falling profits on sugar estates and the prospect of poor sales in the home market, it no longer became viable for the British to keep supplying slaves to the West Indies by the first decade of the nineteenth century. He also suggested that British politicians and traders wished to see a move away from protectionism towards free trade and away from slavery towards free wage labour—arguments clearly stimulated by Adam Smith's *An Inquiry into the Nature and Causes of the Wealth of Nations* (1776), with its emphasis on competition in free markets leading to economic growth. Moreover, by the last two decades of the eighteenth century, Britain was undergoing its first phase of industrialization, with the emergence of factories, machine-based cotton machinery, and steam engines in coal mines. In this new economic climate—a transition from mercantilism to industrial capitalism—the old protectionist framework was no longer appropriate for British overseas expansion and trade. Williams summed up his arguments by stating that 'overproduction in 1807 demanded abolition'.[16]

[16] Eric Williams, *Capitalism and Slavery* (New York, 1944), 152.

Williams, in short, linked together aspects of economic policy with the state of sugar cultivation in the Caribbean. This shifted the argument over abolition from British campaigns to the British government's reaction to West Indian developments. His views have none the less been challenged vigorously by other historians. The consensus is that Williams's critics are nearer the truth than he was himself. The major attack on Williams's interpretation of abolition came in Seymour Drescher's *Econocide: British Slavery in the Era of Abolition* (1977). This established that, though there were economic problems on some Caribbean plantations, the British West Indian share of total British trade increased during the period when Williams suggested that decline occurred. In the period 1763–77, the British Caribbean accounted for 24 per cent of total British imports by value and for 8.4 per cent of exports. The equivalent figures for 1783–7 were 27 per cent and 11 per cent, and for 1803–7 30.5 per cent and 13.1 per cent. The volume of slaves arriving in the West Indies also increased at the time Williams argued that the slave trade was faltering. Philip D. Curtin's figures indicated that 339,000 slaves were loaded on British vessels in Africa in the period 1777–88, and that the number rose to 657,000 slaves in 1789–1807. Drescher's figures, though different, confirmed this trend: 332,000 slaves loaded in Africa on British ships in 1777–88 and 767,000 in 1789–1807.

Other parts of Williams's argument have similarly been challenged. Soil exhaustion did not affect sugar cultivation as irreparably as it did tobacco planting: sugar could drain the soil of its fertility if planted repeatedly on the same ground, but planters had learned techniques whereby this problem was minimized. Profits were still being made on West India sugar plantations in the period 1793–1807, though in some areas these were reduced profits. The one detailed study based on plantation records—admittedly based on limited surviving evidence—shows that the average rate of profit on sugar estates throughout the British Caribbean came to 12.6 per cent for the period 1792–8 but fell to 9.6 per cent between 1799 and 1819. But even where profits were cut back, many planters had experienced such difficulties earlier in the eighteenth century; and there is no reason to believe that they thought that falling profits were anything other than a bad temporary slump. Certainly, it did not suggest that their estates were no longer economically viable. Jamaican sugar prices declined significantly from 1793 to 1807 but there is little evidence to suggest that such prices had sufficiently plummeted to a point where they could not revive or where they would trigger the abandonment of West India plantations.

Other possible economic reasons for abolishing the British slave trade are similarly inconclusive. Four economic tracts were published in 1807 setting forth reasons for abolishing the British slave trade, but it is difficult to determine whether they were written before the decision for prohibition was taken or whether they were read by parliamentarians. It is striking that there was little mention in parliamentary debates in 1806–7 that economic reasons were paramount—with one exception, mentioned below—in seeking abolition of the slave trade. In addition, we now know that the supposed transition from mercantilism to industrial capitalism did not occur swiftly after 1783. Britain retained its Navigation Laws until 1849 and free trade did not inform British policies seriously until almost half a century after Adam Smith first advocated such a system. Furthermore the cultivation of sugar and other crops in the Caribbean expanded in the period 1793–1807, with the acquisition of newly conquered territories in Trinidad, Demerara, Berbice, and Essequibo. From a variety of viewpoints, therefore, Williams's notion that Britain abolished its slave trade primarily for economic reasons cannot be sustained on the evidence available.

If economic reasons were not mainly responsible for getting rid of the British slave trade, why was it dismantled so swiftly in 1806 and 1807? The answer lies in the changed parliamentary and international context of those years, which led politicians to push an abolition bill through Parliament. The younger Pitt's administration was succeeded in 1806 by a wartime coalition administration. Known as the 'Ministry of all the Talents', because it included able politicians from both the Tory and Whig benches, this new government was determined to preserve the national interest in the war against Napoleonic France. As it happened, it also included a number of influential politicians from both major political parties who were privately committed to abolition of the slave trade on moral grounds. Among their number (until his death in September 1806) was Charles James Fox, the scourge of George III, who had once succinctly declared that the movement to abolish the slave trade was a matter of 'humanity on the one side and interest on the other'.[17] The 'Ministry of all the Talents' could act confidently largely because Britain had asserted superiority over the French at the Battle of Trafalgar in October 1805.

Anstey has explained better than anyone else how the new ministry, backed by abolitionists, seized the opportunity to pursue new tactics with

[17] Quoted in *Parliamentary History of England*, xxviii. 100.

regard to the abolition of the British slave trade. Wilberforce introduced a bill in Parliament in 1806, following up a Royal Proclamation of 1805, to prevent the slave trade to foreign powers, arguing that this was in the national interest. This appeal had plenty of emotive resonance because in the period 1800–7 one-third of the slaves supplied by the British to the Caribbean were sold to foreign colonies at high prices—to the French West Indies, Cuba, and Brazil. It was easy to persuade Parliament that Britain should not augment the slave populations of its wartime rivals, the profits in the coffers of Liverpudlian merchants notwithstanding. This line of argument appealed to parliamentarians who supported British Caribbean agricultural production and who were keen to dispel the development of rival colonies by cutting off their supplies of new slaves. In addition, the defeat of Britain's allies at the battles of Austerlitz (December 1805) and Jena (October 1806) and the continental blockage instigated by Napoleon on British shipping helped to persuade politicians that it was patriotic to oppose France by cutting off its supply of slaves while Britain was at war. Naval victories in the period 1793–1802 had established British naval supremacy and the British battle fleet in 1807 greatly exceeded that of the French. This made it virtually impossible for France to restore the productive capacity of Saint-Domingue at this time. Since it was necessary to appeal to the majority of MPs who were uncommitted on the issue of slave trade abolition, a bill to threaten Britain's enemies was one that could win them over. This was achieved by the spring of 1806. The tactics pursued resolved the long-standing problem of persuading sufficient numbers of parliamentarians who were uncommitted on the matter of the slave trade to give their support in the division lobby.

The Foreign Slave Trade Bill was a great achievement for the abolitionists inside and outside Parliament. It was a shrewd move which automatically stopped 33 per cent of the existing British slave trade overnight. After it had passed successfully through both houses of Parliament, the way was clear for a reintroduction of the general motion to abolish the slave trade on the grounds of humanity, justice, and sound policy. The bill was introduced by First Lord of the Treasury William Grenville in the Commons. After its success, a three-hour speech by Lord Sidmouth in the upper chamber won over their lordships. These two achievements were in the bag by February 1807. Some 283 MPs voted in favour of the bill, and it is thought that they included most of the hundred Protestant Irish MPs who entered Parliament as a result of the Act of Union with Ireland in 1801. Those members, ironically, may well have supported prohibition of the slave trade as a better alternative to another reform measure looming on the horizon, namely relief for Roman Catholics. But we do not know why these members voted as they did, or who they were: parliamentary debates were not recorded in full at the time and roll-call votes were similarly not preserved. But it is clear that the issue of the slave trade had attracted much more support across Parliament than had been the case previously. Clearly, the political nation was willing to make the economic sacrifice of abolishing the slave trade.

After both the Commons and the Lords agreed to an abolition of the slave trade, George III consented to the bill becoming law. On 1 May 1807 the bill became an Act of Parliament and the British slave trade had officially ended. The final victory came through a change of government in 1806, brilliant tactical manoeuvring by abolitionist sympathizers, and a fair amount of luck in there being a political and economic conjuncture that was appropriate for resuscitating what seemed a flagging cause. Though he did not present this particular reason for the ending of the British slave trade, Williams's thesis about the economic reasons for its abolition was correct in so far as short-term objectives were concerned; for if there had not been the need to cut off the supply of slaves by British ships to foreign and colonial territories in the national interest, the British slave trade might have taken even longer to dismantle. But ending the slave trade was not perceived at the time as impairing Britain's interest in the Caribbean sugar colonies. Abolitionists, even Wilberforce, considered that slave emancipation would occur at some unspecified time in the future as a result of a gradual process, while supporters of slavery were determined to maintain British property interests in the Caribbean.

# 8

# Slave Emancipation

Be it therefore enacted . . . that from and after the 1st day of May 1807, the *African* slave trade, and all manner of dealing and trading in the purchase, sale, barter or transfer of slaves, or of persons intended to be sold, transferred, used or dealt with as slaves, practised or carried on in, at, to or from any part of the coast or countries of *Africa*, shall be . . . utterly abolished, prohibited and declared to be unlawful.

These words, printed as 47 Geo. III, c. 36 in the *Statutes at Large*, signalled the official end of the British slave trade. They were accompanied by clauses stating that vessels fitted out in Britain and her colonies for transporting slaves would be forfeited; that persons carrying or receiving enslaved Africans would be fined £100 per slave; that insurance arranged to cover slaving voyages would incur a penalty of £100 or treble the amount of the premium; that slaves on foreign ships taken as prizes of war or seized as forfeiture would be condemned as prize captures or forfeited to the monarch and freed from slavery; and that bounties would be paid to the captors of such slaves. Faced with these apparently stringent penalties, Liverpudlians quickly redeployed their slave fleet into other avenues of African and Atlantic trade. Bristolians, whose slave trading activities had effectively collapsed a few years before abolition, concentrated on other European and American trades and on the African palm oil trade. Both ports continued to ship and sell the products cultivated by Africans and by slave labour in the Americas even though the British slave trade had been abolished.

With the demise of the slave trade, the abolitionist battle turned to the problem of dealing with slavery itself. Over a quarter of a century elapsed, however, before slaves in the British Empire were emancipated. This time lag between ending the slave trade and eradicating slavery was common to most European nations that had interests in slavery and the slave trade. Down to 1823, when the British government first adopted an amelioration policy for slaves, the abolitionist strategy largely concentrated on piecemeal efforts. These aimed to improve the lot of enslaved blacks; to tighten up loopholes in the act of 1807; and to oppose the continued existence of an international trade in slaves by other European powers. After 1823 British abolitionism experienced a revival in membership, organization, and impact; governments felt increasingly under pressure on slavery; and in the two years after 1830 a surge of abolitionist petitions, meetings, and publications made emancipation a high priority on the government's agenda. To understand the irregular progress of abolitionism between 1807 and 1834 one has to examine the interplay between private abolitionist endeavours, the changing political scene in Britain, and the role of planters and slaves in the Caribbean.

## REASONS FOR THE DELAY IN ABOLITIONIST CAMPAIGNING

Between 1807 and 1823 there were several reasons for the delay between abolition of the slave trade and a renewed struggle to eradicate slavery. The parliamentary climate was not particularly conducive to the revival of abolitionist activity. The period was dominated by a Tory Party that was inimical to major social changes. The peacetime depression that followed in the years between Waterloo (1815) and Peterloo (1819), with the resurgence of radicalism, a movement for parliamentary reform and government repression of radical associations and meetings, also conspired to keep antislavery off the main political agenda. Preoccupied with winning the war against Napoleon and maintaining the status quo in terms of political power in the aftermath of that conflict, the Tory government did its best to withstand proposals for parliamentary and social reform at a time when the social inequalities and skewed political representation that persisted during Britain's early industrialization led to pressure from outside Westminster for reform.

Within abolitionist ranks, the push for slave emancipation was more muted than one might have anticipated. The leading abolitionists in 1807 were advocates of gradual emancipation rather than immediate freedom for slaves. They believed that preparation was necessary to prepare the enslaved for freedom. William Wilberforce, the leading British antislavery spokesman, strongly advocated gradualism. In *A Letter on the Abolition of the Slave Trade* (1807), he stated that immediate emancipation would be an insane course to follow. In his

view, preparation was needed so that freedom would not be a trau-
matic shock for slaves. Wilberforce argued that the ending of the slave
trade would compel planters to concentrate on breeding and treating
slaves more humanely. Slaves also needed better socialization through
improved medical care, Christian instruction, and education before they
were freed. Thus liberty would be a gradual process requiring effort by
both masters and slaves. These ideas were espoused from a position of
comfortable white superiority. The 'soil and climate' of freedom were
'fruits . . . which our poor degraded Negro Slaves are as yet incapable of
enjoying. To grant it to them immediately, would be to insure not only
their masters ruin, but their own. A certain previous course of discipline is necessary. They must be trained and educated for this most
perfect state of manly maturity.'[1] Joseph Sturge, a Birmingham Quaker corn merchant who played a prominent part in the abolitionist
movement, noted the widespread adherence to gradualism among antislavery leaders. He recalled in his *Memoirs* (1864) that those who had
campaigned so hard for the eradication of the slave trade never 'contem-
plated speedy emancipation as a thing either practicable or safe, though,
no doubt, they expected that the abolition of the slave trade would
ultimately, and by a necessary though very gradual process, lead to the
overthrow of slavery.'[2]

To some extent, the abolitionist movement experienced a lull in its
activities immediately after 1807. It was perhaps to be expected that
the momentum would falter after a twenty-year campaign to eradicate
slave trading. Indeed, already by 1806 most of the sixty or more
provincial anti-slave trade committees had been disbanded once the
goal of slave trade abolition was in sight. For some years, the campaign
against slavery seemed to lose direction. The Society for the Abolition
of the Slave Trade was wound up in 1807, its work completed, and
replaced by a new organization, the African Institution, which drew on a
similar membership. The aims of the African Institution were to ensure
the laws against the slave trade were properly enforced; to encourage
commercial expansion through direct commodity trade between Britain
and Africa; and to persuade other European powers to follow the British
lead in abolishing their slave trades. The first two of these objectives

[1] William Wilberforce, *A Letter on the Abolition of the Slave Trade* (1807), reprinted
in Michael Craton, James Walvin, and David Wright (eds), *Slavery, Abolition and
Emancipation: Black Slaves and the British Empire: A Thematic Documentary* (London,
1976), 286.
[2] *Memoirs of Joseph Sturge* (London, 1864), reprinted ibid., 288.

were pursued, if sometimes with difficulty. The Royal Navy dispatched vessels to patrol the Atlantic sea lanes from Africa to intercept illegal vessels. Direct trade to and from Africa was conducted from London, Liverpool, and Bristol. In fact, a trade in palm oil was consolidated as a part of legitimate trade with Africa. The third aim was taken over by British diplomacy, as shown below. Unfortunately, the African Institution never aroused much popular enthusiasm, possibly because it delayed a direct assault on slavery as an institution in the British Empire. It soon concentrated its activities on trying to run the British Crown territory of Sierra Leone as a progressive colony rather than the broader remit outlined above.

British diplomacy with regard to the international slave trade was only moderately successful. The pressure exerted led to the Dutch being persuaded to end their slave trade in 1814 and to Louis XVIII decreeing that the French slave trade should end (though the latter proved meaningless because France did not enforce it). In addition, diplomatic pressure led to a clause being inserted at the Congress of Vienna (1815), at the conclusion of the Napoleonic Wars, condemning the slave trade and binding the great powers of Europe together to seek its extinction. But subsequent attempts to gain concessions over the international slave trade through diplomatic channels had mixed results. Treaties signed with Spain and Portugal in 1817 prohibited slave trading by those powers north of the Equator and provided for the abolition of Spain's slave trade in 1820; but the extensive Luso-Brazilian slave traffic south of the Equator was sanctioned. An attempt at the Aix la Chapelle Congress (1818) to secure international agreement about the right of search of suspected slave vessels proved fruitless. The failure of British attempts at the Congress of Verona (1822) to secure an international maritime police to suppress the slave trade was the last instance, for the time being, of exerting diplomatic pressure to curb the international slave trade. Soon the pressure on other European powers to act over their slave trade petered out.

## SLAVE REGISTRATION

Parliament dealt with an aspect of abolitionist concern in 1811, when it passed the Scots lawyer Henry Brougham's bill to tighten up penalties for those engaging in the illegal slave trade. Under this legislation, the slave trade was presumed a felony and offenders were liable to fourteen years' transportation to Australia or five years' imprisonment. The impact of this statute was nevertheless weakened by its exclusion of legislation against the intercolonial slave trade transferring blacks among the different Caribbean islands. However, that relatively small-scale phenomenon probably transferred only around 20,000 slaves from one West Indian colony to another by the mid-1820s. The major abolitionist achievement of the period 1807–23 was to secure slave registration by parliamentary Act. The leading figure behind this measure was James Stephen, a Colonial Office lawyer, who started to press for slave registration in 1812. He acted from the premise that only a system of recording the main characteristics of slaves could determine whether planter amelioration was, in fact, taking place, leading to improved slave breeding and better treatment of blacks. Thomas Clarkson was a staunch supporter of Stephen's efforts. After stating that slaves were being treated in a rigid and cruel way, as if the abolition of the slave trade had not taken place, he argued that the British public 'must support the Registry Bill, which is the Foundation-stone of a Constitution' for the 'better treatment of slaves'.[3]

Stephen's work was carried out in an intellectual climate where governments were becoming increasingly interested in gathering statistics on mortality and fertility among the population, as demonstrated in the influence of the Reverend Thomas Malthus's *Essay on the Principle of Population* (1798) and the beginnings of national census-taking by John Rickman in 1801. Stephen persuaded his superior, the Colonial Secretary Lord Bathurst, to put pressure on colonial governors to secure such measures in 1815. This was necessary because, apart from the Crown colonies, the British West Indies consisted of islands with their own legislative assemblies, and the normal practice was to persuade these bodies to accept any internal changes in their islands suggested from Westminster. News of the government's wish to bring in slave registration reached Barbados at the time of Bussa's rebellion in spring 1816. This induced slaves to argue that they had been partly inspired to rebel by thinking that slave registration was a step towards emancipation. Opposition to slave registration came from some older Caribbean territories, notably Jamaica. Eventually this was overcome and the legislatures of West Indian islands were persuaded to accept the

[3] Henry E. Huntington Library, San Marino, Calif., Thomas Clarkson, 'Paper or address to country to interfere for better treatment for Negroes in the West Indies', n.d. but *c.*1815, Clarkson MSS, CN 56.

Colonial Office's plans. A slave registration Act was passed in 1817 and came into effect on 1 January 1820, though registration in Trinidad started in 1813.

Slave registration took place every three years and served four purposes. First, it provided data on the size of slave populations on individual plantations, enumerating blacks by age, name, and skills, to determine whether illegal slave imports were still occurring. Second, it provided accurate statistics on slave fertility and mortality, which would enable the government to gauge whether planters were treating their slaves better and promoting slave breeding. Third, the census data publicized living and working conditions for slaves throughout the British Caribbean. Finally, slave registration served as a platform for further reforms connected with slavery. Stephen hoped that the data compiled would present chapter and verse on the horrors of slavery: the sheer volume of evidence provided by statistics would be incontrovertible proof of the poor treatment of slaves. Once these facts were revealed, planters would have no option but to pursue ameliorative policies towards their slaves; if they failed to do so, government intervention to amend the situation would be justified.

## SLAVE AMELIORATION AND THE REVIVAL OF ANTISLAVERY

Apart from the achievement of slave registration, the antislavery movement was in the doldrums by 1820 for reasons already specified. But a new wave of abolitionist zeal began in 1821 with the formation of the Liverpool Anti-Slavery Society under the leadership of James Cropper, a Quaker philanthropist with a strong involvement in the East India sugar trade, and the establishment of a central Anti-Slavery Society between 1821 and 1823. The latter, heavily backed by the Quakers, was led by Zachary Macaulay, a philanthropist who had been at various times a bookkeeper and estate manager in Jamaica, governor of Sierra Leone, and editor of the *Christian Observer*, the organ of the Clapham Sect. The official title of the new society was 'The Society for the Mitigation and Gradual Abolition of Slavery throughout the British Commonwealth'. This encapsulates the rather mild intentions of its founders. There was no urgency in mainstream antislavery demands in Britain at this time.

The Anti-Slavery Society drew upon many members of the African Institution. Leading representatives for the central antislavery society emerged in Parliament. In the Commons, the leading spokesman was Sir Thomas Fowell Buxton, a Quaker brewer and philanthropist who had taken over from the ageing Wilberforce. In the Lords, Lord Suffield acted as the society's leading spokesman. The members of the Anti-Slavery Society included evangelical businessmen and middling gentry inclined towards social reform based on moral issues. The Society aimed to pressurize Parliament for an improvement in the lot of slaves, with gradual emancipation as its eventual goal. Macaulay and other members of the Anti-Slavery Society did not rest until, as the memorial to the Clapham Sect in Holy Trinity Church puts it, 'the curse of slavery was swept away from all parts of the British dominions.'[4]

Buxton announced the intentions of the society in a parliamentary speech in May 1823, in which he outlined plans to free slave children at birth and stated that slavery was 'repugnant to the principles of the British Constitution and of the Christian Religion; and . . . ought to be gradually abolished throughout the British Colonies with a due regard to the well-being of the parties concerned.'[5] This cautious statement, as the wording suggests, sought to appease planters; it was vague about the timing of gradual emancipation, but this helped to allay alarm among the West India Interest and their sympathizers. But at least the speech was stronger than the amelioration proclamation issued by Governor Somerset in the Cape Colony two months earlier. Buxton's speech convinced the Liberal Tory government that they must quickly formulate their own policy towards improving the plight of slaves, to wrest the initiative from the potentially resurgent abolitionist lobby. Government policy was swiftly announced by George Canning, the foreign secretary, just a few days after Buxton's speech in May 1823. The programme announced focused on amelioration rather than gradual emancipation. Canning stated that it was necessary for 'decisive measures' to be taken to ameliorate the condition of slaves in the British Caribbean. Such measures would be enforced, leading to 'a progressive improvement in the character of the slave population'.[6] Action would be taken as soon as possible. Because of this development, Buxton had no alternative but to withdraw his motion. Canning envisaged that the proposed action could receive binding legislation only for the Crown

    [4] Quoted in Niall Ferguson, *Empire: How Britain made the Modern World* (London, 2003), 122.
    [5] Quoted in Vincent Harlow and A. F. Madden (eds), *British Colonial Developments 1774–1834* (Oxford, 1953), 560.
    [6] Quoted ibid. 560.

colonies; the constitutional right to self-government of older colonies such as Jamaica, Barbados, and the Leewards meant that their island assemblies must be left to decide how to implement amelioration.

Soon afterwards Bathurst sent a circular to the governors of the Crown islands in the Caribbean outlining a detailed government programme of amelioration. This had been drafted in close connection with the views of the Society of West India Merchants and Planters in London. Bathurst's proposals suggested various improvements to the condition of slaves. They emphasized the need for instruction in the main tenets of Christianity to improve the slaves' character, and requested that local assemblies ban Sunday markets to keep the Sabbath for religious observance. Other proposals included offering slaves the right to present evidence in courts of justice; the removal of obstacles to manumission; the prohibition of the sale of slaves from an estate in order to meet proprietors' debts; the setting up of savings banks for slaves; and changes to the laws on punishment. The latter included a call for not meting out punishments to slaves until a day after an offence was committed, entering any more than three lashes in a plantation book, and carrying out the punishment in the presence of one other free person as witness. Bathurst's circular also requested the removal of the whip from slave drivers and banning corporal punishment for female slaves. The circular was given greater weight by an order-in-council of 1824 which required Trinidad to implement these reforms and which advocated compulsory manumission for slaves. Such a constitutional device could be used with regard to Crown colonies but not for colonies with their own legislative assemblies. The Bathurst circular and the order-in-council were absorbed into the handling of slavery in the Cape Colony, where between 1826 and 1832 the governor published various ordinances dealing with slave amelioration. These ordinances included effective provision for mediating in disputes between masters and slaves by setting up Slave Protectors, by bringing in laws to limit allowable punishments, and by giving slaves the right to make complaints against their abuse.

The changes proposed in these government directives fuelled the ire of West Indian planters. 'The slightest breath of the Slave Emancipation Question', the governor of Barbados averred in 1824, 'produces such a Flame, as to render my situation most uncomfortably warm.'[7] The

---

[7] National Archives, Kew, CO323/142P, Henry Warde to Earl Bathurst, 1 Dec. 1824.

planters' fury was based upon attacks on their property rights as slaveowners. They defended their entrenched position in various ways. Some argued that blacks were an inferior race, and thus intended to be kept in a subordinate position. Some, on the contrary, emphasized the humane treatment of slaves on plantations and suggested that their living and working conditions were better than those of mill workers in Britain. Others thought that changes to the West Indian slave system should emanate from assemblies in the Caribbean.

Planters in self-legislating colonies such as Jamaica and Barbados were hostile to many points included in the Bathurst circular. They did their best to delay implementation of the reforms. Thus between 1823 and 1830 a patchy response to amelioration occurred. Some issues were conceded throughout the West Indies, notably the principle that slaves should be allowed to give evidence in court. However, this was implemented fully only in Grenada and Tobago; elsewhere colonial legislatures devised ways of making this impractical. For instance, in Barbados, a slave's testimony in court could not be considered until he had produced statements from his plantation owner and from an Anglican clergyman testifying to his honesty. Compulsory manumission did not make much progress; it was only fully implemented in the Bahamas, which did not have a plantation system. Of the British Caribbean colonies largely based on sugar estates, Trinidad had some relatively frequent compulsory manumission cases. Most planters elsewhere were opposed to manumission because they worried about losing skilled slaves, which would have a deleterious effect on managing estates. The plan to give slaves religious instruction and the encouragement of Christian marriages met hostility from planters, who feared slaves might fall under the influence of dissenting missionaries who had arrived in the Caribbean in great numbers in the 1820s. To remove markets from Sunday also met opposition: any other time of the week would mean releasing slaves from sugar cultivation and thus the productivity of estates was likely to be affected. Most female slaves still received corporal punishment. For male slaves, corporal punishment was limited to twenty-five lashes of the whip by most island assemblies. In St Vincent and Grenada the whip was removed from the field.

The planter interests in the Caribbean were reluctant to implement the proposals suggested by the Colonial Office and many island assemblies saw the ideas put forward as interfering with their legislative autonomy. In taking this attitude, they were reacting not to direct suggestions from the antislavery lobby but to a government that could no longer realistically withstand the pressure from abolitionists about the conditions of slavery. The West India Interest conducted a propaganda campaign in the mid-1820s to convince the British public that most slaveowners were humane Christians who recognized the need for good treatment of slaves; and that proselytization of the Christian faith had made great progress among the black communities of the Caribbean. Their views were undermined by evidence coming back from the West Indies about the poor treatment by planters of some missionaries there.

In Mauritius the implementation of amelioration met greater planter instransigence than in the West Indies. Expatriate French planters dominated the sugar economy there, supplemented by a minority of English merchants and shopkeepers, who held great economic and political authority. They were concerned that new humanitarian measures designed to improve the living and working conditions of slaves on the island would harm economic efficiency at a time when Mauritius's sugar economy was booming partly because of increased production and partly because the British government had removed preferential tariffs on British West Indian sugar imports in 1825. The result was that less was done to put the government amelioration policies into practice than in the Caribbean sugar islands. The British government responded by bringing in a slave ordinance in November 1831 that was intended to enforce a stronger programme of amelioration. But the white plantocracy reacted against this tightening of the screws on their workforce and livelihoods by refusing to pay taxes and by forming local associations with armed bands and meetings for military drill. By January 1833 more planter discontent had abated somewhat but social tensions remained part of everyday life throughout Mauritius.

The antislavery cause in Britain was aided by reports of difficulties associated with slavery in the West Indies. Accounts of the persecution of the Reverend John Smith in Demerara in 1823 made a strong impact. A congregational missionary sent out by the London Missionary Society, Smith spent seven years in Demerara trying to convert 'heathen' slaves by proselytizing the Christian Gospel. 'Your first, your chief, your constant business', Smith was instructed, 'is with the poor negroes. You need not be informed that they are deplorably ignorant; you will probably find them as mere babes in understanding and knowledge; and . . . you must teach them as you would teach children.'[8] Smith

---

[8] Quoted in Emilia Viotti da Costa, *Crowns of Glory, Tears of Blood: The Demerara Slave Rebellion of 1823* (New York, 1994), 131.

worked diligently at his calling but privately he was shocked at the poverty, overwork, and ill treatment of many slaves with whom he had contact. He was caught up in the Demerara slave revolt partly because one of his black deacons, Quamina, was the leader of the insurgence. Accused of inciting the slaves to rebel, Smith was thrown into gaol and sent for trial. He was found guilty of complicity and sentenced to death, but with a recommendation of mercy. George IV signed a reprieve for Smith but it arrived in Demerara several weeks after he had died in gaol of a fever. His death gained wide publicity in the British newspaper press. He was held up as 'the Demerara martyr', someone who had died because of the brutality of the slave system in the British West Indies. Ironically, his death caused more outrage among British public opinion than the death of 250 slaves in the Demerara revolt.

Smith's death and the obstructive methods of West Indian assemblies over amelioration encouraged an upsurge in abolitionist activity from *c*.1825. Many of the tactics used in the 1780s and 1790s resurfaced. Antislavery benefited from extensive newspaper coverage, especially in its own publication, *The Anti-Slavery Reporter*, first issued in 1825. Abolitionists printed and circulated vast numbers of shorter publications. Between 1823 and 1831 the Anti-Slavery Society published 2.8 million copies of tracts, distributed throughout the nation. There were sermons, speeches, and meetings. Lecture tours were undertaken by prominent campaigners. Petitioning of Parliament resumed. Between 1828 and 1830, for example, some 5,000 petitions calling for the gradual abolition of slavery were submitted to Parliament. Probably more than one-fifth of all British males aged over 15 signed the antislavery petitions of 1833.

Various Ladies' Anti-Slavery Associations were formed, in which middle-class women used their energy and spare time to distribute leaflets, cajole people to sign petitions, and publicize antislavery meetings. The first British women's antislavery society was formed by Lucy Townsend in Birmingham. Such associations could be found in Glasgow, Bristol, Sheffield, Manchester, and other cities—not just in the main ports associated with the slave trade. They provided an important outlet for political participation by women at a time when they were excluded from Parliament and public office and were not allowed to be members of national organizations or sign petitions (though they could contribute funds). They drew heavily on nonconformist congregations, in which women had always been prominent in numbers and leadership. The local women's antislavery society in Sheffield, consisting of eighty members in 1825, was just one of several groups that actively propagated the abolitionist message in urban areas. Abolitionist leaders recognized the important contribution made by female efforts in the antislavery cause. The funds raised by women's antislavery societies were reported in the pages of the *Anti-Slavery Reporter*.

## NONCONFORMISTS AND ABOLITIONISTS

Stronger links were forged between nonconformist groups and abolitionists in the late 1820s. But the support varied according to denomination. The Quakers and Unitarians, both relatively small in numbers, made less of an impact on this phase of abolitionism, the Quakers because they had long lost the leadership of a Benezet or a Woolman and the Unitarians because they were more disposed to see the amelioration of slavery rather than its demise. The Baptists, Congregationalists, and the Methodists were more prominent in the antislavery campaigns in the final years of British slavery. Scottish Presbyterians also played their part, though to a lesser extent. The Methodists, in particular, were virtually unanimous in their condemnation of slavery on moral grounds: over 229,000 Methodists signed antislavery petitions presented to Parliament in 1833 when total Methodist membership was just under 233,000 people.

The Baptists, Methodists, and Congregationalists believed in the efficacy of missionary endeavour among slaves; though they admonished missionaries to teach slaves to be obedient to masters, the blacks often used the Christian principles they imbibed to underpin their right to resist tyranny. Missionaries were active in virtually all the Caribbean islands by this time. They were mainly Wesleyan Methodists but included a fair number of Baptists, Congregationalists, and Moravians. In Jamaica, for example, the earliest mission stations were Moravian establishments of 1754 at Carmel and 1760 at Mesopotamia plantation. Another mission station did not appear in the island until 1790, when the Wesleyans arrived at Kingston. Between 1802 and 1834 another fourteen Wesleyan Methodist missions were established in Jamaica along with eleven Baptist, eight Moravian, and six Presbyterian missions. The missionary presence spread to the Cape Colony, where there were six Moravian mission stations by 1834.

The missionaries' presence and their pastoral and evangelical work among the slaves filled a gap left by the relative indifference of the established church and its representatives to the plight of blacks in bondage. While it is true that the Anglican church established bishoprics in Jamaica and Barbados in the aftermath of the Demerara rebellion, the Church establishment looked down upon much missionary activity as smacking of 'enthusiasm'. Dissenting missionaries and abolitionists, however, were imbued with a firm sense that God's Providence upheld the moral order in the world. In order to achieve Salvation, redemption was necessary and this could only be achieved, as far as slavery was concerned, by the destruction of physical bondage.

In 1825 the Wesleyan Conference agreed a resolution that underlined the slave's Christian duty to obey his or her master but also stated that it was the duty of 'the religious public *at home* . . . to promote by legislative measures the ultimate extinction of the system of slavery'.[9] Unfortunately, the political climate for such laws was unpropitious in the mid-1820s: the Liberal Tories had introduced acts dealing with tariff reform, banking reform, and the repeal of the Combination Acts, which were regarded as progressive measures, but had no plans, other than the programme of amelioration, to proceed with antislavery legislation. The one exception to this generalization was the Slave Laws Consolidation Act of 1824. This dealt with a loophole in the Act for the Abolition of the Slave Trade in 1807 by curtailing the inter-colonial trade in slaves between different Caribbean islands.

## FROM GRADUALISM TO IMMEDIATISM

Given the lack of government initiatives on slave emancipation, it is not surprising that the revived antislavery movement faced the problem of maintaining its impetus. By 1828 some abolitionists were turning away from the central desired goal of slave emancipation to other ways of confronting the slave–sugar nexus in the Caribbean. One campaign was waged against the protectionist structure that surrounded West Indian commerce, promoting the notion of 'free sugar', especially from the East Indies. Another campaign was against the illicit slave trade to Mauritius. Contemporary estimates suggest that more than 30,000 slaves were taken illegally to Mauritius from Madagascar and the East African coast between 1811 and the mid-1820s.

---

[9] *Minutes of the Wesleyan Methodist Conference*, 19 vols. (London, 1812–27), vi. 52.

The political atmosphere changed markedly in the two years from 1828 to 1830, however, as Tory administrations experienced leadership problems and faced public clamour for the reform of institutions long untouched that could no longer avoid change. Pressure placed on parliament in those two years led to severe cracks in England's *'ancien régime'*. In 1828 the Test and Corporation Acts were repealed. Enacted as two pieces of separate legislation under Charles II, they had effectively excluded dissenters and Catholics from attending universities, becoming members of Parliament, and holding other public offices. This was followed by Catholic Emancipation in 1829, which gave Roman Catholics, including those in Ireland, the right to the franchise and to take up their seats in Parliament and hold public office. In less than two years, therefore, two pillars of the entrenched political system had been swept away. These changes split the Tory Party severely. The diehards thought this was the beginning of the break-up of the British Constitution, with the indissoluble bond between the State and the Church of England ruptured. The Liberal Tories regarded the situation as one in which, backs to the wall, concessions were necessary to forestall further major political change. The disarray of the Tories, their defeat at the general election in 1830, and the arrival of a Whig government for the first time in half a century gave great impetus and hope for two further reforms—the reform of Parliament, something not dealt with seriously for centuries, and the campaign to emancipate slaves in the British Empire.

Influential members of the establishment were lukewarm, to put it mildly, towards parliamentary reform and the antislavery campaign. The ultra-Tories could not countenance the former measure because it would be the first step towards greater political democracy. But to members of the propertied classes, attempts to rid British territories of slavery seemed similarly misguided. Thus Lord Melbourne, shortly after he became prime minister in July 1834, asked the Archbishop of Canterbury, 'I say, Archbishop, what do you think I would have done about this slavery business if I had my way?' The answer was: 'I would have done nothing at all. It is all a pack of nonsense. There have always been slaves in most civilised countries, the Greeks, the Romans. However they *would* have their own way and we have abolished slavery. But it is all great folly.'[10] This flippant view indicates

---

[10] Quoted in Robin Blackburn, *The Overthrow of Colonial Slavery, 1776–1848* (London, 1988), 458.

the way in which slavery could still seem a normal part of the world order to patrician Englishmen. Yet it was increasingly under attack from committed, zealous, active abolitionists at the very time the remark was made.

The abolitionists sensed that political opportunities now existed to present their case vigorously. They increased substantially their pressure on Parliament in the three years after 1830. Petitions were organized very efficiently and more signatures were attached to those requesting slave emancipation than to those demanding parliamentary reform. Large public meetings were held throughout the country to publicize the abolitionist message. They frequently attracted large audiences; indeed, sometimes the hired accommodation could not hold all who wished to attend. In April 1830, for instance, a meeting convened by the Anti-Slavery committee in Freemason's Hall, Leeds, attracted 3,000 people, with several hundred more unable to gain entrance. Acting with the genuine prospect of their cause gaining a serious airing in Parliament, antislavery campaigners adopted new tactics to add to traditional means of pressure. The establishment of the Agency Committee was instrumental in changing the pace of abolitionist attack, and also the urgency of the arguments deployed. It was a group of radical, often younger, campaigners tired of the procrastination that had been the hallmark of those who advocated gradual emancipation. In the eyes of this group, amelioration had not worked in the Caribbean; persecution of missionaries had continued; and each year fuller data on the poor treatment of black slaves reached the newspapers and public attention. The Agency Committee, led by James Stephen, Joseph Sturge, and James Cropper, organized a network of paid, professional lecturers to tour Britain and put over the abolitionist message as effectively as possible. There were eighteen lecturers in all. They frequently used the techniques of revivalist preachers—stirring up the emotions and conscience of their audience—to promote their message.

The Agency Committee lecturers were committed to an immediate end to slavery. They were responsible for the shift from long-held traditions of gradual emancipation to immediatism. This intellectual change occurred in the early 1830s, though it did not convert those still in favour of gradualism. Underpinning the move to immediatism was a strong evangelical sense that slavery was a grave sin and that for an individual to be at ease in his or her conscience, or to hope for redemption, an immediate cleansing of sin was necessary. The case for an immediate end to slavery had been made in 1824 by an

English Quaker, Elizabeth Heyrick, in her pamphlet *Immediate, not Gradual Emancipation*. This made little impact when it was published. But the Agency Committee quoted extensively from it. The call for immediatism was also put forward in an influential speech by the Reverend Andrew Thomson, a Presbyterian and an advocate of immediatism over gradualism, who addressed the Edinburgh Abolition Society on 19 October 1830, arguing that to engage in slavery was 'to contract guilt in the sight of heaven . . . being aware of this, we are bound to make no delay in hastening out of transgression, and putting an end to it, wherever it has obtained a footing in our dominions.'[11] This speech was printed as a pamphlet and widely circulated. It became an essential reference point for the Agency Committee. In much of the committee's propaganda, there was more emphasis on the sinfulness of British people upholding slavery as a system than on the poor reproductive capacity and high mortality of black people subject to slave regimes. Thus the Agency Committee's campaign was as much concerned with cleansing the souls of British people who acquiesced in the system of slavery as with improving the lot of blacks in the Caribbean.

Not all abolitionists in the early 1830s were convinced about the new tactics of the Agency Committee; it was easy to dismiss its lecturers as attention-grabbing firebrands. In 1832 the Committee issued a report which stated that colonial slavery was a crime in the sight of God, and ought to be immediately abolished. This was contrary to the view held by most British abolitionists. In 1823, a few months after the Abolition Society was first organized, Wilberforce reminded Zachary Macaulay that slave emancipation should be gradual and 'following upon the moral instruction and improvement of the slaves'.[12] Wilberforce and many others still held this position a decade later. In 1832 the rift between the gradualists and the immediatists came to a head and the Agency Committee broke away from the Anti-Slavery Society to form the Agency Anti-Slavery Society.

While the Agency Committee was carrying out its propaganda, the cause of antislavery made great strides throughout Britain. At the General Election of 1830, the pro-slavery Tories lost seats and sixteen out of the thirty-five members of the West India Interest also lost their place in the

---

[11] A. Thomson, *Substance of the Speech Delivered at the Meeting of the Edinburgh Society for the Abolition of Slavery, on October 19, 1830* (Edinburgh, 1830), 4.

[12] Henry E. Huntington Library, San Marino, Calif., William Wilberforce to Zachary Macaulay, 13 Oct. 1823, Macaulay Papers, box 9.

Commons. In many constituencies, slavery was a key issue at the polls. The popularity of antislavery helped the Whigs gain power under Lord Grey's leadership. Antislavery candidates, however, did not succeed in all constituencies. In Bristol two Whig candidates opposed the sitting Tory MP Richard Hart Davis, but the Tories were returned at the election. Both Whigs were members of West Indian trading houses, but they were divided on slave emancipation. Edward Protheroe contested the Bristol constituency in order to promote antislavery, to ensure, as he put it, that West Indian slaves received 'the full enjoyment of the civil rights and immunities of a free-born British subject'.[13] James Evan Baillie, staunch advocate of the West Indian Interest, had supporters who denounced Protheroe as someone who owed every penny to the West Indies: 'His father and grandfather amassed ALL their wealth as West Indian Merchants, and consequently his money is the produce of Slave labour. Tell him then, if he wishes to act in accordance to his **avowed** principles, he should **first** resign ALL wealth derived from such a source!!!'[14] The election campaign in Bristol was marked not just by vituperative remarks in speeches and pamphlets and on election bills and placards. There were armed clashes between the supporters of Protheroe and Baillie and the casualties ended up being treated in the Bristol Infirmary. The excitement and controversy caused by the battle between apologists for slavery and the abolitionist candidates occurred elsewhere, too.

Nevertheless, the abolitionists needed patience in the first eighteen months of the new Whig administration because the government was almost completely dominated by the drive to secure parliamentary reform. Three separate reform bills were introduced in Parliament. The final one was accepted by the Lords only after the prime minister resigned in May 1832, with the prospect of fifty new Whig peers being created if the Tories did not agree to the bill. The Great Reform Act was achieved by June 1832. Though it was a more modest change to the Constitution than its name suggests, it enfranchised significant numbers of the middle classes among whom were a preponderance of people sympathetic to antislavery. Forty of the forty-two new boroughs created by the Act had most features of ideal abolitionist

[13] Bristol Central Library, Address to 'The Friends of Freedom', Bristol Elections, 1830, quoted in Peter Marshall, *Bristol and the Abolition of Slavery: The Politics of Emancipation* (Bristol, 1975), 6.

[14] Bristol Central Library, 'Baillie and Bristol Forever', Placard, Bristol Elections, 1830, quoted ibid. 9.

constituencies: they had a sizeable number of active Dissenters; were medium-sized industrial towns and ports; and had little to lose by slave freedom.

The push for emancipation was helped by the large slave rebellion in Jamaica that broke out after Christmas 1831—a savage conflict between black rebels, largely in the western half of the island, and white militia, aided by black conscripts, that led to the re-establishment of white supremacy but only after three months of almost guerrilla warfare. After the revolt was quashed, a committee appointed by the Jamaican House of Assembly argued that the uprising resulted from interference by Westminster in the Assembly's affairs and antislavery propaganda from Britain filtering through to the Caribbean. Moreover, it alleged that missionary groups had incited slaves to rebel by holding public discussions of freedom based on notions of amelioration, creating the false impression that slaves would be freed after Christmas 1831. The persecution of white missionaries in Jamaica, the burning of their missions, and the savagery with which rebel blacks were tracked down, brought to trial, and either executed or imprisoned, came just at the right time for the Agency Committee to make the most of the oppression.

The Agency Committee's immediatist arguments also gained force from the emerging view that free waged work was superior to slave labour. Adam Smith had famously posited this argument half a century before in *An Inquiry into the Nature and Causes of the Wealth of Nations* (1776), though curiously he offered no cost analysis of colonial slavery. Smith's views on free wage labour were only widely accepted by the later period of slavery in the British Empire. By the 1820s, the prospect of economic growth resulting from free trade and free wage labour had embedded itself among many of the commercial classes. During the final years of British slavery, economic thought was shifting significantly away from protectionism and the inefficiency of slave labour was increasingly claimed. Nevertheless, leading second-generation political economists in Britain, such as Thomas Malthus and David Ricardo, wrote little about slavery to extend Smith's arguments and those ideas were not taken up extensively in the tussle between abolitionist campaigners and proslavery defenders.

The Agency Committee's campaign resulted in antislavery petitions signed by 1.5 million people reaching Westminster by early 1833. The Whigs, who had declared their intention to emancipate slaves when elected in 1830, could not ignore such popular pressure for long.

There were also 104 MPs, nearly all Whigs, elected in September 1832 who had pledged support for a motion for immediate emancipation. Crucially, most of the Cabinet was also prepared to back a scheme for slave emancipation. Yet the Whig government largely consisted of property owners and, as such, they sought to reach accommodation with the West Indian planters who faced ruin from slave freedom. The government preferred this approach to coercion. A special cabinet met almost daily in spring 1833 to work out the details of emancipation. In secret discussions the Whig Cabinet were as mindful of their position as landed gentlemen as they had been when tackling parliamentary reform. Though more committed to slave emancipation than the Tories, they were not radicals. Thus, in government discussions about the labour problem in the British Caribbean, different plans were devised to ensure the continued presence of blacks on the sugar plantations.

The final debates on emancipation began in Parliament on 14 May 1833 when Edward Stanley, the new Colonial Secretary, later to become prime minister as the Earl of Derby, announced a scheme for slave freedom. He prefaced his speech by noting that colonial legislatures had been reluctant to comply with the government's amelioration policy and that parliamentary legislation on emancipation was now vital. He affirmed Parliament's right to intervene in all internal affairs of the colonies except taxation. In his speech in the Commons, Stanley announced that immediate measures would be taken to end slavery in the British Empire: the emancipation scheme provided for all slave children aged under 6 to be freed and for adult slaves to become apprentices for a period of time before attaining full freedom. The system of Apprenticeship was to be overseen by 132 special (or stipendiary) magistrates sent out from Britain to ensure that the new temporary arrangements for blacks worked smoothly. The government would offer a loan of £15 million to planters in compensation for the loss of their slaves' labour. The implementation of the Emancipation Act in the self-governing colonies would be left to their island assemblies.

Some of these arrangements proved uncontroversial, but the proposed system of Apprenticeship and the issue of compensation were deeply contentious issues. Radical abolitionists regarded Apprenticeship as merely a continuation of slavery under another name, while planters feared whether the new system would maintain their sugar output. Antislavery campaigners were outraged that planters should receive compensation. The plantocracy, however, felt a loan was unjustified;

instead, they should receive an outright grant for the loss of their property rights. Stanley's speech did not state the number of years for which Apprenticeship would run, nor did it specify who would repay the compensation loan. Stanley's private preference was that the blacks, once fully freed after Apprenticeship, should pay. It also emerged that the government was thinking of making Apprenticeship last for twelve years, with blacks working for three-quarters of normal working hours.

Buxton led the abolitionist attack in the Commons on the government's emancipation scheme. After all the pressure placed on Parliament, this was not the type of legislation on freedom that antislavery campaigners had anticipated. A compromise was worked out. The amount of compensation paid was increased to £20 million. Moreover, it was an outright grant, not a loan: the government, at the eleventh hour, was convinced by the planters' call for recompense for the loss of their property. In addition, the planters argued convincingly that slave registration had conferred title on their slave chattels. Apprenticeship was to run for six years for field (or praedial) slaves and for four years for domestic slaves, with blacks working on an unpaid basis for anything between 40 and 45 hours a week. Apprentices were to be paid wages for additional work undertaken beyond these set hours. The wage levels were subject to bargaining between planters and apprentices. After their terms were completed, the apprentices would become free blacks. An exception to this was that all slave children aged under 6 were immediately set free under the terms of the 1834 Emancipation Act. Customary food allowances to the enslaved were not given any statutory authority for the future. In most British Caribbean territories apprentices were expected to feed themselves from the produce they cultivated on their provision grounds.

After minor amendments in the Lords, the emancipation bill was passed by a comfortable margin in the Commons on 31 July 1833, a month after the death of Wilberforce. Since a bill becomes law one year after its final passage through Parliament, slavery in the British Empire (including the Caribbean and Mauritius but excluding Ceylon, India, and St Helena) officially ended at midnight on 31 July 1834. Technically, around 775,000 slaves in the British West Indies then became free. There were few celebrations in the Caribbean, however, for the Emancipation Act, though resulting from much pressure from the Agency Committee and their gospel of immediatism, was a gradualist measure, one that tried to appease planters and postpone full freedom

for blacks in the Caribbean. Slavery at the Cape Colony, under the
Emancipation Act's provisions, ended on 1 December 1834.

The Anti-Slavery Society did not like many aspects of the Emancipation Act but agreed to its passage through Parliament rather than see the
issue jettisoned after years of struggle. The veteran abolitionist Thomas
Clarkson was not opposed to compensation for the planters. He viewed
this 'not as an indemnification but as money well paid for procuring the
cooperation of the West India Planters and Legislators, without which
the abolition of slavery might have been materially obstructed and
retarded, if not prevented.'[15] The Caribbean island assemblies promptly
put the Emancipation Act into effect. This was not the result of a
sudden burst of altruism or enlightened thinking. It stemmed from
the fact that planters would not otherwise have been able to claim
their compensation. And so Apprenticeship began on 1 August 1834
throughout the British West Indian islands, with the sole exception
of Antigua. The legislature there opted for immediate freedom on the
grounds that the labour force was sufficiently small to control and the
alternatives to sugar cultivation were minimal; in other words, ex-slaves
would necessarily have to stay working on plantations. Bermuda also
opted to abandon Apprenticeship because most of its slaves worked in
the maritime sector rather than on plantations. Mauritius, however,
implemented the Apprenticeship system and maintained it until 1839.
A four-year Apprenticeship also operated in the Cape Colony, though
the distinction between praedial and non-praedial workers was not
implemented there because slaves, working mainly in vineyards and on
farms growing grain, had rarely been allocated to particular forms of
labour for a fixed time.

Eric Williams in *Capitalism and Slavery* (1944) proposed an alternative view of the ending of slavery in the British West Indies. His argument
was similar to the one he put forward for the abolition of the British
slave trade in 1807: problems with the Caribbean economy caused the
British to pull out of slavery with a view to cutting their losses from
failing investments in sugar cultivation. Williams's argument was that
the overproduction of sugar necessitated emancipation by 1833. He was
correct about the existence of problems with the plantation economy.
The price of West Indian sugar had been falling since 1815. In 1830 the
average price of a hundred weight of muscovado sugar in the London

---

[15] Henry E. Huntington Library, San Marino, Calif., Thomas Clarkson to Sir Thomas
Fowell Buxton, 25 Sept. 1833, Clarkson MSS.

market was, at 24 shillings, exactly the same as the import tariff, implying zero revenue accrued to British sugar importers. Caribbean sugar had to compete with greater worldwide cane sugar production (in Cuba and Brazil, especially) and with successful cultivation of beet sugar in France. Increased world supply of sugar tended, as might be expected, to bring down sale prices. While these trends occurred, the price of acquiring slaves rose steeply in the Caribbean. This was especially the case in newer British Caribbean territories such as Trinidad and British Guiana, where slave prices, based on available fertile soil and labour scarcity, were a third higher in 1830 than they had been in 1823. There was, then, clearly a crisis in the Caribbean economy by 1833.

Despite this situation, most historians have not supported Williams's view of emancipation. There is lack of evidence that such economic considerations were paramount in the minds of MPs and ministers during the extended debates on slavery in the early 1830s. This is not to say that economic thought or the climate of British political opinion favoured the long-term continuance of slavery and a protected system of trade that shored up groups such as sugar planters and merchants (via high import duties) or farmers (through the Corn Laws, introduced in 1815). Ideas of free trade and free labour, as already mentioned, were by then common among many propertied men. However, Grey's government was not planning to implement reforms that would incorporate these ideas in legislation. Economic considerations did affect the decision for slave emancipation but in a different way than Williams envisaged. Rather than debating the economic problems caused by falling sugar prices and greater worldwide competition for sugar, the Whig Cabinet was concerned with protecting property: they wanted the agricultural productivity of the British Caribbean maintained under a protectionist framework for the benefit of the mother country.

The credit for achieving slave emancipation in the British Empire must be given to the continued pressure of the abolitionists inside and outside Parliament; to the greater involvement of nonconformist groups in a moral and humanitarian struggle; to the good fortune of a sea change in the political climate after the Tory Party fell into disarray in the late 1820s; to the election of a Whig government determined to legislate on slave emancipation; to the effective work of the Agency Committee lecturers; and to the role played by missionaries and slaves in the Caribbean, notably in the Jamaican slave revolt in 1831, in demonstrating the urgency of the need for slave emancipation. These various facets of the antislavery movement coalesced in the five years after *c*.1828 to produce the momentum necessary for the rapid demise of slavery in the Caribbean.


## APPRENTICESHIP

Though slavery was abolished in the British West Indies in 1834, its legacy lived on. During the period of Apprenticeship blacks were subject to many of the deprivations they had suffered in the long years of slavery. They could earn overtime wages only after weekly shifts of work for their former owners were completed. They faced discrimination in terms of their allowances. Under slavery, blacks in the British Caribbean had been entitled to allocations of provisions, such as a weekly issue of salt fish. The emphasis on amelioration had also induced planters to withdraw heavily pregnant women from the cane fields. Frequently these 'customary indulgences' were withdrawn under the Apprenticeship system. Most blacks lacked the capital to purchase their freedom and to establish independent lives beyond the plantation nexus. Various measures were implemented, however, that impeded the actions of those who wished to become an independent peasantry. These included taxes brought in to discourage small-scale landholding, high rates for licences for traders and dealers, and laws against vagrancy.

There were additional problems with the operation of Apprenticeship. Too few special magistrates were appointed to supervise the system and many of them were unfit, underpaid, and overburdened with the demands of checking that fair play was followed on scattered rural plantations. Only 132 special magistrates were appointed for the whole of the British Caribbean, half of whom were intended for Jamaica; a number of them were unable to take up their positions immediately; and they were paid the inadequate sum of £400 per year for their work. Only eight special magistrates were allocated to the Cape Colony, and they were also poorly paid. Many apprentices suspected (often unfairly) that the magistrates were hand in glove with the plantocracy. Even where this was not true, which was usually the case, planters defended their property rights and continued to exploit apprentices. Planters needed full gangs to maintain their sugar output; half or two-thirds of a workforce could not cope with the rigours of sugar cultivation. Therefore they did everything in their power to squeeze maximum productivity out of their apprentices.

Lord Sligo, appointed as governor of Jamaica to oversee the Apprenticeship system, hoped to promote cooperation between all the parties concerned. He began his tenure in Jamaica in an optimistic manner. The attorneys and managers of plantations had predicted disaster. But Sligo dismissed their jeremiads:

The first prophecy was blood and destruction on the 1st of August; in this they were wrong. The second, that this scene would take place at Christmas; in this they were wrong. The third, that the apprentices would not work for wages; in this they were wrong, as I know of no instance in which the usual wages were offered and were refused. The fourth was that the crop would not be taken off; in this they were wrong, as it has in many cases been taken off much earlier than usual.[16]

But these early remarks on the working of Apprenticeship, emphasizing what the apprentices could do for planters rather than improvements in the apprentices' condition, proved too sanguine. Sligo's hopes of a liberal implementation of Apprenticeship were ruined by planter opposition. He resigned his appointment in the summer of 1836.

By then the main abuses of Apprenticeship were apparent. The planter-dominated assembly obstructed the work of the special magistrates as best they could. They tried to divert control over Apprenticeship away from the magistrates and towards the justices of the peace and parish vestries over which they had long exercised control. Parish vestries controlled workhouses, and it was to these institutions—modelled on the example of the English poor law—that recalcitrant slaves were sent for discipline after they had caused misdemeanours. Treadmills were already being erected throughout Jamaica when Sligo resigned his commission as governor. These reflected the punishments used in the English prison system in the 1820s after the failure of Elizabeth Fry's attempts at inducing more humane treatment of prisoners. Sligo's successor, Sir Lionel Smith, previously governor of Barbados, battled against the odds in trying to curb the power of the assembly over these mechanisms for controlling Jamaica's apprentices. The condition of apprentices in Mauritius was no better than in the British Caribbean. Mauritian apprentices were given no money, no land, and no special training for occupations other than work in the cane fields. James Backhouse, a Quaker missionary who visited the island in 1838, concluded

---

[16] Despatch of Lord Sligo, Dec. 1834, quoted in *Memoirs of Joseph Sturge* (London, 1864), cited in Craton, Walvin, and Wright (eds), *Slavery, Abolition and Emancipation*, 330.

that 'the idea that they are training to be better prepared for freedom is a complete illusion.'[17]

Given the problematic implementation of Apprenticeship, it is unsurprising that protests against the system occurred. The beginning of the system in Montserrat and Nevis was met by dissatisfaction on the part of apprentices. The unrest in Montserrat led to the military being called upon to maintain order. But in neither island were there prolonged work stoppages, let alone riots. The outset of Apprenticeship created more problems in St Kitts, where riots occurred. A naval force was dispatched from Antigua, martial law was declared, and two weeks of disturbances ensued before the dissatisfaction faded away. One of the major disturbances of the Apprenticeship period occurred in Kingstown, St Vincent, in 1836 when more than a thousand free coloureds rioted against the island authorities' attempts to transfer two ex-slaves to a treadmill. The release of the two prisoners by the Lieutenant-Governor of the island defused the crisis.

The unsatisfactory working out of Apprenticeship led British antislavery campaigners to revive their campaigning. Joseph Sturge assumed a leadership role in this renewed abolitionist activity. Based in Birmingham, Sturge was instrumental in forming a new local committee to publicize the inadequacies of Apprenticeship. This began with a mass meeting at Birmingham Town Hall on 14 October 1835. Firm on-the-spot evidence was needed, however, to make the campaign against Apprenticeship carry conviction. Accordingly, Sturge and an associate, Thomas Harvey, undertook a tour of the West Indies in the summer of 1837 to investigate the system. On their return home they quickly published a book on their observations entitled *The West Indies in 1837*. This thoroughgoing condemnation of the inadequacies of Apprenticehip reported complaints from the black people that they were subject to

compulsory and unrequited labour during crop; frauds of time out of crop; being deprived of their allowances; inattention to the sick; insufficiency of time allowed to pregnant women and nursing mothers; general ill-treatment by their overseers; and, partiality, injustice, and drunkenness of the special magistrate. They said, that all who were sent to the treadmill returned sick and injured, some having to stay in the hospital afterwards for two, three, or even four months.[18]

[17] *Extracts from the letters of James Backhouse when Engaged on a Religious Visit to the Island of Mauritius* (London, 1839), 25.

[18] Joseph Sturge and Thomas Harvey, *The West Indies in 1837* (London, 1838), quoted in Craton, Walvin, and Wright (eds), *Slavery, Abolition and Emancipation*, 330, 341.

Stirred to action by Sturge's and Harvey's findings, the British antislavery movement renewed its agitation in 1837 and 1838 by holding meetings, publishing pamphlets and tracts, and delivering signed petitions to Parliament to bring Apprenticeship to an early end. In November 1837 the Colonial Secretary, Lord Glenelg, sent a circular letter to the West Indian governors in which he praised the operation of Apprenticeship and stated that it had achieved the objectives expected by the Whig ministry. But faced with increased agitation against Apprenticeship, he changed his tune by the spring of 1838. He then sent a private circular to West Indian governors noting that 'the state of public feeling in this Kingdom respecting the apprenticeship system is such as to justify the most serious anxiety as to the possible consequences on the future state of the British West Indies.' To avoid agitation in the colonies, he recommended that the local legislatures should 'bring praedial apprenticeship to an earlier close than that fixed by law for its final termination'.[19]

The deteriorating situation in the West Indies forced politicians to act promptly. By spring 1838, with the ending of Apprenticeship for domestic slaves only a few months away, signs of disaffection among the black people in the British Caribbean became all too apparent. There were many instances of Apprentices not completing work and drifting away of their own accord from sugar estates. Most island assemblies took it upon themselves to declare an early end to Apprenticeship. This forced the British government's hand and on 31 July 1838 the entire system of Apprenticeship in the British Caribbean was brought to an end two years ahead of its intended demise. For Caribbean blacks, the end of Apprenticeship rather than the emancipation of slaves four years earlier marks the real transition to freedom for West Indians once held under bondage.

When apprentices were eventually freed in the British Caribbean in 1838, the only other American territories where slavery had ended permanently were Chile, Mexico, and Bolivia, in which slavery was abolished respectively in 1823, 1829, and 1831. The international growth of abolitionism nevertheless meant that most other powers with slave systems in the Americas freed their enslaved workers over the ensuing half century. Between 1842 and 1854 slavery was abolished in Uruguay, Ecuador, Peru, and Venezuela. Slaves were freed in the Danish and French colonies in 1848–9. The Dutch abolished slavery

[19] Lord Glenelg to Colonial Governors, 2 Apr. 1838, quoted ibid., 343.

in their colonies in 1863. Abraham Lincoln issued his emancipation proclamation to free slaves in the United States during the American Civil War. Latin America held out as the last bastion of slavery in the Atlantic world, but its demise there was achieved by the abolition of slavery in Puerto Rico in 1873, in Cuba in 1886, and in Brazil in 1888.

# Epilogue

The first years of freedom for all blacks in the West Indies brought many problems. Former slaves who remained on plantations now had to face the vicissitudes of market forces. Workers were subject to new terms of oral and written labour contracts, but these were devised with a greater regard for giving planters access to regular labour than to protecting workers' rights. The agreements specified wage levels for work contracted. The penalties for non-fulfilment of the contracts, however, were harsher for black workers than for planters: labourers could be fined a month's wages or placed in prison for a fortnight, whereas masters received orders for redress and distraint orders for non-payment of wages. Efforts to guarantee fair wages proved difficult to bring to fruition because of the wording of contracts but also because free workers were subject to laws of supply and demand for their waged work. There was furthermore a regional dimension to the availability of work for free blacks. In territories such as Trinidad and British Guiana, where insufficient workers were available for plantation employment, black workers could demand good wage levels, but the reverse was true in older, densely settled islands such as most of the Windwards and Leewards, where the supply of available labour outstripped the work offered.

Remuneration for free black workers on plantations also suffered from the importation of cheaper indentured servants after the end of Apprenticeship. Planters wanted to maximize the labour they could secure at low wages. They also needed a regular, compliant workforce to ensure that annual planting and harvest arrangements were not disrupted. The importation of indentured servants from Africa in the 1840s was augmented by a much larger flow of contract labourers from India, Madeira, Europe, Indonesia, and China after 1850. From that date Indian migrants comprised 90 per cent of the intercontinental immigrants to the British Caribbean until 1917, when the Indian contract labour system ended. Most of these imported indentured servants were mainly absorbed into the areas where sugar production was more buoyant after 1838, notably Trinidad and British Guiana. Nearly 250,000 Indian immigrants came to Trinidad, 150,000 went to British Guiana, and over 36,000 ended up in Jamaica. Competition over plantation work occurred between these immigrants and free blacks; the two groups usually remained physically and culturally apart from one another. Racial tension between Indian immigrants and blacks was frequently the result.

After gaining their freedom West Indian blacks had to accommodate themselves to British conceptions of social legislation with regard to marriage laws, the poor law, and education. They experienced considerable difficulties in each of these spheres. The British colonial authorities wanted to promote formal weddings in Christian churches among free blacks but were reluctant to accept the validity of common law unions or those not based on Christian rites. After 1838 planters were no longer compelled to maintain their estate labour force throughout the year, or to provide housing and shelter for black workers. Poor blacks could find themselves placed in parish workhouses, which persisted in the British Caribbean from the era of Apprenticeship. Based on the British New Poor Law of 1834, these workhouses subjected inmates to a harsh institutional regime. A government educational grant of £30,000 to provide elementary education for free blacks was quickly whittled down from 1841 onwards and abolished altogether in 1846. It therefore became more difficult for black children to acquire basic literacy and numeracy than had been the case under Apprenticeship, when each British Caribbean island had Anglican, Catholic, and non-denominational schools supported by the government education grant. It was difficult for blacks to exercise their right to vote at elections after 1838 because assemblies raised the property qualifications to vote in order to prevent existing voters—mainly free white men and some free blacks—being outnumbered and outvoted by former slaves.

But though colonialism persisted, with many obvious warts on display, blacks had at last achieved free status in the British Caribbean. The year 1838 therefore marked the birth of a free peasantry throughout the British West Indies. Positive signs for a better future were evident. Thus by the early 1840s missionaries such as J. M. Philippo in Jamaica were reporting the success of peasants building their own free villages away from the plantations and working hard to survive through the cultivation of provisions for market. By 1846 freed blacks in Jamaica had acquired nearly 100,000 acres by purchase alone and had built nearly 200 free villages. Of course, many black workers had little option other than to remain on estates working for their former owners. They were not educated for anything other than manual, agricultural work and few opportunities existed in the early years of freedom for advancement beyond the peasantry. While there was not a wholesale exodus of workers from sugar estates after 1838, many blacks remained in their former huts on plantations only if they could cultivate provision grounds and market their produce and if they were treated fairly by employers. When planters tried to coerce them into becoming regular estate workers, as in the slavery era, they usually withdrew their labour and joined the free peasantry.

Labour arrangements after Apprenticeship in the Cape Colony and Mauritius only partly replicated what happened in the British Caribbean. The marketing of crops from provision grounds was less well developed in the western Cape than in the West Indies, though in the pastoral eastern districts of the Cape there was more evidence of 'proto-peasant activity'. Thus after 1838 most freed slaves in the Cape Colony continued to work for poor wages or as labour tenants on settler farms. There was no general flight of freed slaves from Cape farms and no significant indentured migrant immigration. However, the fact that the British government's compensation was only payable in London to Cape farmers led many of that group of mainly Boers to migrate into the interior and to take their slaves with them. These were the Vootrekkers, and this mass exodus from the Cape into what became the Transvaal and the Orange Republic was known as 'the great trek'. By contrast, imported Indian labourers were introduced to Mauritius as early as 1829. During the Apprenticeship period this immigration continued on a small scale. It became transformed into large-scale migration after 1842. For many generations indentured Indian labourers became the main workforce on Mauritius sugar plantations.

Though slaves were freed in most British imperial territories by the late 1830s, British antislavery activity continued. In 1839 the creation of the British and Foreign Anti-Slavery Society (BFASS) gave abolitionism an international focus. Spain and Portugal still operated slave trades and plantation slavery and, of course, slavery flourished in the antebellum United States. The BFASS worked to curb the Brazilian and Cuban slave trades and to increase pressure for the elimination of slavery throughout the world. It also supported abolitionists in the United States, welcomed American guests to Britain, and sponsored visits to America. After slaves were emancipated in the United States during the American Civil War, British abolitionists supported the Freedmen's

Aid movement by providing moral support and funds to help the freed blacks in the American South. White southerners regarded these British do-gooders with deep suspicion, but the British abolitionist aid to the United States continued into the 1870s.

In the wider world the Royal Navy played its part in supporting antislavery activity by sending out a British West Africa Squadron to patrol the African coast from Freetown, Sierra Leone. The squadron, created in 1819, predated the creation of the British and Foreign Anti-Slavery Society, but it only became really effective after about 1840. The British West Africa Squadron bolstered British control in parts of West Africa; detained Portuguese and Brazilian slavers; and liberated around 160,000 of the 2.7 million slaves shipped from Africa between 1811 and 1867. No other country matched Britain's record in intercepting slave vessels of various powers along the African coast and in the Atlantic. The British West Africa Squadron helped British forces to destroy the Gallinas slave barracoons in 1840 and to bombard and destroy Lagos in 1851; in the second half of the nineteenth century, it extended its patrols to the eastern coast of Africa. Nevertheless, Spanish and Portuguese merchants were adept at devising ways to avoid the clutches of the squadron, which was stretched in maintaining vigilance against the international slave trade by the sheer amount of territory it covered. It was not until the continental trading powers enacted their own legislation that slavery and the slave trade in the Atlantic world came to an end in the late nineteenth century.

Humanitarian and naval efforts were only one side of the coin as far as the British connection with slavery and the slave trade was concerned. The other side of the coin was a continuing link with slavery and slave systems throughout the world. Britain's involvement with slavery died a slow death, for slavery remained a vital part of British commerce, investment, and empire for many decades. In carrying out legitimate trade with Africa during the nineteenth century, notably in the palm oil trade with Nigeria, British merchants were willing to ship products largely produced by slave labour. In the scramble for Africa in the later Victorian period, Britain and other European powers conquered territories which they defined as 'protectorates' rather than 'colonies'. This enabled Britain to turn a blind eye to slavery in the protectorates on the basis that full-scale abolition was not needed. Moreover, many argued at the time that what appeared to be slavery in these territories in Africa and Asia was better defined as traditional servitude. Thus slavery ended in British-controlled territories at widely scattered points in time. A British Act of Parliament ended the legal status of slavery in India under the India Government Act of 1843. But practices of indigenous slavery continued in India and it was not until 1860 that it became an offence to have slaves there. In 1872-3 Gladstone's ministry produced a new antislavery treaty with Zanzibar, whence Arabs had long dominated the slave trade of East and Central Africa. Under this treaty the sultan of Zanzibar pledged to stop the East African slave trade. In 1874 the Colonial Secretary, Lord Carnarvon, made domestic slavery and other involuntary servitude illegal in the territories on the Gold Coast annexed by Britain. The BFASS and the Aborigines' Protection Society helped the Colonial Office to achieve this goal. In the same year a royal proclamation liberated the slaves imported into the Merina kingdom in Madagascar since the treaty was signed between Britain and that kingdom in 1865.

During the twentieth century, the British connection with slavery and other forms of involuntary servitude continued. It was not until the 1920s that slavery ended in British-held parts of Nepal, Burma, and the Sudan. Slavery continued to flourish in Middle Eastern countries in which Britain had a strong interest. British involvement with slavery in those areas differed markedly. In Nepal slavery had become entrenched as part of the dispossession of low caste Tharu people from the land by other Nepalese. It was difficult for British officials to combat this internal conflict. The Anglo-Egyptian conquest of Sudan (1896-8) was intended to eradicate slavery but the Anglo-Egyptian rulers turned a blind eye to slaveholding practices because of their precarious hold on power in Sudan and their worries about the political and social effects of emancipation. In the 1920s British colonial officials undertook initiatives to eliminate slavery from the unadministered areas of upper Burma but they had to proceed in quasi-secrecy because they feared the international controversy that might arise from their actions. In the Middle East, where British influence was strong after the First World War, the desire to control oil resources led to official British tolerance of the slave trade and slaveholding until the 1930s.

The chequered history of the British involvement with slavery covers four centuries and most parts of the globe. Though the heart of British involvement with slavery and the slave trade lay in the operation of the triangular trade with Africa and the Americas, the British connection with slavery can also be found, as this book has shown, in Asia and the Indian Ocean. The participation of Britain in the abolitionist movement also covered a long stretch of time—over a century and a half of activity—and penetrated many corners of the globe. The 200th anniversary of the abolition of the British slave trade marks a time for reflection on the British connection with slavery and the slave trade, with the role of slavery in the British Empire, and with the legacy of slavery on Britain. The rise in the number of slavery galleries in museums in cities such as Liverpool, Bristol, and London, the recent inclusion of material on the slave trade in the national school curriculum, the statement by Prime Minister Tony Blair of his deep sorrow at Britain's involvement in the slave trade, the call for reparations by activist groups, and the growth of multiculturalism in contemporary British society, will ensure that discussions over the impact of slavery and the slave trade on British society will continue for a long time to come.

# Select Bibliography

## ENCYCLOPAEDIAS, ATLASES, GENERAL WORKS

*Captive Passage: The Transatlantic Slave Trade and the Making of the Americas* (Washington: Smithsonian Institution Press, 2002).

Craton, Michael, *Sinews of Empire: A Short History of British Slavery* (Garden City, NY: Anchor Press/Doubleday, 1974).

Curtin, Philip D., *The Rise and Fall of the Plantation Complex: Essays in Atlantic History* (Cambridge: Cambridge University Press, 1990).

Drescher, Seymour, and Engerman, Stanley L. (eds), *A Historical Guide to World Slavery* (Oxford: Oxford University Press, 1998).

Finkelman, Paul, and Miller, Joseph C. (eds), *Encyclopedia of Slavery* (New York: Macmillan, 1999).

Patterson, Orlando, *Slavery and Social Death* (Cambridge, Mass.: Harvard University Press, 1982).

Rice, C. Duncan, *The Rise and Fall of Black Slavery* (New York: Harper & Row, 1975).

Rodriguez, Junius P. (ed.), *The Historical Encyclopedia of World Slavery*, 2 vols. (Santa Barbara, Calif.: ABC-Clio, 1997).

____ (ed.), *Chronology of World Slavery* (Santa Barbara, Calif.: ABC-Clio, 1999).

Tibbles, Anthony (ed.), *Transatlantic Slavery: Against Human Dignity* (London: Her Majesty's Stationery Office, 1994).

Walvin, James, *An Atlas of Slavery* (Harlow: Pearson Education, 2006).

## CHAPTER 1: SLAVERY AND THE SLAVE TRADE

Axtell, James, 'Colonial America without the Indians', in *After Columbus: Essays in the Ethnohistory of Colonial North America* (New York: Oxford University Press, 1988).

Blackburn, Robin, *The Making of New World Slavery: From the Baroque to the Modern, 1492–1800* (London: Verso, 1997).

Chatterjee, Indrani, *Gender, Slavery and the Law in Colonial India* (Oxford: Oxford University Press, 1999).

Curtin, Philip D., *The Atlantic Slave Trade: A Census* (Madison: University of Wisconsin Press, 1969).

Davis, David Brion, *The Problem of Slavery in Western Culture* (Ithaca, NY: Cornell University Press, 1966).

Eltis, David, *The Rise of African Slavery in the Americas* (Cambridge: Cambridge University Press, 2000).

Eltis, David, Behrendt, Stephen D., Richardson, David, and Klein, Herbert S., *The Trans-Atlantic Slave Trade: A Database on CD-ROM* (Cambridge: Cambridge University Press, 1999).

Jordan, Winthrop D., *White over Black: English and American Attitudes toward the Negro, 1550–1812* (Chapel Hill: University of North Carolina Press, 1968).

Klein, Herbert S., *The Atlantic Slave Trade* (Cambridge: Cambridge University Press, 1999).

Lovejoy, Paul E., *Transformations in Slavery: A History of Slavery in Africa*, 2nd edn (Cambridge: Cambridge University Press, 2000).

McCusker, John J., and Menard, Russell R., *The Economy of British America, 1607–1789* (Chapel Hill: University of North Carolina Press, 1985).

Menard, Russell R., 'Transitions to African Slavery in British America, 1630–1730: Barbados, Virginia and South Carolina', *Indian Historical Review*, 15 (1988–9), 33–49.

Morgan, Edmund S., *American Slavery, American Freedom: The Ordeal of Colonial Virginia* (New York: W. W. Norton, 1975).

Palmer, Colin A., *Human Cargoes: The English Slave Trade to Spanish America, 1700–1739* (Champaign-Urbana: University of Illinois Press, 1981).

Rawley, James A., with Behrendt, Stephen D., *The Trans-Atlantic Slave Trade: A History*, rev. edn (Lincoln: University of Nebraska Press, 2005; orig. pub. 1981).

Richardson, David (ed.), *Bristol, Africa and the Eighteenth-Century Slave Trade to America*, 4 vols (Stroud: Bristol Record Society, 1986–96).

——— 'The British Empire and the Atlantic Slave Trade, 1660–1807', in P. J. Marshall (ed.), *The Oxford History of the British Empire, vii. The Eighteenth Century* (Oxford: Oxford University Press, 1998).

Thomas, Hugh, *The Slave Trade: The Story of the Atlantic Slave Trade*, rev. edn (London: Phoenix, 2006; orig. pub. 1997).

Vaughan, Alden T., *Roots of American Racism: Essays on the Colonial Experience* (New York: Oxford University Press, 1995).

## CHAPTER 2: MERCHANTS AND PLANTERS

Checkland, S. G., *The Gladstones: A Family Biography, 1764–1851* (Cambridge: Cambridge University Press, 1971).

Craton, Michael, 'Reluctant Creoles: The Planters' World in the British West Indies', in Bernard Bailyn and Philip D. Morgan (eds), *Strangers within the Realm: Cultural Margins of the First British Empire* (Chapel Hill: University of North Carolina Press, 1991).

Dresser, Madge, *Slavery Obscured: The Social History of the Slave Trade in an English Provincial Port* (London: Continuum, 2001).

Dunn, Richard S., *Sugar and Slaves: The Rise of the Planter Class in the English West Indies, 1624–1713* (Chapel Hill: University of North Carolina Press, 1972).

Hamilton, Douglas J., *Scotland, the Caribbean and the Atlantic World, 1750–1820* (Manchester: Manchester University Press, 2005).

Harlow, Vincent T., *Christopher Codrington, 1668–1710* (Oxford: Clarendon Press, 1928).

Higman, B. W., 'The West India "Interest" in Parliament, 1807–1833', *Historical Studies*, 13 (1967), 1–19.

Morgan, Kenneth, 'Bristol West India Merchants in the Eighteenth Century', *Transactions of the Royal Historical Society*, 6th series, 3 (1993), 185–208.

—— (ed.), *The Bright–Meyler Papers: A Bristol–West India Connection, 1732–1837* (Oxford: Oxford University Press, 2007).

O'Shaughnessy, Andrew Jackson, *An Empire Divided: The American Revolution and the British Caribbean* (Philadelphia: University of Pennsylvania Press, 2000).

Pares, Richard, *A West-India Fortune* (London: Longman, 1950).

—— *Merchants and Planters, Economic History Review*, suppl. 4 (Cambridge: Cambridge University Press, 1960).

Penson, L. M., *The Colonial Agents of the British West Indies: A Study in Colonial Administration, Mainly in the Eighteenth Century* (London: University of London Press, 1924).

Ragatz, Lowell Joseph, *The Fall of the Planter Class in the British West Indies, 1763–1834* (New York: Octagon Books, 1963; orig. pub. 1928).

Richardson, David, *The Bristol Slave Traders: A Collective Portrait* (Bristol: Bristol Branch of the Historical Association, 1985).

Ryden, David (ed.), *The British Transatlantic Slave Trade*, iv. *The Abolitionist Struggle: Promoters of the Slave Trade* (London: Pickering & Chatto, 2003).

Sheridan, Richard B., *Sugar and Slavery: An Economic History of the British West Indies, 1623–1775* (Baltimore: Johns Hopkins University Press, 1973).

Smith, S. D., *Slavery, Family and Gentry Capitalism in the British Atlantic: The World of the Lascelles, 1648–1834* (Cambridge: Cambridge University Press, 2006).

## CHAPTER 3: THE TRIANGULAR TRADE

Anstey, Roger, *The Atlantic Slave Trade and British Abolition, 1760–1810* (London: Macmillan, 1975).

—— and Hair, P. E. H. (eds), *Liverpool, the African Slave Trade and Abolition*, rev. edn (n.p.: Historic Society of Lancashire and Cheshire, 1989).

Burnard, Trevor, and Morgan, Kenneth, 'The Dynamics of the Slave Market and Slave Purchasing Patterns in Jamaica, 1655- 1788', *William and Mary Quarterly*, 3rd series, 58 (2001), 205–28.

Coughtry, Jay, *The Notorious Triangle: Rhode Island and the African Slave Trade, 1700–1807* (Philadelphia: Temple University Press, 1981).

Davies, K. G., *The Royal African Company* (London: Longman, 1957).

Eltis, David, *The Rise of African Slavery in the Americas* (Cambridge: Cambridge University Press, 2000).

Gemery, Henry A., and Hogendorn, Jan S. (eds), *The Uncommon Market: Essays on the Atlantic Slave Trade* (New York: Academic Press, 1978).

Inikori, Joseph E., *Africans and the Industrial Revolution: A Study in International Trade and Economic Development* (Cambridge: Cambridge University Press, 2002).

Law, Robin, *The Slave Coast of West Africa 1550–1750: The Impact of the Atlantic Slave Trade on an African Society* (Oxford: Oxford University Press, 1991).

Lovejoy, Paul E., *Transformations in Slavery*, 2nd edn (Cambridge: Cambridge University Press, 2000).

Manning, Patrick, *Slavery and African Life: Occidental, Oriental and African Slave Trades* (Cambridge: Cambridge University Press, 1990).

Morgan, Kenneth, *Slavery, Atlantic Trade and the British Economy, 1660–1800* (Cambridge: Cambridge University Press, 2000).

Richardson, David, Schwarz, Suzanne, and Tibbles, Anthony (eds), *Liverpool and Transatlantic Slavery* (Liverpool: Liverpool University Press, 2007).

St Clair, William, *The Door of No Return: Cape Coast Castle and the Slave Trade* (New York: BlueBridge, 2007).

Sheridan, Richard B., 'The Commercial and Financial Organization of the British Slave Trade, 1750–1807', *Economic History Review*, 2nd series, 11 (1958), 249–63.

—— 'The Slave Trade to Jamaica, 1702–1808', in B. W. Higman (ed.), *Trade, Government and Society: Caribbean History 1700–1920* (Kingston: University of the West Indies Press, 1983).

Solow, Barbara (ed.), *Slavery and the Atlantic System* (Cambridge: Cambridge University Press, 1991).

—— and Engerman, Stanley L. (eds), *British Capitalism and Caribbean Slavery: The Legacy of Eric Williams* (Cambridge: Cambridge University Press, 1987).

Williams, Eric, *Capitalism and Slavery* (Chapel Hill: University of North Carolina Press, 1944).

## CHAPTER 4: SLAVE DEMOGRAPHY AND FAMILY LIFE

Berlin, Ira, and Morgan, Philip D. (eds), *Cultivation and Culture: Labor and the Shaping of Slave Life in the Americas* (Charlottesville: University of Virginia Press, 1993).

Bush, Barbara, *Slave Women in Caribbean Society, 1650–1838* (Kingston: Heinemann Publishers [Caribbean], 1990).

Craton, Michael, *Searching for the Invisible Man: Slaves and Plantation Life in Jamaica* (Cambridge, Mass.: Harvard University Press, 1978).

Dirks, Robert, *The Black Saturnalia: Conflict and its Ritual Expression on British West Indian Slave Plantations* (Gainesville: University of Florida Press, 1987).

Dunn, Richard S., *Sugar and Slaves: The Rise of the Planter Class in the English West Indies, 1624–1713* (Chapel Hill: University of North Carolina Press, 1972).

Engerman, Stanley L., and Higman, B. W., 'The Demographic Structure of the Caribbean Slave Societies in the Eighteenth and Nineteenth Centuries', in Franklin W. Knight (ed.), *General History of the Caribbean*, iii. *The Slave Societies of the Caribbean* (London: Macmillan, 1997).

Fogel, Robert W., *Without Consent or Contract: The Rise and Fall of American Slavery* (New York: W. W. Norton, 1989).

Higman, B. W., 'The Slave Family and Household in the British West Indies, 1800–1834', *Journal of Interdisciplinary History*, 6 (1975), 261–87.

——*Slave Population and Economy in Jamaica, 1807–1834* (Cambridge: Cambridge University Press, 1976).

——*Slave Populations of the British Caribbean, 1807–1834* (Baltimore: Johns Hopkins University Press, 1984).

Kiple, Kenneth F., *The Caribbean Slave: A Biological History* (Cambridge: Cambridge University Press, 1984).

Kulikoff, Allan, *Tobacco and Slaves: The Development of Southern Cultures in the Chesapeake, 1680–1800* (Chapel Hill: University of North Carolina Press, 1986).

Menard, Russell R., 'Slave Demography in the Lowcountry, 1670–1740: From Frontier Society to Plantation Regime', *South Carolina Historical Magazine*, 96 (1995), 280–303.

Morgan, Kenneth, 'Slave Women and Reproduction in Jamaica, c.1776–1834', *History*, 91 (2006), 231–53.

Morgan, Philip D., *Slave Counterpoint: Black Culture in the Eighteenth-Century Chesapeake and Lowcountry* (Chapel Hill: University of North Carolina Press, 1998).

Sheridan, Richard B., *Doctors and Slaves: A Medical and Demographic History of Slavery in the British West Indies, 1680–1834* (Cambridge: Cambridge University Press, 1985).

Wood, Peter H., *Black Majority: Negroes in South Carolina from 1670 through the Stono Rebellion* (New York: W. W. Norton, 1974).

## CHAPTER 5: WORK, LAW, AND CULTURE

Allen, Richard B., *Slaves, Freedmen, and Indentured Laborers in Colonial Mauritius* (Cambridge: Cambridge University Press, 1999).

Barker, Anthony J., *Slavery and Antislavery in Mauritius, 1810–33: The Conflict between Economic Expansion and Humanitarian Reform under British Rule* (Basingstoke: Macmillan, 1996).

Berlin, Ira, *Many Thousands Gone: The First Two Centuries of Slavery in North America* (Cambridge, Mass.: Harvard University Press, 1998).

Brathwaite, Edward, *The Development of Creole Society in Jamaica, 1770–1820* (Oxford: Oxford University Press, 1971).

Burnard, Trevor, *Mastery, Tyranny, and Desire: Thomas Thistlewood and his Slaves in the Anglo-Jamaican World* (Chapel Hill: University of North Carolina Press, 2004).

Craton, Michael, *Searching for the Invisible Man: Slaves and Plantation Life in Jamaica* (Cambridge, Mass.: Harvard University Press, 1978).

Frey, Sylvia R., and Wood, Betty, *Come Shouting to Zion: African American Protestantism in the American South and British Caribbean to 1830* (Chapel Hill: University of North Carolina Press, 1998).

Hall, Gwendolyn Midlo, *Slavery and African Ethnicities in the Americas* (Chapel Hill: University of North Carolina Press, 2005).

Handler, Jerome S., and Lange, Frederick, *Plantation Slavery in Barbados: An Archeological and Historical Investigation* (Cambridge, Mass.: Harvard University Press, 1978).

Higman, B. W., *Montpelier, Jamaica: A Plantation Community in Slavery and Freedom, 1739–1912* (Kingston: University of the West Indies Press, 1998).

Littlefield, Daniel C., *Rice and Slaves: Ethnicity and the Slave Trade in Colonial South Carolina* (Baton Rouge: Louisiana State University Press, 1981).

Mason, John Edwin, *Social Death and Resurrection: Slavery and Emancipation in South Africa* (Charlottesville: University of Virginia Press, 2003).

Morgan, Philip D., *Slave Counterpoint: The Development of Slavery in the Eighteenth-Century Chesapeake and Lowcountry* (Chapel Hill: University of North Carolina Press, 1998).

―― 'The Black Experience in the British Empire, 1680–1810', in P. J. Marshall (ed.), *The Oxford History of the British Empire*, ii. *The Eighteenth Century* (Oxford: Oxford University Press, 1998).

Morris, Thomas D., *Southern Slavery and the Law, 1619–1860* (Chapel Hill: University of North Carolina Press, 1996).

Shell, Robert C.-H., *Children of Bondage: A Social History of the Slave Society at the Cape of Good Hope, 1652–1834* (Hanover, NH: University of New England Press, 1994).

Sobel, Mechal, *The World they made Together: Black and White Values in Eighteenth-Century Virginia* (Princeton: Princeton University Press, 1987).

Turner, Mary, 'Religious Beliefs', in Franklin W. Knight (ed.), *General History of the Caribbean*, iii. *The Slave Societies of the Caribbean* (London: Macmillan, 1997).

Walsh, Lorena S., *From Calabar to Carter's Grove: The History of a Virginia Slave Community* (Charlottesville: University of Virginia Press, 1997).

Walvin, James, *Black Ivory: A History of British Slavery* (New York: Fontana, 1992).

Ward, J. R., *British West Indian Slavery: The Process of Amelioration, 1750–1834* (Oxford: Oxford University Press, 1988).


CHAPTER 6: SLAVE RESISTANCE AND REBELLION

Beckles, Hilary, *Black Rebellion in Barbados: The Struggle against Slavery, 1627–1838* (Bridgetown: Antilles Publications, 1984).
Campbell, Mavis, *The Maroons of Jamaica 1655–1796: A History of Resistance, Collaboration and Betrayal* (Granby, Mass.: Bergin and Garvey Publishers, 1988).
Craton, Michael, *Testing the Chains: Resistance to Slavery in the British West Indies* (Ithaca, NY: Cornell University Press, 1982).
Geggus, David, 'The Enigma of Jamaica in the 1790s: New Light on the Causes of Slave Rebellions', *William and Mary Quarterly*, 3rd series, 44 (1987), 274–99.
Genovese, Eugene D., *From Rebellion to Revolution: Afro-American Slave Revolts in the Making of the Modern World* (Baton Rouge: Louisiana State University Press, 1979).
Heuman, Gad, 'Runaway Slaves in Nineteenth-Century Barbados', in Gad Heuman (ed.), *Out of the House of Bondage: Runaways, Resistance and Marronage in Africa and the New World* (London: Frank Cass, 1986).
Mullin, G. W., *Flight and Rebellion: Slave Resistance in Eighteenth-Century Virginia* (New York: Oxford University Press, 1972).
Mullin, Michael, *Africa in America: Slave Acculturation and Resistance in the American South and British Caribbean, 1736–1831* (Urbana and Chicago: University of Illinois Press, 1992).
Teelock, Vijaya, *Bitter Sugar: Sugar and Slavery in 19th Century Mauritius* (Moka, Mauritius: Mahatma Gandhi Institute, 1998).
John K., Thornton, 'African Dimensions of the Stono Rebellion', *American Historical Review*, 96 (1991), 1101–13.
Viotti da Costa, Emilia, *Crowns of Glory, Tears of Blood: The Demerara Slave Rebellion of 1823* (New York: Oxford University Press, 1994).
Wood, Peter H., *Black Majority: Negroes in Colonial South Carolina from 1670 through the Stono Rebellion* (New York: W. W. Norton, 1975).


CHAPTER 7: THE ABOLITION OF THE BRITISH SLAVE TRADE

Anstey, Roger, *The Atlantic Slave Trade and British Abolition, 1760–1810* (London: Macmillan, 1975).
Brown, Christopher Leslie, *Moral Capital: Foundations of British Abolitionism* (Chapel Hill: University of North Carolina Press, 2006).

Carrington, Selwyn H. H., *The Sugar Industry and the Abolition of the Slave Trade, 1775–1810* (Gainesville: University of Florida Press, 2002).

Davis, David Brion, *The Problem of Slavery in the Age of Revolution* (Ithaca, NY: Cornell University Press, 1975).

Drescher, Seymour, *Econocide: British Slavery in the Era of Abolition* (Pittsburgh: Pittsburgh University Press, 1977).

—— *Capitalism and Antislavery: British Mobilization in Comparative Perspective* (New York: Oxford University Press, 1986).

Duffy, Michael, 'The French Revolution and British Attitudes to the West Indian Colonies', in David Barry Gaspar and David Patrick Geggus (eds), *A Turbulent Time: The French Revolution and the Greater Caribbean* (Bloomington: Indiana University Press, 1997).

Eltis, David, *Economic Growth and the Ending of the Transatlantic Slave Trade* (New York: Oxford University Press, 1987).

Howse, E. M., *Saints in Politics: the 'Clapham Sect' and the Growth of Freedom* (London: Allen and Unwin, 1971).

Oldfield, J. R., *Popular Politics and British Anti-Slavery: The Mobilisation of Public Opinion against the Slave Trade, 1787–1807* (Manchester: Manchester University Press, 1995).

Porter, Dale H., *The Abolition of the Slave Trade in England, 1784–1807* (Hamden, Conn.: Archon Books, 1970).

Walvin, James, *An African's Life: The Life and Times of Olaudah Equiano, 1745–1797* (London: Cassell, 1998).

Ward, J. R., 'The British West Indies in the Age of Abolition, 1748–1815', in P. J. Marshall (ed.), *The Oxford History of the British Empire*, ii. *The Eighteenth Century* (Oxford: Oxford University Press, 1998).

Williams, Eric, *Capitalism and Slavery* (Chapel Hill: University of North Carolina Press, 1944).

## CHAPTER 8: SLAVE EMANCIPATION

Blackburn, Robin, *The Overthrow of Colonial Slavery, 1776–1848* (London: Verso, 1988).

Bolt, Christine, and Drescher, Seymour (eds), *Antislavery, Religion and Reform: Essays in Memory of Roger Anstey* (Folkestone: W. Dawson, 1980).

Burroughs, Peter, 'The Mauritius Rebellion of 1832 and the Abolition of British Colonial Slavery', *Journal of Imperial and Commonwealth History*, 4 (1976), 243–66.

Craton, Michael, *Testing the Chains: Resistance to Slavery in the British West Indies* (Ithaca, NY: Cornell University Press, 1982).

Davis, David Brion, *Slavery and Human Progress* (New York: Oxford University Press, 1984).

Drescher, Seymour, *The Mighty Experiment: Free Labor versus Slavery in British Emancipation* (New York: Oxford University Press, 2002).

Dresser, Madge, *Slavery Obscured: The Social History of the Slave Trade in an English Provincial Port* (London: Continuum, 2001).

Engerman, Stanley L., 'The Land and Labour Problem at the time of the Legal Emancipation of British West Indian Slaves', in Roderick A. McDonald (ed.), *West Indies Accounts: Essays on the History of the British Caribbean and the Atlantic Economy in Honour of Richard Sheridan* (Kingston: University of the West Indies Press, 1996).

Fladeland, Betty, *Men & Brothers: Anglo-American Antislavery Cooperation* (Urbana: University of Illinois Press, 1972).

Green, William A., *British Slave Emancipation: The Sugar Colonies and the Great Experiment, 1830–1865* (Oxford: Oxford University Press, 1976).

Midgley, Clare, *Women against Slavery: The British Campaigns, 1780–1870* (New York: Routledge, 1992).

Miers, Suzanne, *Britain and the Ending of the Slave Trade* (London: Longman, 1975).

Rice, C. Duncan, *The Rise and Fall of Black Slavery* (Baton Rouge: Louisiana State University Press, 1975).

Sherwood, Marika, *After Abolition: Britain and the Slave Trade since 1807* (London: I. B. Tauris, 2007).

Temperley, Howard, *British Antislavery, 1833–1870* (New Haven: Yale University Press, 1972).

Turner, Mary, *Slaves and Missionaries: The Disintegration of Jamaican Slave Society, 1787–1834* (Champaign-Urbana: University of Illinois Press, 1984).

Viotta da Costa, Emilia, *Crowns of Glory, Tears of Blood: The Demerara Slave Rebellion of 1823* (New York: Oxford University Press, 1994).

Walvin, James, *England, Slaves and Freedom, 1776–1838* (Jackson and London: University Press of Mississippi, 1986).

Williams, Eric, *Capitalism and Slavery* (Chapel Hill: University of North Carolina Press, 1944).

# Index